Leo Brodie

THINKING FORTH

A Language
and Philosophy
for Solving Problems

A SPECTRUM BOOK

Prentice-Hall, Inc.
Englewood Cliffs, New Jersey 07632

Library of Congress Cataloging in Publication Data

Brodie, Leo.
　Thinking FORTH.

　"A Spectrum book."
　Includes index.
　1. FORTH (Computer program language)　I. Title.
QA76.73.F24B763　1984　　　001.64'24　　　84-8362
ISBN 0-13-917576-8
ISBN 0-13-917568-7 (pbk.)

This book is available at a special discount when ordered
in bulk quantities. Contact Prentice-Hall, Inc., General
Publishing Division, Special Sales, Englewood Cliffs, N.J. 07632.

A SPECTRUM BOOK

10　9　8　7　6　5　4　3　2　1

Editorial/production supervision by Peter Jordan
Manufacturing buyer: Joyce Levatino
Cover design by Hal Siegel

ISBN 0-13-917568-7 {PBK.}

ISBN 0-13-917576-8

Prentice-Hall International, Inc., *London*
Prentice-Hall of Australia Pty. Limited, *Sydney*
Prentice-Hall Canada Inc., *Toronto*
Prentice-Hall of India Private Limited, *New Delhi*
Prentice-Hall of Japan, Inc., *Tokyo*
Prentice-Hall of Southeast Asia Pte. Ltd., *Singapore*
Whitehall Books Limited, *Wellington, New Zealand*
Editora Prentice-Hall do Brasil Ltda., *Rio de Janeiro*

To Stephanie, Brandon, and Ryan

It is impossible to disassociate language from science or science from language, because every natural science always involves three things: the sequence of phenomena on which the science is based, the abstract concepts which call these phenomena to mind, and the words in which the concepts are expressed. To call forth a concept, a word is needed; to portray a phenomenon, a concept is needed. All three mirror one and the same reality.

Antoine Lavoisier, 1789

CONTENTS

List of Program Examples

PREFACE

Programming computers can be crazy-making. Other professions give you the luxury of seeing tangible proof of your efforts. A watchmaker can watch the cogs and wheels; a seamstress can watch the seams come together with each stitch. But programmers design, build, and repair the stuff of imagination, ghostly mechanisms that escape the senses. Our work takes place not in RAM, not in an editor, but within our own minds.

Building models in the mind is both the challenge and the joy of programming. How should we prepare for it? Arm ourselves with better debuggers, decompilers, and disassemblers? They help, but our most essential tools and techniques are mental. We need a consistent and practical methodology for *Thinking about* software problems. That is what I have tried to capture in this book. *Thinking FORTH* is meant for anyone interested in writing software to solve problems. It focuses on design and implementation: deciding what you want to accomplish, designing the components of the system, and finally building the program.

The book stresses the importance of writing programs that not only work, but that are also readable, logical, and that express the best solution in the simplest terms.

Although most of the principles described here can be applied to any language, I've presented them in the context of FORTH. FORTH is a language, an operating system, a set of tools, and a philosophy. It is an ideal means for thinking because it corresponds to the way our minds work. Thinking FORTH is thinking simple, thinking elegant, thinking flexible. It is *not* restrictive, *not* complicated, *not* over-general. You don't have to know FORTH to benefit from this book. *Thinking FORTH* synthesizes the FORTH approach with many principles taught by modern computer science. The marriage of FORTH's simplicity with the traditional disciplines of analysis and style will give you a new and better way to look at software problems and will be helpful in all areas of computer application.

If you want to learn more about FORTH, another book of mine, *Starting FORTH,* covers the language aspects of FORTH. Otherwise, Appendix A of this book introduces FORTH fundamentals.

A few words about the layout of the book: After devoting the first chapter to fundamental concepts, I've patterned the book after the software development cycle: from initial specification up through implementation. The appendixes in back include an overview of FORTH for those new to the language, code for several of the utilities described, answers to problems, and a summary of style conventions.

Many of the ideas in this book are unscientific. They are based on subjective experience and observations of our own humanity. For this reason, I've included interviews with a variety of FORTH professionals, not all of whom completely agree with one another, or with me. All these opinions are subject to change without notice. The book also offers suggestions called "tips." They are meant to be taken only as they apply to your situation. FORTH thinking accepts no inviolable rules. To ensure the widest possible conformity to available FORTH systems, all coded examples in this book are consistent with the FORTH-83 Standard.

One individual who greatly influenced this book is the man who invented FORTH, Charles Moore. In addition to spending several days interviewing him for this book, I've been privileged to watch him at work. He is a master craftsman, moving with speed and deftness, as though he were physically altering the conceptual models inside the machine—building, tinkering, playing. He accomplishes this with a minimum of tools (the result of an ongoing battle against insidious complexity) and few restrictions other than those imposed by his own techniques. I hope this book captures some of his wisdom. Enjoy!

Acknowledgments

Many thanks to all the good people who gave their time and ideas to this book, including: Charles Moore, Dr. Mark Bernstein, Dave Johnson, John Teleska, Dr. Michael Starling, Dr. Peter Kogge, Tom Dowling, Donald Burgess, Cary Campbell, Dr. Raymond Dessy, Michael Ham, and Kim Harris.

Another of the interviewees, Michael LaManna, passed away while this book was in production. He is deeply missed by those of us who loved him.

THINKING
FORTH

ONE

The Philosophy of FORTH

FORTH is a language and an operating system. But that's not all: It's also the embodiment of a philosophy. The philosophy is not generally described as something apart from FORTH. It did not precede FORTH, nor is it described anywhere apart from discussions of FORTH, nor does it even have a name other than "FORTH."

What is this philosophy? How can you apply it to solve your software problems?

Before we can answer these questions, let's take 100 steps backwards and examine some of the major philosophies advanced by computer scientists over the years. After tracing the trajectory of these advances, we'll compare—and contrast—FORTH with these state-of-the-art programming principles.

An Armchair History of Software Elegance

In the prehistoric days of programming, when computers were dinosaurs, the mere fact that some genius could make a program run correctly provided great cause for wonderment. As computers became more civilized, the wonder waned. Management wanted more from programmers and from their programs.

As the cost of hardware steadily dropped, the cost of software soared. It was no longer good enough for a program to run correctly. It also had to be developed quickly and maintained easily. A new demand began to share the spotlight with correctness. The missing quality was called "elegance."

In this section we'll outline a history of the tools and techniques for writing more elegant programs.

Memorability

The first computer programs looked something like this:

```
00110101
11010011
11011001
```

Programmers entered these programs by setting rows of switches—"on" if the digit was "1," "off" if the digit was "0." These values were the "machine instructions" for the computer, and each one caused the computer to perform some mundane operation like "Move the contents of Register B to Register A," or "Add the contents of Register C into the contents of Register A."

This proved a bit tedious.

Tedium being the stepmother of invention, some clever programmers realized that the computer itself could be used to help. So they wrote a program that translated easy-to-remember abbreviations into the hard-to-remember bit patterns. The new language looked something like this:

```
MOV B,A
ADD C,A
JMC REC1
```

The translator program was called an *assembler*, the new language *assembly language*. Each instruction "assembled" the appropriate bit pattern for that instruction, with a one-to-one correspondence between assembly instruction and machine instruction. But names are easier for programmers to remember. For this reason the new instructions were called *mnemonics*.

Power

Assembly-language programming is characterized by a one-for-one correspondence between each command that the programmer types and each command that the processor performs.

In practice, programmers found themselves often repeating the same *sequence* of instructions over and again to accomplish the same thing in different parts of the program. How nice it would be to have a name which would represent each of these common sequences.

This need was met by the "macro assembler," a more complicated assembler that could recognize not only normal instructions, but also special names ("macros"). For each name, the macro assembler assembles the five or ten machine instructions represented by the name, just as though the programmer had written them out in full.

Abstraction

A major advance was the invention of the "high-level language." Again this was a translator program, but a more powerful one. High-level languages make it possible for programmers to write code like this:

```
X = Y(456/A) - 2
```

So then I typed GOTO 500—and here I am!

which looks a lot like algebra. Thanks to high-level languages, engineers, not just bizarre bit-jockeys, could start writing programs. BASIC and FORTRAN are examples of high-level languages.

High-level languages are clearly more "powerful" than assembly languages in the sense that each instruction might compile dozens of machine instructions. But more significantly, high-level languages eliminate the linear correspondence between source code and the resulting machine instructions.

The actual instructions depend on each entire "statement" of source code taken as a whole. Operators such as + and = have no meaning by themselves. They are merely part of a complex symbology that depends upon syntax and the operator's location in the statement.

This nonlinear, syntax-dependent correspondence between source and object code is widely considered to be an invaluable step in the progress of programming methodology. But as we'll see, the approach ultimately offers more restriction than freedom.

Manageability

Most computer programs involve much more than lists of instructions to work down from start to finish. They also involve testing for various conditions and then "branching" to the appropriate parts of the code depending upon the outcome. They also involve "looping" over the same sections of code repeatedly, usually testing for the moment to branch out of the loop.

Both assembler and high-level languages provide branching and looping capabilities. In assembly languages you use "jump instructions"; in some high-level languages you use "GO TO" commands. When these capabilities are used in the most brute-force way, programs tend to look like the jumble you see in Figure 1-1.

This approach, still widely used in languages like FORTRAN and BASIC, suffers from being difficult to write and difficult to change if corrections need to be made. In this "bowl-of-spaghetti" school of programming, it's impossible to test a single part of the code or to figure out how something is getting executed that isn't supposed to be getting executed.

Difficulties with spaghetti programs led to the discovery of "flow charts." These were pen-and-ink drawings representing the "flow" of execution used by the programmer as an aid to understanding the code being written. Unfortunately the programmer had to make the translation from code to flow chart and back by hand. Many programmers found old-fashioned flow charts less than useful.

Modularity

A significant advance arose with the invention of "Structured Programming," a methodology based on the observation that large problems

Figure 1-1. *Unstructured code, using jumps or "GOTOs."*

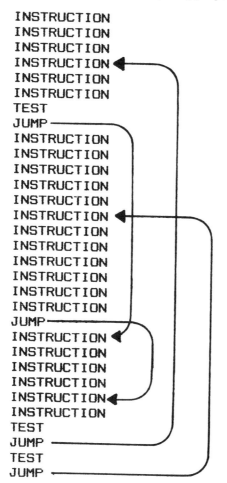

```
INSTRUCTION
INSTRUCTION
INSTRUCTION
INSTRUCTION
INSTRUCTION
INSTRUCTION
TEST
JUMP
INSTRUCTION
INSTRUCTION
INSTRUCTION
INSTRUCTION
INSTRUCTION
INSTRUCTION
INSTRUCTION
INSTRUCTION
INSTRUCTION
INSTRUCTION
INSTRUCTION
INSTRUCTION
JUMP
INSTRUCTION
INSTRUCTION
INSTRUCTION
INSTRUCTION
INSTRUCTION
INSTRUCTION
TEST
JUMP
TEST
JUMP
```

are more easily solved if treated as collections of smaller problems [1].
Each piece is called a *module*. Programs consist of modules within
modules.

Structured programming eliminates spaghetti coding by insisting
that control flow can be diverted only within a module. You can't jump
out from the middle of one module into the middle of another module.

For example, Figure 1-2 shows a structured diagram of a module to
"Make Breakfast," which consists of four submodules. Within each sub-
module you'll find a whole new level of complexity which needn't be
shown at this level.

A branching decision occurs in this module to choose between the

Figure 1-2. *Design for a structured program.*

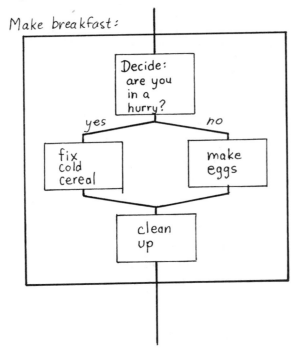

Make breakfast:

"cold cereal" module and the "eggs" module, but control flow stays within the outer module.

Structured programming has three premises:

1. Every program is described as a linear sequence of self-contained functions, called *modules*. Each module has exactly one entry point and one exit point.
2. Each module consists of one or more functions, each of which has exactly one entry point and one exit point and can itself be described as a module.
3. A module can contain:
   a. operations or other modules
   b. decision structures (IF THEN statements)
   c. looping structures

The idea of modules having "one-entry, one-exit" is that you can unplug them, change their innards, and plug them back in, without screwing up the connections with the rest of the program. This means you can test each piece by itself. That's only possible if you know exactly where you stand when you start the module, and where you stand when you leave it.

In "Make Breakfast" you'll either fix cereal or make eggs, not both. And you'll always clean up. (Some programmers I know circumvent this last module by renting a new apartment every three months.)

Structured programming was originally conceived as a design approach. Modules were imaginary entities that existed in the mind of the

Figure 1-3. *Structured programming with a non-structured language.*

```
10        INSTRUCTION
20        INSTRUCTION         } Decide -- in a hurry?
30    IF H=TRUE THEN  GOTO 80   If yes, go to instr.#
40        INSTRUCTION
50        INSTRUCTION         } Make eggs
60        INSTRUCTION
70    GOTO 110                  Go to instr.# 110
80        INSTRUCTION
90        INSTRUCTION         } Make cereal
100       INSTRUCTION
110       INSTRUCTION
120       INSTRUCTION         } Clean up
130       INSTRUCTION
```

programmer or designer, not actual units of source code. When structured programming design techniques are applied to non-structured languages like BASIC, the result looks something like Figure 1–3.

Writeability

Yet another breakthrough encouraged the use of structured programs: structured programming languages. These languages include control structures in their command sets, so you can write programs that have a more modular appearance. Pascal is such a language, invented by Niklaus Wirth to teach the principles of structured programming to his students.

Figure 1–4 shows how this type of language would allow "Make Breakfast" to be written.

Figure 1-4. *Using a structured language.*

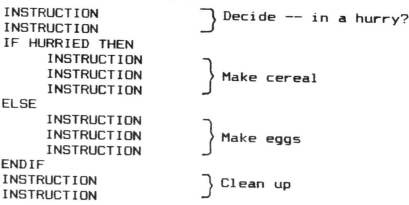

```
INSTRUCTION
INSTRUCTION                } Decide -- in a hurry?
IF HURRIED THEN
        INSTRUCTION
        INSTRUCTION        } Make cereal
        INSTRUCTION
ELSE
        INSTRUCTION
        INSTRUCTION        } Make eggs
        INSTRUCTION
ENDIF
INSTRUCTION                } Clean up
INSTRUCTION
```

Structured programming languages include control structure operators such as IF and THEN to ensure a modularity of control flow. As you can see, indentation is important for readability, since all the instructions within each module are still written out rather than being referred to by name (e.g., "MAKE-CEREAL"). The finished program might take ten pages, with the ELSE on page five.

Designing from the Top

How does one go about designing these modules? A methodology called "top-down design" proclaims that modules should be designed in order starting with the most general, overall module and working down to the nitty-gritty modules.

Proponents of top-down design have witnessed shameful wastes of time due to lack of planning. They've learned through painful experience that trying to correct programs after they've been written—a practice known as "patching"—is like locking the barn door after the horse has bolted.

So they offer as a countermeasure this official rule of top-down programming:

Write no code until you have planned every last detail.

Because programs are so difficult to change once they've been written, any design oversight at the preliminary planning stage should be revealed before the actual code-level modules are written, according to the top-down design. Otherwise, man-years of effort may be wasted writing code that cannot be used.

Subroutines

We've been discussing "modules" as abstract entities only. But all high-level programming languages incorporate techniques that allow modules of design to be coded as modules of code—discrete units that can be given names and "invoked" by other pieces of code. These units are called subroutines, procedures, or functions, depending on the particular high-level language and on how they happen to be implemented.

Suppose we write "MAKE-CEREAL" as a subroutine. It might look something like this:

```
procedure make-cereal
    get clean bowl
    open cereal box
    pour cereal
    open milk
    pour milk
    get spoon
end
```

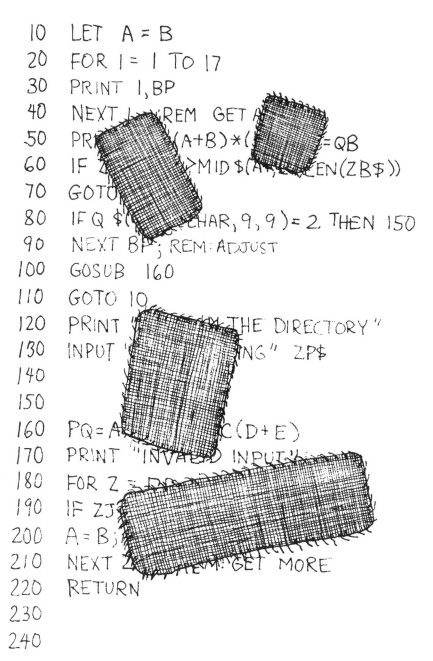

```
10    LET A = B
20    FOR I = 1 TO 17
30    PRINT I, BP
40    NEXT I ; REM  GET
50    PR        (A+B)*(        =QB
60    IF Z       >MID $(A,    EN(ZB$))
70    GOTO
80    IF Q $(     HAR, 9, 9 )= 2  THEN 150
90    NEXT BP ; REM: ADJUST
100   GOSUB  160
110   GOTO 10
120   PRINT          THE DIRECTORY "
130   INPUT             NG "  ZP$
140
150
160   PQ= A        C(D+E)
170   PRINT "INVALID INPUT"
180   FOR Z =
190   IF ZJ
200   A = B ;
210   NEXT Z       GET MORE
220   RETURN
230
240
```

Software patches are ugly and conceal structural weaknesses.

We can also write "MAKE-EGGS" and "CLEANUP" as subroutines. Elsewhere we can define "MAKE-BREAKFAST" as a simple routine that invokes, or calls, these subroutines:

```
procedure make-breakfast
    var h: boolean (indicates hurried)
    test for hurried
    if h = true then
      call make-cereal
    else
      call make-eggs
    end
    call cleanup
end
```

The phrase "call make-cereal" causes the subroutine named "make-cereal" to be executed. When the subroutine has finished being executed, control returns back to the calling program at the point following the call. Subroutines obey the rules of structured programming.

As you can see, the effect of the subroutine call is as if the subroutine code were written out in full within the calling module. But unlike the code produced by the macro assembler, the subroutine can be compiled elsewhere in memory and merely referenced. It doesn't necessarily have to be compiled within the object code of the main program (Figure 1-5).

Over the years computer scientists have become more forceful in favoring the use of many small subroutines over long-winded, continuous programs. Subroutines can be written and tested independently. This

Figure 1-5. *A main program and a subroutine in memory.*

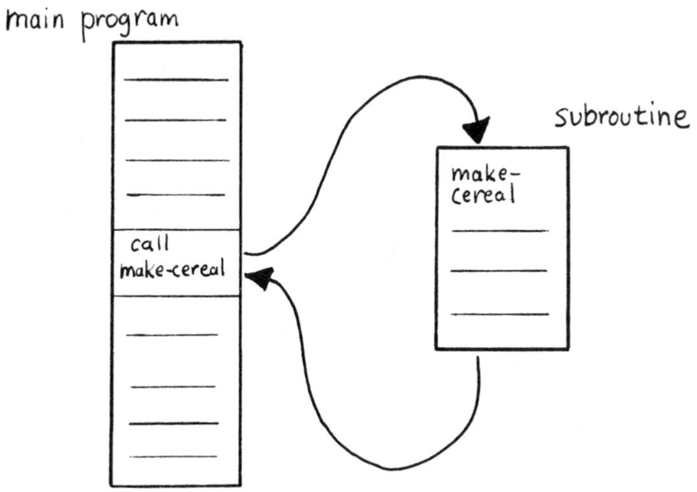

makes it easier to reuse parts of previously written programs, and easier to assign different parts of a program to different programmers. Smaller pieces of code are easier to think about and easier to verify for correctness.

When subroutines are compiled in separate parts of memory and referred to, you can invoke the same subroutine many times throughout a program without wasting space on repeated object code. Thus the judicious use of subroutines can also decrease program size.

Unfortunately, there's a penalty in execution speed when you use a subroutine. One problem is the overhead in saving registers before jumping to the subroutine and restoring them afterwards. Even more time-consuming is the invisible but significant code needed to pass parameters to and from the subroutine.

Subroutines are also fussy about how you invoke them, and particularly how you pass data to and from them. To test them independently, you need to write a special testing program to call them from.

For these reasons, computer scientists recommend their use in moderation. In practice, subroutines are usually fairly large, between a half page to a full page of source code in length.

Successive Refinement

An approach that relies heavily on subroutines is called "Successive Refinement" [2]. The idea is that you begin by writing a skeletal version of your program using natural names for procedures for data structures. Then you write versions of each of the named procedures. You continue this process to greater levels of detail until the procedures can only be written in the computer language itself.

At each step, the programmer must make decisions about the algorithms being used and about the data structures they're being used on. Decisions about the algorithms and associated data structures should be made in parallel.

If an approach doesn't work out, the programmer is encouraged to backtrack as far as necessary and start again.

Notice this about successive refinement: You can't actually run any part of the program until its lowest-level components are written. Typically this means you can't test the program until after you've completely designed it.

Also notice: Successive refinement forces you to work out all details of control structure on each level before proceeding to the next lower level.

Structured Design

By the middle of late '70s, the computing industry had tried all the concepts we've described, and it was still unhappy. The cost of maintaining software—keeping it functional in the face of change—accounted for

"*Dr. Tobias, I think you've carried the successive refinement of that module far enough.*"

more than half of the total cost of software, in some estimates as much as ninety percent!

Everyone agreed that these atrocities could usually be traced back to incomplete analysis of the program, or poorly thought-out designs. Not that there was anything wrong with structured programming *per se.* When projects came in late, incomplete, or incorrect, the designers took the blame for not anticipating the unforeseen.

Scholars naturally responded by placing more emphasis on design. "Next time let's think things out better."

About this time a new philosophy arose, described in an article called "Structured Design" [3]. One of its principles is stated in this paragraph:

> Simplicity is the primary measurement recommended for evaluating alternative designs relative to reduced debugging and modification time. Simplicity can be enhanced by dividing the system into separate pieces in such a way that pieces can be considered, implemented, fixed, and changed with minimal consideration or effect on the other pieces of the system.

By dividing a problem into simple modules, programs were expected to be easier to write, easier to change, and easier to understand.

But what is a module, and on what basis does one make the divisions? "Structured Design" outlines three factors for designing modules.

Functional Strength

One factor is something called "functional strength," which is a measure of the uniformity of purpose of all the statements within a module. If all the statements inside the module collectively can be thought of as performing a single task, they are functionally bound.

You can generally tell whether the statements in a module are functionally bound by asking the following questions: First, can you describe its purpose in one sentence? If not, the module is probably not functionally bound. Next, ask these four questions about the module:

1. Does the description have to be a compound sentence?
2. Does it use words involving time, such as "first", "next", "then," etc.?
3. Does it use a general or nonspecific object following the verb?
4. Does it use words like "initialize" which imply a lot of different functions being done at the same time?

If the answer to any of these four questions is "yes," you're looking at some less cohesive type of binding than functional binding. Weaker forms of binding include:

> *Coincidental binding:* (the statements just happen to appear in the same module)

Logical binding: (the module has several related functions and requires a flag or parameter to decide which particular function to perform)

Temporal binding: (the module contains a group of statements that happen at the same time, such as initialization, but have no other relationship)

Communicational binding: (the module contains a group of statements that all refer to the same set of data)

Sequential binding: (where the output of one statement serves as input for the next statement).

Our "MAKE-CEREAL" module exhibits functional binding, because it can be thought of as doing one thing, even though it consists of several subordinate tasks.

Coupling

A second tenet of structured design concerns "coupling," a measure of how modules influence the behavior of other modules. Strong coupling is considered bad form. The worst case is when one module actually modifies code inside another module. Even passing control flags to other modules with the intent to control their function is dangerous.

An acceptable form of coupling is "data coupling," which involves passing data (not control information) from one module to another. Even then, systems are easiest to build and maintain when the data interfaces between modules are as simple as possible.

When data can be accessed by many modules (for instance, global variables), there's stronger coupling between the modules. If a programmer needs to change one module, there's a greater danger that the other modules will exhibit "side effects."

The safest kind of data coupling is the passing of local variables as parameters from one module to another. The calling module says to the subordinate module, in effect, "I want you to use the data I've put in these variables named X and Y, and when you're done, I expect you to have put the answer in the variable named Z. No one else will use these variables."

As we said, conventional languages that support subroutines include elaborate methods of passing arguments from one module to another.

Hierarchical Input-Process-Output Designing

A third precept of structured design concerns the design process. Designers are advised to use a top-down approach, but to pay less attention initially to control structures. "Decision designing" can wait until the later, detailed design of modules. Instead, the early design should focus on the program's hierarchy (which modules call which modules) and to the passing of data from one module to another.

To help designers think along these new lines, a graphic representation was invented, called the "structure chart." (A slightly different form

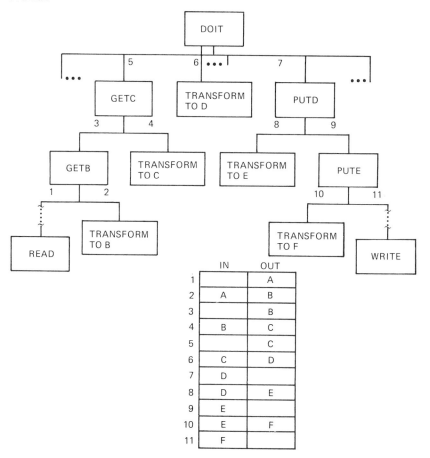

is called the "HIPO chart," which stands for "hierarchical input-process-output.") Structure charts include two parts, a hierarchy chart and an input-output chart.

Figure 1–6 shows these two parts. The main program, called DOIT, consists of three subordinate modules, which in turn invoke the other modules shown below them. As you can see, the design emphasizes the transformation of input to output.

The tiny numbers of the hierarchy chart refer to the lines on the in-out chart. At point 1 (the module READ), the output is the value A. At point 2 (the module TRANSFORM-TO-B), the input is A, and the output is B.

Perhaps the greatest contribution of this approach is recognizing that decisions about control flow should not dominate the emerging design. As we'll see, control flow is a superficial aspect of the problem. Minor changes in the requirements can profoundly change the program's control structures, and "deep-six" years of work. But if programs are designed around other concerns, such as the flow of data, then a change in plan won't have so disastrous an effect.

Information-Hiding

In a paper [4] published back in 1972, Dr. David L. Parnas showed that the criteria for decomposing modules should not be steps in the process, but rather pieces of information that might possibly change. Modules should be used to hide such information.

Let's look at this important idea of "information-hiding": Suppose you're writing a Procedures Manual for your company. Here's a portion:

> Sales Dept. takes order
> sends blue copy to Bookkeeping
> orange copy to Shipping
>
> Jay logs the orange copy in the red binder on his desk, and completes packing slip.

Everyone agrees that this procedure is correct, and your manual gets distributed to everyone in the company.

Then Jay quits, and Marilyn takes over. The new duplicate forms have green and yellow sheets, not blue and orange. The red binder fills up and gets replaced with a black one.

Your entire manual is obsolete. You could have avoided the obsolescence by using the term "Shipping Clerk" instead of the name "Jay," the terms "Bookkeeping Dept. copy" and "Shipping Dept. copy" instead of "blue" and "orange," etc.

This example illustrates that in order to maintain correctness in the face of a changing environment, arbitrary details should be excluded from procedures. The details can be recorded elsewhere if necessary. For instance, every week or so the personnel department might issue a list of employees and their job titles, so anyone who needed to know who the shipping clerk was could look it up in this single source. As the personnel changes, this list would change.

This technique is very important in writing software. Why would a program ever need to change, once it's running? For any of a million reasons. You might want to run an old program on new equipment; the program must be changed just enough to accommodate the new hardware. The program might not be fast enough, or powerful enough, to suit the people who are using it. Most software groups find themselves writing "families" of programs; that is, many versions of related programs in their particular application field, each a variant on an earlier program.

To apply the principle of information-hiding to software, certain details of the program should be confined to a single location, and any useful piece of information should be expressed only once. Programs that ignore this maxim are guilty of redundancy. While hardware redundancy (backup computers, etc.) can make a system more secure, redundancy of information is dangerous.

As any knowledgeable programmer will tell you, a number that a program uses and that might conceivably change should be made into a "constant" and referred to throughout the program by name, not by value. For instance, the number of columns representing the width of your computer paper forms should be expressed as a constant. Even assembly languages provide "EQU"'s and labels for associating values such as addresses and bit-patterns with names.

Any good programmer will also apply the concept of information-hiding to the development of subroutines, ensuring that each module knows as little as possible about the insides of other modules. Contemporary programming languages such as C, Modula 2, and Edison apply this concept to the architecture of their procedures.

But Parnas takes the idea much further. He suggests that the concept should be extended to algorithms and data structures. In fact, hiding information—not decision-structure or calling-hierarchy—should be the primary basis for design!

The Superficiality of Structure

Parnas proposes two criteria for decomposition:

    a. possible (though currently unplanned) reuse, and
    b. possible (though unplanned) change.

This new view of a "module" is different than the traditional view. This "module" is a collection of routines, usually very small, which together hide information about some aspect of the problem.

Two other writers describe the same idea in a different way, using the term "data abstraction" [5]. Their example is a push-down stack. The stack "module" consists of routines to initialize the stack, push a value onto the stack, pop a value from the stack, and determine whether the stack is empty. This "multiprocedure module" hides the information of how the stack is constructed from the rest of the application. The procedures are considered to be a single module because they are interdependent. You can't change the method for pushing a value without also changing the method for popping a value.

The word *uses* plays an important role in this concept. Parnas writes in a later paper [6]:

> Systems that have achieved a certain "elegance"... have done so by having parts of the system "use" other parts ...

> If such a hierarchical ordering exists, then each level offers a testable and usable subset of the system ...

The design of the "uses" hierarchy should be one of the major milestones in a design effort. The division of the system into independently callable subprograms has to go in parallel with the decisions about *uses,* because they influence each other.

A design in which modules are grouped according to control flow or sequence will not readily allow design changes. Structure, in the sense of control-flow hierarchy, is superficial.

A design in which modules are grouped according to things that may change can readily accommodate change.

Looking Back, and FORTH

In this section we'll review the fundamental features of FORTH and relate them to what we've seen about traditional methodologies.

Here's an example of FORTH code:

```
: BREAKFAST
    HURRIED?  IF  CEREAL  ELSE  EGGS  THEN    CLEAN ;
```

This is structurally identical to the procedure MAKE-BREAKFAST on page 8. (If you're new to FORTH, refer to Appendix A for an explanation.)

The words HURRIED?, CEREAL, EGGS, and CLEAN are (most likely) also defined as colon definitions.

Up to a point, FORTH exhibits all the traits we've studied: mnemonic value, abstraction, power, structured control operators, strong functional binding, limited coupling, and modularity. But regarding modularity, we encounter what may be FORTH's most significant breakthrough:

> The smallest atom of a FORTH program is not a module or a subroutine or a procedure, but a "word."

Furthermore, there are no subroutines, main programs, utilities, or executives, each of which must be invoked differently. *Everything* in FORTH is a word.

Before we explore the significance of a word-based environment, let's first study two FORTH inventions that make it possible.

Implicit Calls

First, calls are implicit. You don't have to say CALL CEREAL, you simply say CEREAL. In FORTH, the definition of CEREAL "knows" what kind of word it is and what procedure to use to invoke itself.

Thus variables and constants, system functions, utilities, as well as any user-defined commands or data structures can all be "called" simply by name.

Implicit Data Passing

Second, data passing is implicit. The mechanism that produces this effect is FORTH's data stack. FORTH automatically pushes numbers onto the stack; words that require numbers as input automatically pop them off the stack; words that produce numbers as output automatically push them onto the stack. The words PUSH and POP do not exist in high-level FORTH.

Thus we can write

```
: DOIT
     GETC   TRANSFORM-TO-D   PUT-D ;
```

confident that GETC will get "C", and leave it on the stack. TRANSFORM—TO—D will pick up "C" from the stack, transform it, and leave "D" on the stack. Finally, PUT—D will pick up "D" on the stack and write it. FORTH eliminates the act of passing data from our code, leaving us to concentrate on the functional steps of the data's transformation.

Because FORTH uses a stack for passing data, words can nest within words. Any word can put numbers on the stack and take them off without upsetting the flow of data between words at a higher level (provided, of course, that the word doesn't consume or leave any unexpected values). Thus the stack supports structured, modular programming while providing a simple mechanism for passing local arguments.

FORTH eliminates from our programs the details of *how* words are invoked and *how* data are passed. What's left? Only the words that describe our problem.

Having words, we can fully exploit the recommendations of Parnas—to decompose problems according to things that may change, and have each "module" consist of many small functions, as many as are needed to hide information about that module. In FORTH we can write as many words as we need to do that, no matter how simple each of them may be.

A line from a typical FORTH application might read:

```
20 ROTATE LEFT TURRET
```

Few other languages would encourage you to concoct a subroutine called LEFT, merely as a modifier, or a subroutine called TURRET, merely to name part of the hardware.

Since a FORTH word is easier to invoke than a subroutine (simply by being named, not by being called), a FORTH program is likely to be decomposed into more words than a conventional program would be into subroutines.

Component Programming

Having a larger set of simpler words makes it easy to use a technique we'll call "component programming." To explain, let's first reexamine these collections we have vaguely described as "things that may change." In a typical system, just about everything is subject to change: I/O devices such as terminals and printers, interfaces such as UART chips, the operating system, any data structure or data representation, any algorithm, etc.

The question is: "How can we minimize the impact of any such change? What is the smallest set of other things that must change along with such a change?"

The answer is: "The smallest set of interacting data structures and algorithms that share knowledge about how they collectively work." We'll call this unit a "component."

A component is a resource. It may be a piece of hardware such as a UART or a hardware stack. Or the component may be a software resource such as a queue, a dictionary, or a software stack.

All components involve data objects and algorithms. It doesn't matter whether the data object is physical (such as a hardware register), or abstract (such as a stack location or a field in a data base). It doesn't matter whether the algorithm is described in machine code or in problem-oriented words such as CEREAL and EGGS.

Figure 1–7 contrasts the results of structured design with the results of designing by components. Instead of *modules* called READ–RECORD, EDIT–RECORD, and WRITE–RECORD, we're concerned with *components* that describe the structure of records, provide a set of editor commands, and provide read/write routines to storage.

What have we done? We've inserted a new stage in the development process: We decomposed by components in our *design*, then we described the sequence, hierarchy, and input-process-output in our *implementation*. Yes, it's an extra step, but we now have an extra dimension for decomposition—not just slicing but *dicing*.

Suppose that, after the program is written, we need to change the record structure. In the sequential, hierarchical design, this change would affect all three modules. In the design by components, the change would be confined to the record-structure component. No code that uses this component needs to know of the change.

Aside from maintenance, an advantage to this scheme is that programmers on a team can be assigned components individually, with less interdependence. The principle of component programming applies to team management as well as to software design.

Figure 1-7. *Structured design vs. component design.*

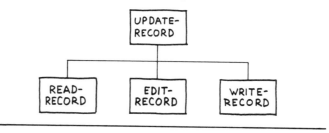

Sequential/Hierarchical Design:

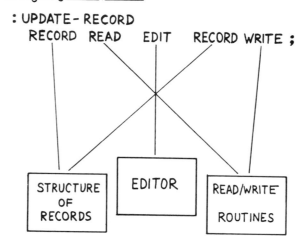

Design by Components:

We'll call the set of words which describe a component a "lexicon." (One meaning of lexicon is "a set of words pertaining to a particular field of interest.") The lexicon is your interface with the component from the outside (Figure 1-8).

In this book, the term "lexicon" refers only to those words of a component that are used by name outside of a component. A component may also contain definitions written solely to support the externally visible lexicon. We'll call the supporting definitions "internal" words.

The lexicon provides the logical equivalents to the data objects and algorithms in the form of names. The lexicon veils the component's data structures and algorithms—the "how it works." It presents to the world only a "conceptual model" of the component described in simple words—the "what it does."

These words then become the language for describing the data structures and algorithms of components written at a higher level. The "what" of one component becomes the "how" of a higher component.

Written in FORTH, an entire application consists of nothing but components. Figure 1-9 shows how a robotics application might be decomposed.

Figure 1-8. *A lexicon describes a component.*

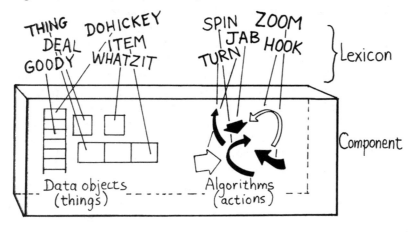

Figure 1-9. *The entire application consists of components.*

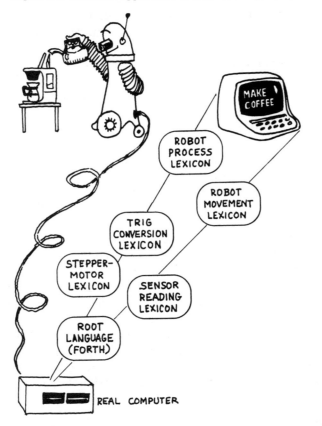

You could even say that each lexicon is a special-purpose compiler, written solely for the purpose of supporting higher-level application code in the most efficient and reliable way.

By the way, FORTH itself doesn't support components. It doesn't need to. Components are the product of the program designer's decomposition. (FORTH does have "screens," however—small units of mass storage for saving source code. A component can usually be written in one or two screens of FORTH.)

It's important to understand that a lexicon can be used by any and all of the components at higher levels. Each successive component does *not* bury its supporting components, as is often the case with layered approaches to design. Instead, each lexicon is free to use all of the commands beneath it. The robot-movement command relies on the root language, with its variables, constants, stack operators, math operators, and so on, as heavily as any other component.

An important result of this approach is that the entire application employs a single syntax, which makes it easy to learn and maintain. This is why I use the term "lexicon" and not "language." Languages have unique syntaxes.

This availability of commands also makes the process of testing and debugging a whole lot easier. Because FORTH is interactive, the programmer can type and test the primitive commands, such as

```
RIGHT SHOULDER 20 PIVOT
```

from the "outside" as easily as the more powerful ones like

```
LIFT COFFEE-POT
```

At the same time, the programmer can (if he or she wants) deliberately seal any commands, including FORTH itself, from being accessed by the end user, once the application is complete.

Now FORTH's methodology becomes clear. FORTH programming consists of extending the root language toward the application, providing new commands that can be used to describe the problem at hand.

Programming languages designed especially for particular applications such as robotics, inventory control, statistics, etc., are known as "application-oriented languages." FORTH is a programming environment for *creating* application-oriented languages. (That last sentence may be the most succinct description of FORTH that you'll find.)

In fact, you shouldn't write any serious application in FORTH; as a language it's simply not powerful enough. What you *should* do is write your own languages in FORTH (lexicons) to model your understanding of the problem, in which you can elegantly describe its solution.

Hide From Whom?

Because modern mainstream languages give a slightly different meaning to the phrase "information-hiding," we should clarify. From what, or whom, are we hiding the information?

The newest traditional languages (such as Modula 2) bend over backwards to ensure that modules hide internal routines and data structures from other modules. The goal is to achieve module independence (a minimum of coupling). The fear seems to be that modules strive to attack each other like alien antibodies. Or else, that evil bands of marauding modules are out to clobber the precious family data structures.

This is *not* what we're concerned about. The purpose of hiding information, as we mean it, is simply to minimize the effects of a possible design-change by localizing things that might change within each component.

FORTH programmers generally prefer to keep the program under their own control and not to employ any techniques to physically hide data structures. (Nevertheless a brilliantly simple technique for adding Modula-type modules to FORTH has been implemented, in only three lines of code, by Dewey Val Shorre [7].)

Hiding the Construction of Data Structures

We've noted two inventions of FORTH that make possible the methodology we've described—implicit calls and implicit data passing. A third feature allows the data structures within a component to be described in terms of previously-defined components. This feature is direct access of memory.

Suppose we define a variable called APPLES, like this:

```
VARIABLE APPLES
```

We can store a number into this variable to indicate how many apples we currently have:

```
20 APPLES !
```

We can display the contents of the variable:

```
APPLES ? 20 ok
```

We can up the count by one:

```
1 APPLES +!
```

(The newcomer can study the mechanics of these phrases in Appendix A.)

The word APPLES has but one function: to put on the stack the *address* of the memory location where the tally of apples is kept. The tally can be thought of as a "thing," while the words that set the tally, read the tally, or increment the tally can be considered as "actions."

FORTH conveniently separates "things" from "actions" by allowing addresses of data structures to be passed on the stack and providing the "fetch" and "store" commands.

We've discussed the importance of designing around things that may change. Suppose we've written a lot of code using this variable APPLES. And now, at the eleventh hour, we discover that we must keep track of two different kinds of apples, red and green!

We needn't wring our hands, but rather remember the function of APPLES: to provide an address. If we need two separate tallies, APPLES can supply two different addresses depending on which kind of apple we're currently talking about. So we define a more complicated version of APPLES as follows:

```
VARIABLE COLOR   ( pointer to current tally)
VARIABLE REDS    ( tally of red apples)
VARIABLE GREENS  ( tally of green apples)
: RED   ( set apple-type to RED)   REDS COLOR ! ;
: GREEN  ( set apple-type to GREEN)  GREENS COLOR ! ;
: APPLES  (  -- adr of current apple tally)   COLOR @
```

Figure 1-10. *Changing the indirect pointer.*

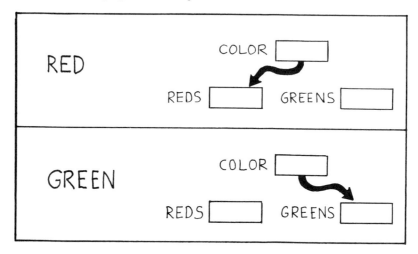

Here we've redefined APPLES. Now it fetches the contents of a variable called COLOR. COLOR is a pointer, either to the variable REDS or to the variable GREENS. These two variables are the real tallies.

If we first say RED, then we can use APPLES to refer to red apples. If we say GREEN, we can use it to refer to green apples (Figure 1-10).

We didn't need to change the syntax of any of the existing code that uses APPLES. We can still say

```
20 APPLES !
```

and

```
1 APPLES +!
```

Look again at what we did. We changed the definition of APPLES from that of a variable to a colon definition, without affecting its usage. FORTH allows us to hide the details of how APPLES is defined from the code that uses it. What appears to be a "thing" (a variable) to the original code is actually defined as an "action" (a colon definition) within the component.

FORTH encourages the use of abstract data types by allowing data structures to be defined in terms of lower level components. Only FORTH, which eliminates the CALLs from procedures, which allows addresses and data to be implicitly passed via the stack, and which provides direct access to memory locations with @ and !, can offer this level of information-hiding.

FORTH pays little attention to whether something is a data structure or an algorithm. This indifference allows us programmers incredible freedom in creating the parts of speech we need to describe our applications.

I tend to think of any word which returns an address, such as APPLES, as a "noun," regardless of how it's defined. A word that performs an obvious action is a "verb."

Words such as RED and GREEN in our example can only be called "adjectives" since they modify the function of APPLES. The phrase

```
RED APPLES ?
```

is different from

```
GREEN APPLES ?
```

FORTH words can also serve as adverbs and prepositions. There's little value in trying to determine what part of speech a particular word is, since FORTH doesn't care anyway. We need only enjoy the ease of describing an application in natural terms.

But Is It a High-Level Language?

In our brief historical overview, we noted that traditional high-level languages broke away from assembly language by eliminating not only the *one-for-one* correspondence between commands and machine operations, but also the *linear* correspondence. Clearly FORTH lays claim to the first difference; but regarding the second, the order of words that you use in a definition is the order in which those commands are compiled.

Two points of view.

Does this disqualify FORTH from the ranks of high-level languages? Before we answer, let's explore the advantages of the FORTH approach.

Here's what Charles Moore, the inventor of FORTH, has to say:

> You define each word so that the computer knows what it means. The way it knows is that it executes some code as a consequence of being invoked. The computer takes an action on every word. It doesn't store the word away and keep it in mind for later.
>
> In a philosophical sense I think this means that the computer "understands" a word. It understands the word **DUP**, perhaps more profoundly than you do, because there's never any question in its mind what **DUP** means.
>
> The connection between words that have meaning to you and words that have meaning to the computer is a profound one. The computer becomes the vehicle for communication between human being and concept.

One advantage of the correspondence between source code and machine execution is the tremendous simplification of the compiler and interpreter. This simplification improves performance in several ways, as we'll see in a later section.

From the standpoint of programming methodology, the advantage to the FORTH approach is that *new* words and *new* syntaxes can easily be added. FORTH cannot be said to be "looking" for words—it finds words and executes them. If you add new words FORTH will find and execute them as well. There's no difference between existing words and words that you add.

What's more, this "extensibility" applies to all types of words, not just action-type functions. For instance, FORTH allows you to add new *compiling* words—like **IF** and **THEN** that provide structured control flow. You can easily add a case statement or a multiple-exit loop if you need them, or, just as importantly, take them out if you don't need them.

By contrast, any language that depends on word order to understand a statement must "know" all legal words and all legal combinations. Its chances of including all the constructs you'd like are slim. The language exists as determined by its manufacturer; you can't expand its knowledge.

Laboratory researchers cite flexibility and extensibility as among FORTH's most important benefits in their environment. Lexicons can be developed to hide information about the variety of test equipment attached to the computer. Once this work has been done by a more experienced programmer, the researchers are free to use their "software toolbox" of small words to write simple programs for experimentation. As new equipment appears, new lexicons are added.

Mark Bernstein has described the problem of using an off-the-shelf special-purpose procedure library in the laboratory [8]: "The computer, not the user, dominates the experiment." But with FORTH, he writes, "the computer actually encourages scientists to modify, repair, and improve software, to experiment with and characterize their equipment.

Two solutions to the problem of security.

Initiative becomes once more the prerogative of the researcher."

For those purists who believe FORTH isn't fit to be called a high-level language, FORTH makes matters even worse. While strong syntax checking and data typing are becoming one of the major thrusts of contemporary programming languages, FORTH does almost no syntax checking at all. In order to provide the kind of freedom and flexibility we have described, it cannot tell you that you meant to type RED APPLES instead of APPLES RED. You have just invented that syntax!

Yet FORTH more than makes up for its omission by letting you compile each definition, one at a time, with turnaround on the order of seconds. You discover your mistake soon enough when the definition doesn't work. In addition, you can add appropriate syntax checking in your definitions if you want to.

An artist's paintbrush doesn't notify the artist of a mistake; the painter will be the judge of that. The chef's skillet and the composer's piano remain simple and yielding. Why let a programming language try to outthink you?

So, is FORTH a high-level language? On the question of syntax checking, it strikes out. On the question of abstraction and power, it seems to be of *infinite* level—supporting everything from bit manipulation at an output port to business applications.

You decide. (FORTH doesn't care.)

The Language of Design

FORTH is a design language. To the student of traditional computer science, this statement is self-contradictory. "One doesn't design with a language, one implements with a language. Design precedes implementation."

Experienced FORTH programmers disagree. In FORTH you can write abstract, design-level code and still be able to test it at any time by taking advantage of decomposition into lexicons. A component can easily be rewritten, as development proceeds, underneath any components that use it. At first the words in a component may print numbers on your terminal instead of controlling stepper motors. They may print their own names just to let you know they've executed. They may do nothing at all.

Using this philosophy you can write a simple but testable version of your application, then successively change and refine it until you reach your goal.

Another factor that makes designing in code possible is that FORTH, like some of the newer languages, eliminates the "batch-compile" development sequence (edit-compile-test-edit-compile-test). Because the feedback is instantaneous, the medium becomes a partner in the creative process. The programmer using a batch-compiler language can seldom achieve the productive state of mind that artists achieve when the creative current flows unhindered.

For these reasons, FORTH programmers spend less time planning than their classical counterparts, who feel righteous about planning. To them, not planning seems reckless and irresponsible. Traditional environments force programmers to plan because traditional programming languages do not readily accommodate change.

Unfortunately, human foresight is limited even under the best conditions. Too much planning becomes counterproductive.

Of course FORTH doesn't eliminate planning. It allows prototyping. Constructing a prototype is a more refined way to plan, just as breadboarding is in electronic design.

As we'll see in the next chapter, experimentation proves more reliable in arriving at the truth than the guesswork of planning.

The Language of Performance

Although performance is not the main topic of this book, the newcomer to FORTH should be reassured that its advantages aren't purely philosophical. Overall, FORTH outdoes all other high-level languages in speed, capability and compactness.

Speed

Although FORTH is an interpretive language, it executes compiled code. Therefore it runs about ten times faster than interpretive BASIC.

FORTH is optimized for the execution of words by means of a technique known as "threaded code" [9], [10], [11]. The penalty for modularizing into very small pieces of code is relatively slight.

It does not run as fast as assembler code because the inner interpreter (which interprets the list of addresses that comprise each colon definition) may consume up to 50% of the run time of primitive words, depending on the processor.

But in large applications, FORTH comes very close to the speed of assembler. Here are three reasons:

First and foremost, FORTH is simple. FORTH's use of a data stack greatly reduces the performance cost of passing arguments from word to word. In most languages, passing arguments between modules is one of the main reasons that the use of subroutines inhibits performance.

Second, FORTH allows you to define words either in high-level or in machine language. Either way, no special calling sequence is needed. You can write a new definition in high level and, having verified that it is correct, rewrite it in assembler without changing any of the code that uses it. In a typical application, perhaps 20% of the code will be running 80% of the time. Only the most often used, time-critical routines need to be machine coded. The FORTH system itself is largely implemented in machine-code definitions, so you'll have few application words that need to be coded in assembler.

The best top-down designs of mice and young men.

Third, FORTH applications tend to be better designed than those written entirely in assembler. FORTH programmers take advantage of the language's prototyping capabilities and try out several algorithms before settling on the one best suited for their needs. Because FORTH encourages change, it can also be called the language of optimization.

FORTH doesn't guarantee fast applications. It does give the programmer a creative environment in which to design fast applications.

Capability

FORTH can do anything any other language can do—usually easier.

At the low end, nearly all FORTH systems include assemblers. These support control-structure operators for writing conditionals and loops using structured programming techniques. They usually allow you to write interrupts—you can even write interrupt code in high level if desired.

Some FORTH systems are multitasked, allowing you to add as many foreground or background tasks as you want.

FORTH can be written to run on top of any operating system such as RT-11, CP/M, or MS-DOS—or, for those who prefer it, FORTH can be written as a self-sufficient operating system including its own terminal drivers and disk drivers.

With a FORTH cross-compiler or target compiler, you can use FORTH to recreate new FORTH systems, for the same computer or for different computers. Since FORTH is written in FORTH, you have the otherwise unthinkable opportunity to rewrite the operating system according to the needs of your application. Or you can transport streamlined versions of applications over to embedded systems.

Size

There are two considerations here: the size of the root FORTH system, and the size of compiled FORTH applications.

The FORTH nucleus is very flexible. In an embedded application, the part of FORTH you need to run your application can fit in as little as 1K. In a fuel development environment, a multitasked FORTH system including interpreter, compiler, assembler, editor, operating system, and all other support utilities averages 16K. This leaves plenty of room for applications. (And some FORTHs on the newer processors handle 32-bit addressing, allowing unimaginably large programs.)

Similarly, FORTH compiled applications tend to be very small—usually smaller than equivalent assembly language programs. The reason, again, is threaded code. Each reference to a previously defined word, no matter how powerful, uses only two bytes.

One of the most exciting new territories for FORTH is the production of FORTH chips such as the Rockwell R65F11 FORTH-based microprocessor [12]. The chip includes not only hardware features but also the run-time portions of the FORTH language and operating system for dedicated applications. Only FORTH's architecture and compactness make FORTH-based micros possible.

Summary

FORTH has often been characterized as offbeat, totally unlike any other popular language in structure or in philosophy. On the contrary, FORTH incorporates many principles now boasted by the most contemporary languages. Structured design, modularity, and information-hiding are among the buzzwords of the day.

Some newer languages approach even closer to the spirit of FORTH. The language C, for instance, lets the programmer define new functions either in C or in assembly language, as does FORTH. And as with FORTH, most of C is defined in terms of functions.

But FORTH extends the concepts of modularity and information-hiding further than any other contemporary language. FORTH even hides the manner in which words are invoked and the way local arguments are passed.

The resulting code becomes a concentrated interplay of words, the purest expression of abstract though. As a result, FORTH programmers tend to be more productive and to write tighter, more efficient, and better maintainable code.

FORTH may not be the ultimate language. But I believe the ultimate language, if such a thing is possible, will more closely resemble FORTH than any other contemporary language.

References

1. O.J. Dahl, E.W. Dijkstra, and C.A.R. Hoare, *Structured Programming*, London, Academic Press, 1972.
2. Niklaus Wirth, "Program Development by Stepwise Refinement," *Communications of ACM, 14*, No. 4 (1971), 221-27.
3. W.P. Stevens, G.J. Myers, and L.L. Constantine, "Structured Design," *IBM Systems Journal*, Vol. 13, No. 2, 1974.
4. David L. Parnas, "On the Criteria To Be Used in Decomposing Systems into Modules," *Communications of the ACM*, December 1972.
5. Barbara H. Liskov and Stephen N. Zilles, "Specification Techniques for Data Abstractions," *IEEE Transactions on Software Engineering*, March 1975.
6. David L. Parnas, "Designing Software for Ease of Extension and Contraction," *IEEE Transactions on Software Engineering*, March 1979.
7. Dewey Val Shorre, "Adding Modules to FORTH," 1980 FORML Proceedings, p. 71.

8. Mark Bernstein, "Programming in the Laboratory," unpublished paper, 1983.

9. James R. Bell, "Threaded Code," *Communications of ACM*, Vol. 16, No. 6, 370-72.

10. Robert B.K. DeWar, "Indirect Threaded Code," *Communications of ACM*, Vol. 18, No. 6, 331.

11. Peter M. Kogge, "An Architectural Trail to Threaded-Code Systems," *Computer*, March, 1982.

12. Randy Dumse, "The R65F11 FORTH Chip," *FORTH Dimensions*, Vol. 5, No. 2, p. 25.

TWO

Analysis

Anyone who tells you there is some definite number of phases to the software development cycle is a fool.

Nevertheless . . .

The Nine Phases of the Programming Cycle

As we've seen, FORTH integrates aspects of design with aspects of implementation and maintenance. As a result, the notion of a "typical development cycle" makes as much sense as a "typical noise."

But any approach is better than no approach, and indeed, some approaches have worked out better than others. Here is a development cycle that represents an "average" of the most successful approaches used in software projects:

Analysis
1. Discover the Requirements and Constraints
2. Build a Conceptual Model of the Solution
3. Estimate Cost/Schedule/Performance

Engineering
4. Preliminary Design
5. Detailed Design
6. Implementation

Usage
7. Optimization
8. Validation and Debugging
9. Maintenance

In this book we'll treat the first six stages of the cycle, focusing on analysis, design, and implementation.

In a FORTH project the phases occur on several levels. Looking at a project from the widest perspective, each of these steps could take a month or more. One step follows the next, like seasons.

But FORTH programmers also apply these same phases toward defining each word. The cycle then repeats on the order of minutes.

Developing an application with this rapid repetition of the programming cycle is known as using the "Iterative Approach."

The Iterative Approach

The iterative approach was explained eloquently by Kim Harris [1]. He begins by describing the scientific method:

> . . . a never-ending cycle of discovery and refinement. It first studies a natural system and gathers observations about its behavior. Then the observations are modeled to produce a theory about the natural system. Next, analysis tools are applied to the model, which produces predictions about the real system's behavior. Experiments are devised to compare actual behavior to the predicted behavior. The natural system is again studied, and the model is revised.
>
> The *goal* of the method is to produce a model which accurately predicts all observable behavior of the natural system.

Harris then applies the scientific method to the software development cycle, illustrated in Figure 2-1:

1. A problem is analyzed to determine what functions are required in the solution.
2. Decisions are made about how to achieve those functions with the available resources.
3. A program is written which attempts to implement the design.
4. The program is tested to determine if the functions were implemented correctly.

Figure 2-1. *The iterative approach to the software development cycle, from "The FORTH Philosophy," by Kim Harris,* Dr. Dobb's Journal.

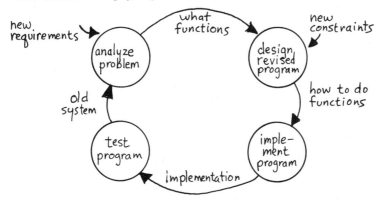

Mr. Harris adds:

> Software development in FORTH seeks first to find the simplest solution to a given problem. This is done by implementing selected parts of the problem separately and by ignoring as many constraints as possible. Then one or a few constraints are imposed and the program is modified.

An excellent testimonial to the development/testing model of design is evolution. From protozoa to tadpoles to people, each species along the way has consisted of functional, living beings. The Creator does not appear to be a top-down designer.

TIP

Start simple. Get it running. Learn what you're trying to do. Add complexity gradually, as needed to fit the requirements and constraints. Don't be afraid to restart from scratch.

The Value of Planning

In the nine phases at the start of this chapter we listed five steps *before* "implementation." Yet in Chapter One we saw that an overindulgence in planning is both difficult and pointless.

Clearly you can't undertake a significant software project—regardless of the language—without some degree of planning. Exactly what degree is appropriate?

More than one FORTH programmer has expressed high regard for Dave Johnson's meticulous approach to planning. Johnson is supervisor at Moore Products Co. in Springhouse, Pennsylvania. The firm specializes in industrial instrumentation and process control applications. Dave has been using FORTH since 1978.

He describes his approach:

> Compared with many others that use FORTH, I suppose we take a more formal approach. I learned this the hard way, though. My lack of discipline in the early years has come back to haunt me.
>
> We use two tools to come up with new products: a functional specification and a design specification. Our department of Sales & Applications comes up with the functional specification, through customer contact.
>
> Once we've agreed on what we're going to do, the functional specification is turned over to our department. At that point we work through a design, and come up with the design specification.
>
> Up to this point our approach is no different from programming in any language. But with FORTH, we go about designing somewhat differently. With FORTH you don't have to work 95% through your design before you can start coding, but rather 60% before you can get into the iterative process.

A typical project would be to add a functional enhancement to one of our products. For example, we have an intelligent terminal with disk drives, and we need certain protocols for communicating with another device. The project to design the protocols, come up with displays, provide the operator interfaces, etc. may take several months. The functional specification takes a month; the design specification takes a month; coding takes three months; integration and testing take another month.

This is the typical cycle. One project took almost two years, but six or seven months is reasonable.

When we started with FORTH five years ago, it wasn't like that. When I received a functional specification, I just started coding. I used a cross between top-down and bottom-up, generally defining a structure, and as I needed it, some of the lower level, and then returning with more structure.

The reason for that approach was the tremendous pressure to show something to management. We wound up never writing down what we were doing. Three years later we would go back and try to modify the code, without any documentation. FORTH became a disadvantage because it allowed us to go in too early. It was fun to make the lights flash and disk drives hum. But we didn't go through the nitty-gritty design work. As I said, our "free spirits" have come back to haunt us.

Now for the new programmers, we have an established requirement: a thorough design spec that defines in detail all the high-level FORTH words—the tasks that your project is going to do. No more reading a few pages of the functional specification, answering that, reading a few more, answering that, etc.

No living programmer likes to document. By ensuring the design ahead of time, we're able to look back several years later and remember what we did.

I should mention that during the design phase there is some amount of coding done to test out certain ideas. But this code may not be part of the finished product. The idea is to map out your design.

Johnson advises us to complete the design specification before starting to code, with the exception of needed preliminary tests. The next interview backs up this point, and adds some additional reasons.

John Teleska has been an independent software consultant since 1976, specializing in custom applications for academic research environments. He enjoys providing research tools "right at the edge of what technology is able to do." Teleska works in Rochester, New York:

I see the software development process as having two phases. The first is making sure I understand what the problem is. The second is implementation, including debugging, verification, etc.

My goal in Phase One is an operational specification. I start with a problem description, and as I proceed it becomes the operational specification. My understanding of the problem metamorphoses into a solution. The better the understanding, the more complete the solution. I look for closure; a sense of having no more questions that aren't answered in print.

I've found that on each project I've been putting more time into Phase One, much to the initial dismay of many of my clients. The limiting factor is how much I can convince the client it's necessary to spend that time up front. Customers generally don't know the specifications for the job they want done. And they don't have the capital—or don't feel they do—to spend on good specs. Part of my job is to convince them it will end up costing more time and money not to.

Some of Phase One is spent on feasibility studies. Writing the spec unearths uncertainties. I try to be as uncertain about uncertainties as possible. For instance, they may want to collect 200,000 samples a second to a certain accuracy. I first need to find out if it's even possible with the equipment they've got. In this case I've got to test its feasibility by writing a patch of code.

Another reason for the spec is to cover myself. In case the application performs to the spec but doesn't fully satisfy the customer, it's the customer's responsibility. If the customer wants more, we'll have to renegotiate. But I see it as the designer's responsibility to do whatever is necessary to generate an operational specification that will do the job to the customer's satisfaction.

I think there are consultants who bow to client pressure and limit the time they spend on specs, for fear of losing the job. But in these situations nobody ends up happy.

We'll return to the Teleska interview momentarily.

The Limitations of Planning

Experience has taught us to map out where we're going before we begin coding. But planning has certain limitations. The following interviews give different perspectives to the value of planning.

Despite Teleska's preference for a well-planned project, he suggests that the choice between a top-down and bottom-up approach may depend on the situation:

On two recent projects involving a lot of technical interface work, I did the whole thing bottom-up. I milled around in a bunch of data-sheets and technical descriptions of little crannies of the operating system I was dealing with. I felt lost most of the time, wondering why I ever took the job on. Then finally I reached a critical mass of some sort and began putting small programs together that made small things happen. I continued, bottom-up, until I matched the target application.

My top-down sense was appalled at this procedure. But I've seen me go through this process successfully too many times to discount it for any pedagogical reasons. And there is always this difficult phase which it seems no amount of linear thinking will penetrate. Programming seems a lot more intuitive than we, in this business, tell each other it ought to be.

I think if the application elicits this sense of being lost, I proceed bottom-up. If the application is in familiar territory then I'll probably use a more traditional by-the-book approach.

And here's another view:

At the time I interviewed him, Michael Starling of Union Carbide was putting the final touches on two applications involving user-configurable laboratory automation and process control automation systems. For the pilot plant system, Starling designed both the hardware and software to known requirements; on the laboratory automation system he also defined the requirements himself.

His efforts were extremely successful. On one project, the new system typically costs only 20% as much as the equivalent system and requires days, instead of months, to install and configure.

I asked him what techniques of project management he employed.

On both of these projects much design was needed. I did not follow the traditional analysis methods, however. I did employ these steps:

First, I clearly defined the boundaries of the problem.

Second, I determined what the smaller functional pieces, the software subsystems, had to be.

Third, I did each piece, put them together, and the system ran.

Next, I asked the users "Does this meet your requirements?" Sometimes it didn't, and in ways that neither the users nor the specification designers could have anticipated.

For instance, the designers didn't realize that the original specification wouldn't produce pleasing, human-oriented graphics displays. After working with the interactive graphics on the first version, users were applying arbitrary scales and coming up with oddball displays.

So even after the basic plot algorithm was designed, we realized we needed auto-scaling. We went back in and analyzed how human beings plot data and wrote a first level plot function that evaluates the x and y data and how much will fit on the graph.

After that, we realized that not all the data taken will be of interest to experimenters. So we added a zoom capability.

This iterative approach resulted in cleaner code and better thought out code. We established a baseline set of goals and built a minimal system to the users' known requirements. Then we'd crank in the programmer's experience to improve it and determine what the users forgot they needed when they generated the specs.

The users did not invent most of the new ideas. The programmers did, and they would bounce these ideas off the users. The problem definition was a two-way street. In some cases they got things they didn't know they could do on such a small computer, such as applying digital filters and signal processing to the data.

One of the things about FORTH that makes this approach possible is that primitives are easily testable. It takes some experience with FORTH to learn how to take advantage of this. Guys from traditional environments want to write ten pages of code at their desk, then sit down to type it in and expect it to work.

To summarize my approach: I try to find out from the users what they need, but at the same time recognizing its incompleteness. Then I keep them involved in the design during the implementation, since they have the expertise in the application.

When they see the result, they feel good because they know their ideas were involved.

The iterative approach places highest value on producing a good solution to the real problem. It may not always give you the most predictable software costs. The route to a solution may depend upon your priorities. Remember:

Good
Fast
Cheap

Pick any two!

As Starling observes, you don't know completely what you're doing till you've done it once. In my own experience, the best way to write an application is to write it twice. Throw away the first version and chalk it up to experience.

Peter Kogge is Senior Technical Staff in the IBM Federal Systems Division, Oswego, New York:

One of the key advantages I find in FORTH is that it allows me to very quickly prototype an application without all the bells and whistles, and often with significant limitations, but enough to wring out the "human interface" by hands-on trial runs.

When I build such a prototype, I do so with the firm constraint that I will use not a single line of code from the prototype in the final program. This enforced "do-over" almost always results in far simpler and more elegant final programs, even when those programs are written in something other than FORTH.

Our conclusions? In the FORTH environment planning is necessary. But it should be kept short. Testing and prototyping are the best ways to discover what is really needed.

A word of caution to project managers: If you're supervising any experienced FORTH programmers, you won't have to worry about them spending too much time on planning. Thus the following tip has two versions:

TIP

For newcomers to FORTH (with "traditional" backgrounds): Keep the analysis phase to a minimum.

For FORTH addicts (without a "traditional" background): Hold off on coding as long as you can possibly stand it.

Or, as we observed in Chapter One:

TIP

Plan for change (by designing components that can be changed).

Or, simply:

TIP

Prototype.

The Analysis Phase

In the remainder of this chapter we'll discuss the analysis phase. Analysis is an organized way of understanding and documenting what the program should do.

With a simple program that you write for yourself in less than an hour, the analysis phase may take about 250 microseconds. At the other extreme, some projects will take many man-years to build. On such a project, the analysis phase is critical to the success of the entire project.

We've indicated three parts to the analysis phase:

1. Discovering the requirements and constraints
2. Building a conceptual model of the solution
3. Estimating cost, scheduling, and performance

Let's briefly describe each part:

Discovering the Requirements

The first step is to determine what the application should do. The customer, or whoever wants the system, should supply a "requirements specification." This is a modest document that lists the minimum capabilities for the finished product.

The analyst may also probe further by conducting interviews and sending out questionnaires to the users.

Discovering the Constraints

The next step is to discover any limiting factors. How important is speed? How much memory is available? How soon do you need it?

No matter how sophisticated our technology becomes, programmers will always be bucking limitations. System capacities inexplicably diminish over time. The double-density disk drives that once were the answer to my storage prayers no longer fill the bill. The double-sided, double-density drives I'll get next will seem like a vast frontier—for a while. I've heard guys with 10-megabyte hard disks complain of feeling cramped.

Whenever there's a shortage of something—and there always will be—tradeoffs have to be made. It's best to use the analysis phase to anticipate most limitations and decide which tradeoffs to make.

On the other hand, you should *not* consider other types of constraints during analysis, but should instead impose them gradually during implementation, the way one stirs flour into gravy.

The type of constraint to consider during analysis includes those that might affect the overall approach. The type of defer includes those that can be handled by making iterative refinements to the planned software design.

As we heard in our earlier interviews, finding out about *hardware* constraints often requires writing some test code and trying things out. Finding out about the *customer's* constraints is usually a matter of asking the customer, or of taking written surveys. "How fast do you need such-and-such, on a scale of one to ten?", etc.

Building a Conceptual Model of the Solution

A conceptual model is an imaginary solution to the problem. It is a view of how the system *appears* to work. It is an answer to all the requirements and constraints.

If the requirements definition is for "something to stand on to paint the ceiling," then a description of the conceptual model is "a device that is free-standing (so you can paint the center of the room), with several steps spaced at convenient intervals (so you can climb up and down), and having a small shelf near the top (to hold your paint can)."

A conceptual model is not quite a design, however. A design begins to describe how the system *really* works. In design, the image of a step ladder would begin to emerge.

FORTH blurs the distinction a little, because all definitions are written in conceptual terms, using the lexicons of lower level components. In fact, later in this chapter we'll use FORTH "pseudocode" to describe conceptual model solutions.

Nevertheless, it's useful to make the distinction. A conceptual model is more flexible than a design. It's easier to fit the requirements and constraints into the model than into a design.

TIP

Strive to build a solid conceptual model before beginning the design.

Refining the conceptual model to meet requirements and constraints.

Analysis consists of expanding the requirements definition into a conceptual model. The technique involves two-way communication with the customer in successive attempts to describe the model.

Like the entire development cycle, the analysis phase is best approach iteratively. Each new requirement will tend to suggest something in your mental model. Your job is to juggle all the requirements and constraints until you can weave a pattern that fits the bill.

Figure 2–2 illustrates the iterative approach to the analysis phase. The final step is one of the most important: show the documented model to the customer. Use whatever means of communication are necessary—diagrams, tables, or cartoons—to convey your understanding to the customer and get the needed feedback. Even if you cycle through this loop a hundred times, it's worth the effort.

In the next three sections we'll explore three techniques for defining and documenting the conceptual model:

1. defining the interfaces
2. defining the rules
3. defining the data structures.

Defining the Interfaces

TIP

First, and most importantly, the conceptual model should describe the system's interfaces.

Teleska:

The "spec" basically deals with WHAT. In its most glorious form, it describes what the system would look like to the user—you might call it the user's manual. I find I write more notes on the human interaction—what it

Figure 2-2. *An iterative approach to analysis.*

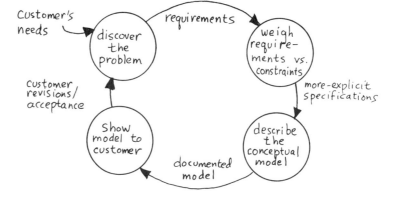

will look like on the outside—than on the part that gets the job done. For instance, I'll include a whole error-action listing to show what happens when a particular error occurs. Oddly, this is the part that takes the most time to implement anyway.

I'm currently working on a solid-state industrial washing-machine timer. In this case, the user interface is not that complex. What is complex is the interface to the washing machine, for which I must depend on the customer and the documentation they can provide.

The significant interface is whatever is the arms and legs of the product. I don't make the distinction between hardware and software at this early stage. They can be interchanged in the implementation.

The process of designing hardware and the process of designing software are analogous. The way I design hardware is to treat it as a black box. The front panel is input and output. You can do the same with software.

I use any techniques, diagrams, etc., to show the customer what the inputs and outputs look like, using his description of what the product has to do. But in parallel, in my own mind, I'm imagining how it will be implemented. I'm evaluating whether I can do this efficiently. So to me it's not a black box, it's a grey box. The designer must be able to see inside the black boxes.

When I design a system that's got different modules, I try to make the coupling as rational and as little as possible. But there's always give and take, since you're compromising the ideal.

For the document itself, I use DFDs [data-flow diagrams, which we'll discuss later], and any other kind of representation that I can show to my client. I show them as many diagrams as I can to clarify my understanding. I don't generally use these once it comes to implementation. The prose must be complete, even without reference to the diagrams.

TIP

Decide on error- and exception-handling early as part of defining the interface.

It's true that when coding for oneself, a programmer can often concentrate first on making the code run correctly under *normal* conditions, then worry about error-handling later. When working for someone else, however, error-handling should be worked out ahead of time. This is an area often overlooked by the beginning programmer.

The reason it's so important to decide on error-handling at this stage is the wide divergence in how errors can be treated. An error might be:

- ignored
- made to set a flag indicating that an error occurred, while processing continues
- made to halt the application immediately
- designed to initiate procedures to correct the problem and keep the program running.

There's room for a serious communications gap if the degree of complexity required in the error-handling is not nailed down early. Obviously, the choice bears tremendous impact on the design and implementation of the application.

TIP

Develop the conceptual model by imagining the data traveling through and being acted upon by the parts of the model.

A discipline called *structured analysis* [2] offers some techniques for describing interfaces in ways that your clients will easily understand. One of these techniques is called the "data-flow diagram" (DFD), which Teleska mentioned.

A data-flow diagram, such as the one depicted in Figure 2-3, emphasizes what happens to items of data as they travel through the system. The circles represent "transforms," functions that act upon information. The arrows represent the inputs and outputs of the transforms.

The diagram depicts a frozen moment of the system in action. It ignores initialization, looping structures, and other details of programming that relate to time.

Three benefits are claimed for using DFDs:

First, they speak in simple, direct terms to the customer. If your

Figure 2-3. *A data-flow diagram.*

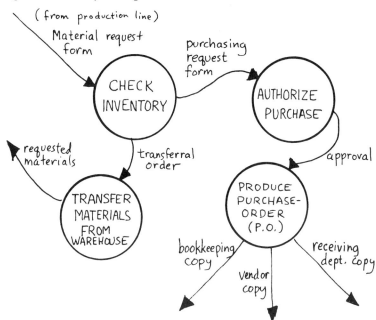

customer agrees with the contents of your data-flow diagram, you know you understand the problem.

Second, they let you think in terms of the logical "whats," without getting caught up in the procedural "hows," which is consistent with the philosophy of hiding information as we discussed in the last chapter.

Third, they focus your attention on the interfaces to the system and between modules.

FORTH programmers, however, rarely use DFDs except for the customer's benefit. FORTH encourages you to think in terms of the conceptual model, and FORTH's implicit use of a data stack makes the passing of data among modules so simple it can usually be taken for granted. This is because FORTH, used properly, approaches a functional language.

For anyone with a few days' familiarity with FORTH, simple definitions convey at least as much meaning as the diagrams:

```
: REQUEST  ( quantity part# -- )
   ON-HAND?  IF  TRANSFER  ELSE  REORDER  THEN ;
: REORDER   AUTHORIZATION?  IF  P.O.  THEN ;
: P.O.   BOOKKEEPING COPY   RECEIVING COPY
   VENDOR MAIL-COPY ;
```

This if FORTH pseudocode. No effort has been made to determine what values are actually passed on the stack, because that is an implementation detail. The stack comment for REQUEST is used only to indicate the two items of data needed to initiate the process.

(If I were designing this application, I'd suggest that the user interface be a word called NEED, which has this syntax:

```
NEED 50 AXLES
```

NEED converts the quantity into a numeric value on the stack, translates the string AXLES into a part number, also on the stack, then calls REQUEST. Such a command should be defined only at the outermost level.)

Johnson of Moore Products Co. has a few words on FORTH pseudocode:

IBM uses a rigorously documented PDL (program design language). We use a PDL here as well, although we call it FDL, for FORTH design language. It's probably worthwhile having all those standards, but once you're familiar with FORTH, FORTH itself can be a design language. You just have to leave out the so-called "noise" words: C@, DUP, OVER, etc., and show only the basic flow. Most FORTH people probably do that informally. We do it purposefully.

During one of our interviews I asked Moore if he used diagrams of any sort to plan out the conceptual model, or did he code straight into FORTH? His reply:

> The conceptual model *is* FORTH. Over the years I've learned to think that way.

Can everyone learn to think that way?

> I've got an unfair advantage. I codified my programming style and other people have adopted it. I was surprised that this happened. And I feel at a lovely advantage because it is my style that others are learning to emulate. Can they learn to think like I think? I imagine so. It's just a matter of practice, and I've had more practice.

Defining the Rules

Most of your efforts at defining a problem will center on describing the interface. Some applications will also require that you define the set of application rules.

All programming involves rules. Usually these rules are so simple it hardly matters how you express them: "If someone pushes the button, ring the bell."

Some applications, however, involve rules so complicated that they can't be expressed in a few sentences of English. A few formal techniques can come in handy to help you understand and document these more complicated rules.

Here's an example. Our requirements call for a system to compute the charges on long-distance phone calls. Here's the customer's explanation of its rate structure. (I made this up; I have no idea how the phone company actually computes their rates except that they overcharge.)

> All charges are computed by the minute, according to distance in hundreds of miles, plus a flat charge. The flat charge for direct dial calls during weekdays between 8 A.M. and 5 P.M. is .30 for the first minute, and .20 for each additional minute; in addition, each minute is charged .12 per 100 miles. The flat charge for direct calls during weekdays between 5 P.M. and 11 P.M. is .22 for the first minute, and .15 for each additional minute; the distance rate per minute is .10 per 100 miles. The flat charge for direct calls late during weekdays between 11 P.M. or anytime on Saturday, Sundays, or holidays is .12 for the first minute, and .09 for each additional minute; the distance rate per minute is .06 per 100 miles. If the call requires assistance from the operator, the flat charge increases by .90, regardless of the hour.

This description is written in plain old English, and it's quite a mouthful. It's hard to follow and, like an attic cluttered with accumulated belongings, it may even hide a few bugs.

In building a conceptual model for this system, we must describe the rate structure in an unambiguous, useful way. The first step towards cleaning up the clutter involves factoring out irrelevant pieces of information—that is, applying the rules of limited redundancy. We can improve this statement a lot by splitting it into two statements. First there's the time-of-day rule:

> Calls during weekdays between 8 A.M. and 5 P.M. are charged at "full" rate. Calls during weekdays between 5 P.M. and 11 P.M. are charged at "lower" rate. Calls placed during weekdays between 11 P.M. or anytime on Saturday, Sundays, or holidays are charged at the "lowest" rate.

Then there's the rate structure itself, which should be described in terms of "first-minute rate," "additional minute rate," "distance rate," and "operator-assistance rate."

TIP

Factor the fruit. (Don't confuse apples with oranges.)

These prose statements are still difficult to read, however. System analysts use several techniques to simplify these statements: structured English, decision trees, and decision tables. Let's study each of these techniques and evaluate their usefulness in the FORTH environment.

Structured English

Structured English is a sort of structured pseudocode in which our rate statement would read something like this:

```
IF full rate
   IF direct-dial
      IF first-minute
         .30 + .12/100miles
      ELSE ( add'l- minute)
         .20 + .12/100miles
      ENDIF
   ELSE ( operator)
      IF first-minute
         1.20 + .12/100miles
      ELSE ( add'l- minute)
         .20 + .12/100miles
      ENDIF
   ENDIF
ELSE   ( not-full-rate)
   IF lower-rate
      IF direct-dial
```

```
                IF first-minute
                    .22 + .10/100miles
                ELSE ( add'l- minute)
                    .15 + .10/100miles
                ENDIF
            ELSE ( operator)
                IF first-minute
                    1.12 + .10/100miles
                ELSE ( add'l- minute)
                    .15 + .10/100miles
                ENDIF
            ENDIF
        ELSE ( lowest-rate)
            IF direct-dial
                IF first-minute
                    .12 + .06/100miles
                ELSE ( add'l- minute)
                    .09 + .06/100miles
                ENDIF
            ELSE ( operator)
                IF first-minute
                    1.02 + .06/100miles
                ELSE ( add'l- minute)
                    .09 + .06/100miles
                ENDIF
            ENDIF
        ENDIF
    ENDIF
ENDIF
```

This is just plain awkward. It's hard to read, harder to maintain, and hardest to write. And for all that, it's worthless at implementation time. I don't even want to talk about it anymore.

The Decision Tree

Figure 2-4 illustrates the telephone rate rules by means of a decision tree. The decision tree is the easiest method of any to "follow down" to determine the result of certain conditions. For this reason, it may be the best representation to show the customer.

Unfortunately, the decision tree is difficult to "follow up," to determine which conditions produce certain results. This difficulty inhibits seeing ways to simplify the problem. The tree obscures the fact that additional minutes cost the same, whether the operator assists or not. You can't see the facts for the tree.

Figure 2-4. *Example of a decision tree.*

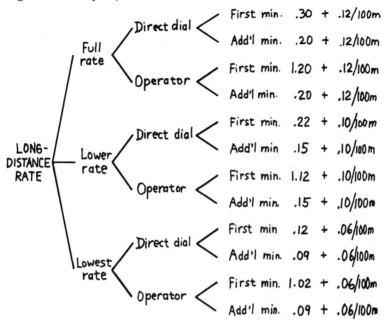

The Decision Table

The decision table, described next, provides the most usable graphic representation of compound rules for the programmer, and possibly for the customer as well. Figure 2–5 shows our rate structure rules in decision-table form.

In Figure 2–5 there are three dimensions: the rate discount, whether an operator intervenes, and initial minute vs. additional minute.

Drawing problems with more than two dimensions gets a little tricky. As you can see, these additional dimensions can be depicted on

Figure 2-5. *The decision table.*

	FULL RATE		LOWER RATE		LOWEST RATE	
	FIRST MIN.	ADD'L MIN	FIRST MIN.	ADD'L MIN.	FIRST MIN.	ADD'L MIN.
Direct Dial	.30 + .12/100m	.20 + .12/100m	.22 + .10/100m	.15 + .10/100m	.12 + .06/100m	.09 + .06/100m
Operator Assist	1.20 + .12/100m	.20+ .12/100m	1.12 + .10/100m	.15+ .10/100m	1.02 + .06/100m	.09 + .06/100m

paper as subdimensions within an outer dimension. All of the subdimension's conditions appear within every condition of the outer dimension. In software, any number of dimensions can be easily handled, as we'll see.

All the techniques we've described force you to analyze which conditions apply to which dimensions. In factoring these dimensions, two rules apply:

First, all the elements of each dimension must be mutually exclusive. You don't put "first minute" in the same dimension as "direct dial," because they are not mutually exclusive.

Second, all possibilities must be accounted for within each dimension. If there were another rate for calls made between 2 A.M. to 2:05 A.M., the table would have to be enlarged.

But our decision tables have other advantages all to themselves. The decision table not only reads well to the client but actually benefits the implementor in several ways:

Transferability to actual code. This is particularly true in FORTH, where decision tables are easy to implement in a form very similar to the drawing.

Ability to trace the logic upwards. Find a condition and see what factors produced it.

Clearer graphic representation. Decision tables serve as a better tool for understanding, both for the implementor and the analyst.

Unlike decision trees, these decision tables group the *results* together in a graphically meaningful way. Visualization of ideas helps in understanding problems, particularly those problems that are too complex to perceive in a linear way.

For instance, Figure 2–5 clearly shows that the charge for additional minutes does not depend on whether an operator assisted or not. With this new understanding we can draw a simplified table, as shown in Figure 2–6.

Figure 2-6. *A simplified decision table.*

	FULL RATE		LOWER RATE		LOWEST RATE	
	FIRST MIN.	ADD'L MIN	FIRST MIN.	ADD'L MIN.	FIRST MIN.	ADD'L MIN.
Direct Dial	.30 + .12/100m	.20 + .12/100m	.22 + .10/100m	.15 + .10/100m	.12 + .06/100m	.09 + .06/100m
Operator Assist	1.20 + .12/100m		1.12 + .10/100m		1.02 + .06/100m	

It's easy to get so enamored of one's analytic tools that one forgets about the problem. The analyst must do more than carry out all possibilities of a problem to the nth degree, as I have seen authors of books on structured analysis recommend. That approach only increases the amount of available detail. The problem solver must also try to simplify the problem.

TIP

You don't understand a problem until you can simplify it.

If the goal of analysis is not only understanding, but simplification, then perhaps we've got more work to do.

Our revised decision table (Figure 2-6) shows that the per-mile charge depends only on whether the rate is full, lower, or lowest. In other words, it's subject to only one of the three dimensions shown in the table. What happens if we split this table into two tables, as in Figure 2-7?

Now we're getting the answer through a combination of table look-up and calculation. The formula for the per-minute charge can be expressed as a pseudoFORTH definition:

```
: PER-MINUTE-CHARGE ( -- per-minute-charge)
      CONNECT-CHARGE  MILEAGE-CHARGE  + ;
```

The "+" now appears once in the definition, not nine times in the table.

Taking the principle of calculation one step further, we note (or remember from the original problem statement) that operator assistance merely adds a one-time charge of .90 to the total charge. In this sense, the operator charge is not a function of any of the three dimensions. It's more

Figure 2-7. *The sectional decision table.*

		FULL RATE		LOWER RATE		LOWEST RATE	
		FIRST MIN.	ADD'L MIN	FIRST MIN.	ADD'L MIN.	FIRST MIN.	ADD'L MIN.
Connection charge	Direct Dial	.30	.20	.22	.15	.12	.09
	Operator Assist	1.20		1.12		1.02	
PLUS							
Mileage Charge		.12/100m		.10/100m		.06/100m	

appropriately expressed as a "logical calculation"; that is, a function that combines logic with arithmetic:

```
: ?ASSISTANCE
  ( direct-dial-charge -- total-charge)
  OPERATOR? IF  .90 +  THEN ;
```

(But remember, this charge applies only to the first minute.)

This leaves us with the simplified table shown in Figure 2-8, and an increased reliance on expressing calculations. Now we're getting somewhere.

Let's go back to our definition of PER—MINUTE—CHARGE:

```
: PER-MINUTE-CHARGE ( -- per-minute-charge)
  CONNECT-CHARGE  MILEAGE-CHARGE  + ;
```

Let's get more specific about the rules for the connection charge and for the mileage charge.

The connection charge depends on whether the minute is the first or an additional minute. Since there are two kinds of per-minute charges, perhaps it will be easiest to rewrite PER—MINUTE—CHARGE as two different words.

Let's assume we will build a component that will fetch the appropriate rates from the table. The word 1MINUTE will get the rate for the first minute; +MINUTES will get the rate for each additional minute. Both of these words will depend on the time of day to determine whether to use the full, lower, or lowest rates.

Now we can define the pair of words to replace PER—MINUTE—CHARGE:

Figure 2-8. *The decision table without operator involvement depicted.*

	FULL RATE	LOWER RATE	LOWEST RATE
Connect-ion charge { First Minute	.30	.22	.12
Connect-ion charge { Add'l. Minute	.20	.15	.09
PLUS			
Mileage Charge	.12/ 100m	.10 /100 m	.06 /100 m

```
: FIRST   ( -- charge)
   1MINUTE  ?ASSISTANCE  MILEAGE-CHARGE + ;
: PER-ADDITIONAL  ( -- charge)
   +MINUTES  MILEAGE-CHARGE + ;
```

What is the rule for the mileage charge? Very simple. It is the rate (per hundred miles) times the number of miles (in hundreds). Let's assume we can define the word MILEAGE—RATE, which will fetch the mileage rate from the table:

```
: MILEAGE-CHARGE  ( -- charge)
   #MILES ∂  MILEAGE-RATE * ;
```

Finally, if we know the total number of minutes for a call, we can now calculate the total direct-dial charge:

```
: TOTAL  ( -- total-charge)
   FIRST                         ( first minute rate)
   ( #minutes) 1-                ( additional minutes)
      PER-ADDITIONAL *           ( times the rate)
   + ;                           ( added together)
```

We've expressed the rules to this particular problem through a combination of simple tables and logical calculations.

(Some final notes on this example: We've written something very close to a running FORTH application. But it is only pseudocode. We've avoided stack manipulations by assuming that values will somehow be on the stack where the comments indicate. Also, we've used hyphenated names because they might be more readable for the customer. Short names are preferred in real code—see Chapter Five.)

We'll unveil the finished code for this example in Chapter Eight.

Defining the Data Structures

After defining the interfaces, and sometimes defining the rules, occasionally you'll need to define certain data structures as well. We're not referring here to the implementation of the data structures, but rather to a description of their conceptual model.

If you're automating a library index, for instance, a crucial portion of your analysis will concern developing the logical data structure. You'll have to decide what information will be kept for each book: title, author, subject, etc. These "attributes" will comprise an "entity" (set of related records) called BOOKS. Then you'll have to determine what other data structures will be required to let the users search the BOOKS efficiently.

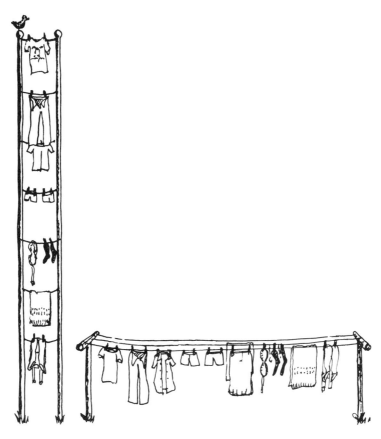

Given two adequate solutions, the correct one is the simpler.

You may need another entity consisting of authors' names in alphabetical order, along with "attribute pointers" to the books each author has written.

Certain constraints will also affect the conceptual model of the data structure. In the library index example, you need to know not only *what* information the users need, but also how long they're willing to *wait* to get it.

For instance, users can request listings of topics by year of publication—say everything on ladies' lingerie between 1900 and 1910. If they expect to get this information in the snap of a girdle, you'll have to index on years and on topics. If they can wait a day, you might just let the computer search through all the books in the library.

Achieving Simplicity

TIP

Keep it simple.

While you are taking these crucial first steps toward understanding the problem, keep in mind the old saying:

Given two solutions to a problem, the correct one is the simpler.

This is especially true in software design. The simpler solution is often more difficult to discover, but once found, it is:

- easier to understand
- easier to implement
- easier to verify and debug
- easier to maintain
- more compact
- more efficient
- more fun

One of the most compelling advocates of simplicity is Moore:

You need a feeling for the size of the problem. How much code should it take to implement the thing? One block? Three? I think this is a very useful design tool. You want to gut-feel whether it's a trivial problem or a major problem, how much time and effort you should spend on it.

When you're done, look back and say, "Did I come up with a solution that is reasonable?" If your solution fills six screens, it may seem you've used a sledgehammer to kill a mosquito. Your mental image is out of proportion to the significance of the problem.

I've seen nuclear physics programs with hundreds of thousands of lines of FORTRAN. Whatever that code does, it doesn't warrant hundreds of thousands of lines of code. Probably its writers have overgeneralized the problem. They've solved a large problem of which their real needs are a subset. They have violated the principle that the solution should match the problem.

TIP

Generality usually involves complexity. Don't generalize your solution any more than will be required; instead, keep it changeable.

Moore continues:

Given a problem, you can code a solution to it. Having done that, and found certain unpleasantnesses to it, you can go back and change the problem, and end up with a simpler solution.

There's a class of device optimization—minimizing the number of gates in a circuit—where you take advantage of the "don't care" situation. These occur either because a case won't arise in practice or because you really don't care. But the spec is often written by people who have no appreciation for programming. The designer may have carefully specified all the cases, but hasn't told you, the programmer, which cases are really important.

If you are free to go back and argue with him and take advantage of the "don't cares," you can come up with a simpler solution.

Take an engineering application, such as a 75-ton metal powder press, stamping out things. They want to install a computer to control the valves in place of the hydraulic control previously used. What kind of spec will you get from the engineer? Most likely the sensors were placed for convenience from an electromechanical standpoint. Now they could be put somewhere else, but the engineer has forgotten. If you demand explanations, you can come closer to the real world and further from their model of the world.

Another example is the PID (proportional integration and differentiation) algorithm for servos. You have one term that integrates, another term that differentiates, and a third term that smoothes. You combine those with 30% integration, 10% differentiation, or whatever. But it's only a digital filter. It used to be convenient in analog days to break out certain terms of the digital filter and say, "This is the integrator and this is the differentiator. I'll make this with a capacitor and I'll make that with an inductor."

Again the spec writers will model the analog solution which was modeling the electromechanical solution, and they're several models away from reality. In fact, you can replace it all with two or three coefficients in a digital filter for a much cleaner, simpler and more efficient solution.

TIP

Go back to what the problem was before the customer tried to solve it. Exploit the "don't cares."

An overgeneralized solution.

Moore continues:

> Sometimes the possibilities for simplification aren't immediately obvious. There's this problem of zooming in a digitized graphics display, such as CAD systems. You have a picture on the screen and you want to zoom in on a portion to see the details.
>
> I used to implement it so that you move the cursor to the position of interest, then press a button, and it zooms until you have a window of the desired size. That was the way I've always done it. Until I realized that that was stupid. I never needed to zoom with such fine resolution.
>
> So instead of moving the cursor a pixel at a time, I jump the cursor by units of, say, ten. And instead of increasing the size of box, I jump the size of the box. You don't have a choice of sizes. You zoom by a factor of four. The in-between sizes are not interesting. You can do it as many times as you like.
>
> By quantitizing things fairly brutally, you make it easier to work with, more responsive, and simpler.

TIP

To simplify, quantitize.

Moore concludes:

> It takes arrogance to go back and say "You didn't really mean this," or "Would you mind if I took off this page and replaced it with this expression?" They get annoyed. They want you to do what they told you to do.
>
> LaFarr Stuart took this attitude when he redesigned FORTH [3]. He didn't like the input buffer, so he implemented FORTH without it, and discovered he didn't really need an input buffer.
>
> If you can improve the problem, it's a great situation to get into. It's much more fun redesigning the world than implementing it.

Effective programmers learn to be tactful and to couch their approaches in non-threatening ways: "What would be the consequences of replacing that with this?" etc.

Yet another way to simplify a problem is this:

TIP

To simplify, keep the user out of trouble.

Suppose you're designing part of a word processor that displays a directory of stored documents on the screen, one per line. You plan that the user can move the cursor next to the name of any document, then type a one-letter command indicating the chosen action: "p" for print, "e" for edit, etc.

Initially it seems all right to let the user move the cursor anywhere on the screen. This means that those places where text already appears must be protected from being overwritten. This implies a concept of "protected fields" and special handling. A simpler approach confines the cursor to certain fields, possibly using reverse video to let the user see the size of the allowable field.

Another example occurs when an application prompts the user for a numeric value. You often see such applications that don't check input until you press "return," at which time the system responds with an error message such as "invalid number." It's just as easy—probably easier—to check each key as it's typed and simply not allow non-numeric characters to appear.

TIP

To simplify, take advantage of what's available.

Michael LaManna, a FORTH programmer in Long Island, New York, comments:

> I always try to design the application on the most powerful processor I can get my hands on. If I have a choice between doing development on a 68000-based system and a 6809-based system, I'd go for the 68000-based system. The processor itself is so powerful it takes care of a lot of details I might otherwise have to solve myself.
>
> If I have to go back later and rewrite parts of the application for a simpler processor, that's okay. At least I won't have wasted my time.

A word of caution: If you're using an existing component to simplify your prototype, don't let the component affect your design. You don't want the design to depend on the internals of the component.

Budgeting and Scheduling

Another important aspect of the analysis phase is figuring the price tag. Again, this process is much more difficult than it would seem. If you don't know the problem till you solve it, how can you possibly know how long it will take to solve it?

Careful planning is essential, because things always take longer than you expect. I have a theory about this, based on the laws of probability:

Conventional wisdom reveres complexity.

Imagine the following scenario: You're in the middle of writing a large application when suddenly it strikes you to add some relatively simple feature. You think it'll take about two hours, so without further planning, you just do it. Consider: That's two hours coding time. The design time you don't count because you perceived the need—and the design—in a flash of brilliance while working on the application. So you estimate two hours.

But consider the following possibilities:

1. Your implementation has a bug. After two hours it doesn't work. So you spend another two hours recoding. (Total 4.)
2. OR, before you implemented it, you realized your initial design wouldn't work. You spend two hours redesigning. *These* two hours count. Plus another two hours coding it. (Total 4.)
3. OR, you implement the first design before you realize the design wouldn't work. So you redesign (two more hours) and reimplement (two more). (Total 6.)
4. OR, you implement the first design, code it, find a bug, rewrite the code, find a design flaw, redesign, recode, find a bug in the new code, recode again. (Total 10.)

You see how the thing snowballs?

5. Now you have to document your new feature. Add two hours to the above. (Total 12.)
6. After you've spent anywhere from 2 to 12 hours installing and debugging your new feature, you suddenly find that element Y of your application bombs out. Worst yet, you have no idea why. You spend two hours reading memory dumps trying to divine the reason. Once you do, you spend as many as 12 additional hours redesigning element Y. (Total 26.) Then you have to document the syntax change you made to element Y. (Total 27.)

That's a total of over three man-days. If all these mishaps befell you at once, you'd call for the men with the little white coats. It rarely gets that bad, of course, but the odds are decidedly *against* any project being as easy as you think it will be.

How can you improve your chances of judging time requirements correctly? Many fine books have been written on this topic, notably *The Mythical Man-Month* by Frederick P. Brooks, Jr. [4]. I have little to add to this body of knowledge except for some personal observations.

1. Don't guess on a total. Break the problem up into the smallest possible pieces, then estimate the time for each piece. The sum of the pieces is always greater than what you'd have guessed the total would be. (The whole appears to be less than the sum of the parts.)

2. In itemizing the pieces, separate those you understand well enough to hazard a guess from those you don't. For the second category, give the customer a range.

3. A bit of psychology: always give your client some options. Clients *like* options. If you say, "This will cost you $6,000," the client will probably respond "I'd really like to spend $4,000." This puts you in the position of either accepting or going without a job.

But if you say, "You have a choice: for $4,000 I'll make it *walk* through the hoop; for $6,000 I'll make it *jump* through the hoop. For $8,000 I'll make it *dance* through the hoop waving flags, tossing confetti and singing "Roll Out the Barrel."

Most customers opt for jumping through the hoop.

TIP

Everything takes longer than you think, including thinking.

Reviewing the Conceptual Model

The final box on our iterative analytic wheel is labelled "Show Model to Customer." With the tools we've outlined in this chapter, this job should be easy to do.

In documenting the requirements specification, remember that specs are like snowmen. They may be frozen now, but they shift, slip, and melt away when the heat is on. Whether you choose data-flow diagrams or straight FORTH pseudocode, prepare yourself for the great thaw by remembering to apply the concepts of limited redundancy.

Show the documented conceptual model to the customer. When the customer is finally satisfied, you're ready for the next big step: the design!

References

1. Kim Harris, "The FORTH Philosophy," *Dr. Dobb's Journal*, Vol. 6, Iss. 9, No. 59 (Sept. 81), pp. 6-11.

2. Victor Weinberg, *Structured Analysis*, Englewood Cliffs, N.J.: Prentice-Hall, Inc., 1980.

3. LaFarr Stuart, "LaFORTH," 1980 FORML Proceedings, p. 78.

4. Frederick P. Brooks, Jr., *The Mythical Man-Month*, Reading, Massachusetts, Addison-Wesley, 1975.

THREE

Preliminary Design/ Decomposition

Assuming you have some idea of what your program should accomplish, it's time to begin the design. The first stage, preliminary design, focuses on shrinking your mountainous problem into manageable molehills.

In this chapter we'll discuss two ways to decompose your FORTH application.

Decomposition by Component

Has this sort of thing ever happened to you? You've been planning for three months to take a weekend vacation to the mountains. You've been making lists of what to bring, and daydreaming about the slopes.

Meanwhile you're deciding what to wear to your cousin's wedding next Saturday. They're informal types, and you don't want to overdress. Still, a wedding's a wedding. Maybe you should rent a tuxedo anyway.

For all this planning, it's not until Thursday that you realize the two events coincide. You have expletives for such moments.

How is such a mental lapse possible, in one so intelligent as yourself? Apparently the human mind actually makes links between memories. New ideas are somehow added onto existing paths of related thoughts.

Figure 3-1. *Pools of thought not yet linked.*

In the mishap just described, no connection was ever made between the two separately-linked pools of thought until Thursday. The conflict probably occurred when some new input (something as trivial as hearing Saturday's weather report) got linked into both pools of thought. A lightning flash of realization arced between the pools, followed inexorably by thunderous panic.

A simple tool has been invented to avoid such disasters. It's called a calendar. If you had recorded both plans in the same calendar, you would have seen the other event scheduled, something your brain failed to do for all its intricate magnificence.

TIP

To see the relationship between two things, put them close together. To remind yourself of the relationship, *keep* them together.

These truisms apply to software design, particularly to the preliminary design phase. This phase is traditionally the one in which the designer dissects a large application into smaller, programmer-sized modules.

In Chapter One we discovered that applications can be conveniently decomposed into components.

TIP

The goal of preliminary design is to determine what components are necessary to accomplish the requirements.

For instance, you might have an application in which events must occur according to some predetermined schedule. To manage the scheduling, you might first design a few words to constitute a "schedule-building lexicon." With these words you'll be able to describe the order of events that must occur within your application.

Thus within a single component, you'll not only share information, but also work out potential conflicts. The wrong approach would be to let each functional module "know" things about its schedule that could potentially conflict with another module's schedule.

How can you know, in designing a component, what commands the using components will need? Admittedly, this is something of a "chicken vs. egg" problem. But FORTH programmers handle it the same way chickens and eggs do: iteratively.

If the component is well-designed, completeness doesn't matter. In fact, a component need only suffice for the current iteration's design. No component should be considered a "closed book" until the application has been completed—which, in the case of maintained applications, is never.

As an example, imagine that your product needs to "talk" to other machines in the outside world via a universal I/O chip that is part of your system. This particular chip has a "control register" and a "data register." In a badly designed application, pieces of code throughout the program would access the communication chip by simply invoking the OUT instruction to put an appropriate command byte into the command register. This makes the entire application needlessly dependent on that particular chip—very risky.

Instead, FORTH programmers would write a component to control the I/O chip. These commands would have logical names and a convenient interface (usually FORTH's stack) to allow usage by the rest of the application.

For any iteration of your product's design, you would implement only the commands needed so far—not all the valid codes that could be sent to the "control register." If later in the project cycle you realize that you need an additional command, say one to change the baud rate, the new command would be added to the I/O chip lexicon, not to the code that needed to set the baud rate. There's no penalty for making this change except the few minutes (at most) it takes to edit and recompile.

TIP

Within each component, implement only the commands needed for the current iteration. (But don't preclude future additions.)

What goes on inside a component is pretty much its own business. It's not necessarily bad style for definitions within the component to share redundant information.

For instance, a record in a certain data structure is fourteen bytes long. One definition in the component advances a pointer 14 bytes to point to the next record; another definition decrements the pointer 14 bytes.

As long as that number 14 remains a "secret" to the component and won't be used elsewhere, you don't need to define it as constant. Just use the number 14 in both definitions:

```
: +RECORD    14 RECORD# +! ;
: -RECORD   -14 RECORD# +! ;
```

On the other hand, if the value will be needed outside of the component, or if it's used several times within the component and there's a good chance that it will change, you're better off hiding it behind a name:

```
14 CONSTANT /RECORD
: +RECORD    /RECORD RECORD# +! ;
: -RECORD    /RECORD NEGATE RECORD# +! ;
```

(The name /RECORD, by convention, means "bytes per record.")

Let's apply decomposition by component to a real problem. It would be nice to design a large application right here in Chapter Three, but alas, we don't have the room and besides, we'd get sidetracked in trying to understand the application.

Instead, we'll take a component from a large application that has already been decomposed. We'll design this component by decomposing it further, into subcomponents.

Imagine that we must create a tiny editor that will allow users to change the contents of input fields on their terminal screen. For instance, the screen might look like this:

Name of Member   Justine Time

The editor will provide three modes for users to change the contents of the input field:

Overwrite. Typing ordinary characters overwrites any characters that were there before.

Delete. Pressing the combination of keys "Ctrl D" deletes the character under the cursor and slides the remaining characters leftwards.

Insert. Pressing the combination of keys "Ctrl I" switches the editor into "Insert Mode," where subsequently typing ordinary characters inserts them at the cursor position, sliding the remaining characters rightwards.

As part of the conceptual model we should also consider the error or exception-handling; for instance, what is the limit of the field? what happens in insert mode when characters spill off the right? etc.

That's all the specification we have right now. The rest is up to us.

Let's try to determine what components we'll need. First, the editor will react to keys that are typed at the keyboard. Therefore we'll need a keystroke interpreter—some kind of routine that awaits keystrokes and matches them up with a list of possible operations. The keystroke interpreter is one component, and its lexicon will consist of a single word. Since that word will allow the editing of a field, let's call the word EDIT.

The operations invoked by the keystroke interpreter will comprise a second lexicon. The definitions in this lexicon will perform the various functions required. One word might be called DELETE, another INSERT, etc. Since each of these commands will be invoked by the interpreter, each of them will process a single keystroke.

Below these commands should lie a third component, the set of words that implement the data structure to be edited.

Finally, we'll need a component to display the field on the video

Figure 3-2. *Generalized decomposition of the Tiny Editor problem.*

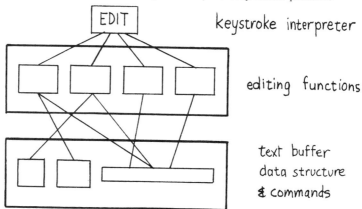

keystroke interpreter

editing functions

text buffer
data structure
& commands

screen. For the sake of simplicity, let's plan on creating one word only, REDISPLAY, to redisplay the entire field after each key is pressed.

```
: EDITOR    BEGIN  KEY  REVISE   REDISPLAY  ... UNTIL ;
```

This approach separates revising the buffer from updating the display. For now, we'll only concentrate on revising the buffer.

Let's look at each component separately and try to determine the words each will need. We can begin by considering the events that must occur within the three most important editing functions: overwriting, deleting, and inserting. We might draw something like the following on the back of an old pizza menu (we won't pay much attention to exception-handling in the present discussion):

To Overwrite:

Store new character into byte pointed to by pointer

Advance pointer (unless at end of field)

```
F U N K T I O N A L I T Y
       ^
F U N C T I O N A L I T Y
       ^
F U N C T I O N A L I T Y
         ^
```

To Delete:

Copy leftwards, by one place, the string beginning one place to the right of the pointer.

Store a "blank" into the last position on the line.

```
F U N C T I O N S A L I T Y
               ^
F U N C T I O N A L I T Y Y
               ^
F U N C T I O N A L I T Y □
               ^
```

To Insert:

Copy rightwards by one place the string beginning at the pointer

Store new character into byte pointed to by pointer

Advance pointer (unless at end of field)

```
F U N T I O N A L I T Y
F U N T T I O N A L I T Y
F U N C T I O N A L I T Y
F U N C T I O N A L I T Y
```

We've just developed the algorithms for the problem at hand.

Our next step is to examine these three essential procedures, looking for useful "names"—that is procedures or elements which can either:

1. possibly be reused, or
2. possibly change

We discover that all three procedures use something called a "pointer." We need two procedures:

1. to get the pointer (if the pointer itself is relative, this function will perform some computation).
2. to advance the pointer

Wait, three procedures:

3. to move the pointer backwards

because we will want "cursor keys" to move the cursor forward and back without editing changes.

These three operators will all refer to a physical pointer somewhere in memory. Where it is kept and how (relative or absolute) should be hidden within this component.

Let's attempt to rewrite these algorithms in code:

```
: KEY#   ( returns value of key last pressed ) ... ;
: POSITION   (returns address of character pointed-to) ;
: FORWARD   (advance pointer, stopping at last position) ;
: BACKWARD   (decrement pointer, stopping at first position) ;
: OVERWRITE   KEY# POSITION C!  FORWARD ;
: INSERT   SLIDE>  OVERWRITE ;
: DELETE   SLIDE<   BLANK-END ;
```

To copy the text leftwards and rightwards, we had to invent two new names as we went along, SLIDE < and SLIDE > (pronounced "slide-backwards" and "slide-forwards" respectively). Both of them will certainly use POSITION, but they also must rely on an element we've deferred considering: a way to "know" the length of the field. We can tackle that aspect when we get to writing the third component.

But look at what we found out already: we can describe "Insert" as simply "SLIDE > OVERWRITE".

In other words, "Insert" actually *uses* "Overwrite" even though they appear to exist on the same level (at least to a Structured Programmer).

Instead of probing deeper into the third component, let's lay out what we know about the first component, the key interpreter. First we must solve the problem of "insert mode." It turns out that "insert" is not just something that happens when you press a certain key, as delete is. Instead it is a *different way of interpreting* some of the possible keystrokes.

For instance in "overwrite" mode, an ordinary character gets stored into the current cursor position; but in "insert mode" the remainder of the line must first be shifted right. And the backspace key works differently when the editor is in Insert Mode as well.

Since there are two modes, "inserting" and "not-inserting," the keystroke interpreter must associate the keys with two possible sets of named procedures.

We can write our keystroke interpreter as a decision table (worrying about the implementation later):

Key	Not-inserting	Inserting
Cntrl-D	DELETE	INSERT-OFF
Cntrl-I	INSERT-ON	INSERT-OFF
backspace	BACKWARD	INSERT<
left-arrow	BACKWARD	INSERT-OFF
right-arrow	FORWARD	INSERT-OFF
return	ESCAPE	INSERT-OFF
any printable	OVERWRITE	INSERT

We've placed the possible types of keys in the left column, what they do normally in the middle column, and what they do in "insert mode" in the right column.

To implement what happens when "backspace" is pressed while in Insert Mode, we add a new procedure:

```
: INSERT<   BACKWARD  SLIDE< ;
```

(move the cursor backwards on top of the last character typed, then slide everything to the right leftward, covering the mistake).

This table seems to be the most logical expression of the problem at the current level. We'll save the implementation for later (Chapter Eight).

Now we'll demonstrate the tremendous value of this approach in terms of maintainability. We'll throw ourselves a curve—a major change of plans!

Maintaining a Component-based Application

How well will our design fare in the face of change? Envision the following scenario:

We originally assumed that we could refresh the video display simply by retyping the field every time a key is pressed. We even implemented the code on our personal computer, with its memory-mapped video that refreshes an entire line in the blink of a scan cycle. But now our customer wants the application to run on a telephone-based network, with all I/O being done at a not-so-fast baud rate. Since some of our input fields are almost as wide as the video screen, maybe 65 characters, it just takes too long to refresh the entire line on every key stroke.

We've got to change the application so that we only refresh that part of the field that actually changes. In "insert" and "delete," this would mean the text to the right of the cursor. In "overwrite" it would mean changing just the single character being overwritten.

This change is significant. The video refresh function, which we cavalierly relegated to the key interpreter, now must depend on which editing functions occur. As we've discovered, the most important names needed to implement the key interpreter are:

```
FORWARD
BACKWARD
OVERWRITE
INSERT
DELETE
< INSERT
```

None of their descriptions make any reference to the video refresh process, because that was originally assumed to happen later.

But things aren't as bad as they seem. Looking at it now, the process OVERWRITE could easily include a command to type the new character where the terminal's cursor is. And SLIDE< and SLIDE> could include commands to type everything to the right of, and including, POSITION, then reset the terminal's cursor to its current position.

Here are our revised procedure names. The commands just added are in boldface:

```
: OVERWRITE  KEY# POSITION C!  KEY# EMIT  FORWARD ;
: RETYPE  ( type from current position to
    end of field and reset cursor) ;
: INSERT  SLIDE>  RETYPE  OVERWRITE ;
: DELETE  SLIDE<  BLANK-END  RETYPE ;
```

Since these are the only three functions which change memory, they are the only three functions that need to refresh the screen. This idea is critical. We must be able to make such assertions to assure program correctness. The assertion is intrinsic to the nature of the problem.

Note that the additional problem of video refresh adds an additional "pointer": the current cursor position on the screen. But decomposition by component has encouraged us to view the OVERWRITE process as changing both the data field and the video vision of it; similarly with SLIDE< and SLIDE>. For this reason it seems natural now to maintain

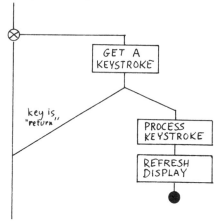

Figure 3-3. *The traditional approach: view from the top.*

GET A KEYSTROKE

key is "return"

PROCESS KEYSTROKE

REFRESH DISPLAY

only one real pointer—a relative one—from which we can compute either the data address in memory, or the column number on the screen.

Since the nature of the pointer is wholly hidden within the three processes POSITION, FORWARD, and BACKWARD, we can readily accommodate this approach, even if it wasn't our first approach.

This change may have seemed simple enough here—even obvious. If so, it's because the technique ensures flexible design. If we had used a traditional approach—if we had designed according to structure, or according to data transformation through sequential processes—our brittle design would have been shattered by the change.

To prove this assertion, we'll have to start all over again from scratch.

Designing and Maintaining a Traditional Application

Let's pretend we haven't studied the Tiny Editor problem yet, and we're back with a minimal set of specs. We'll also start with our initial assumption, that we can refresh the display by retyping the entire field after each keystroke.

According to the dictum of top-down design, let's take the widest-angle view possible and examine the problem. Figure 3-3 depicts the program in its simplest terms. Here we've realized that the editor is actually a loop which keeps getting keystrokes and performing some editing function, until the user presses the return key.

Inside the loop we have three modules: getting a character from the keyboard, editing the data, and finally refreshing the display to match the data.

Clearly most of the work will go on inside "Process a Keystroke."

Applying the notion of successive refinement, Figure 3-4 shows the editor problem redrawn with "Process a Keystroke" expanded. We find it

Figure 3-4. *A structure for "Process a Keystroke."*

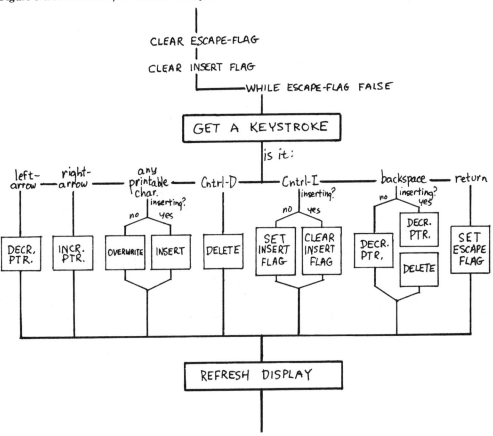

takes several attempts before we arrive at this configuration. Designing this level forces us to consider many things at once that we had deferred till later in the previous try.

For instance, we must determine all the keys that might be pressed. More significantly, we must consider the problem of "insert mode." This realization forces us to invent a flag called INSERT–MODE which gets toggled by the "Cntrl I" key. It's used within several of the structural lines to determine how to process a type of key.

A second flag, called ESCAPE, seems to provide a nice structured way of escaping the editor loop if the user presses the return key while not in insert mode.

Having finished the diagram, we're bothered by the multiple tests for Insert Mode. Could we test for Insert Mode once, at the beginning? Following this notion, we draw yet another chart (Figure 3-5).

As you can see, this turns out even more awkward than the first figure. Now we're testing for each key twice. It's interesting though, how the two structures are totally different, yet functionally equivalent. It's enough to make one wonder whether the control structure is terribly relevant to the problem.

Figure 3-5. *Another structure for "Process a Keystroke."*

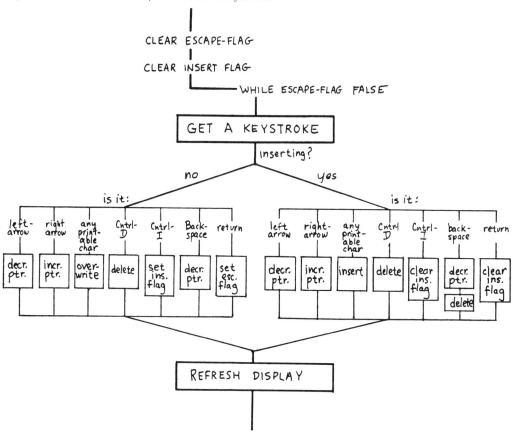

Having decided on the first structure, we've finally arrived at the most important modules—the ones that do the work of overwriting, inserting, and deleting. Take another look at our expansion of "Process a Character" in Figure 3-4. Let's consider just one of the seven possible execution paths, the one that happens if a printable character is pressed.

In Figure 3-6(a) we see the original structural path for a printable character.

Once we figure out the algorithms for overwriting and inserting characters, we might refine it as shown in Figure 3-6(b). But look at that embarrassing redundancy of code (circled portions). Most competent structured programmers would recognize that this redundancy is unnecessary, and change the structure as shown in Figure 3-6(c).

Not too bad so far, right?

Change in Plan

Okay, everyone, now act surprised. We've just been told that this application won't run on a memory-mapped display. What does this change do to our design structure?

Figure 3-6. *The same section, "refined" and "optimized."*

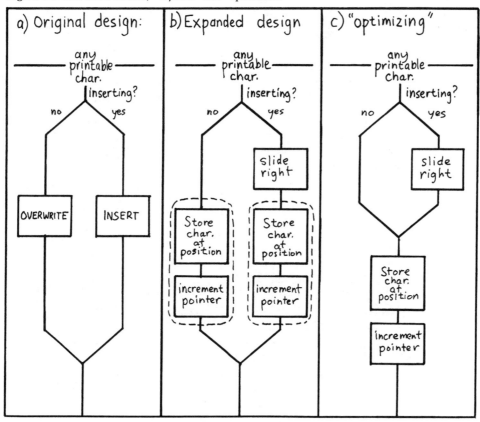

Well, for one thing it destroys "Refresh Display" as a separate module. The function of "Refresh Display" is now scattered among the various structural lines inside "Process a Keystroke." The structure of our entire application has changed. It's easy to see how we might have spent weeks doing top-down design only to find we'd been barking down the wrong tree.

What happens when we try to change the program? Let's look again at the path for any printable character.

Figure 3-7 (a) shows what happens to our first-pass design when we add refresh. Part (b) shows our "optimized" design with the refresh modules expanded. Notice that we're now testing the Insert flag twice within this single leg of the outer loop.

But worse, there's a bug in this design. Can you find it?

In both cases, overwriting and inserting, the pointer is incremented *before* the refresh. In the case of overwrite, we're displaying the new character in the wrong position. In the case of insert, we're typing the remainder of the line but not the new character.

Granted, this is an easy problem to fix. We need only move the refresh modules up before "Increment Pointer." The point here is: How did

Figure 3-7. *Adding refresh.*

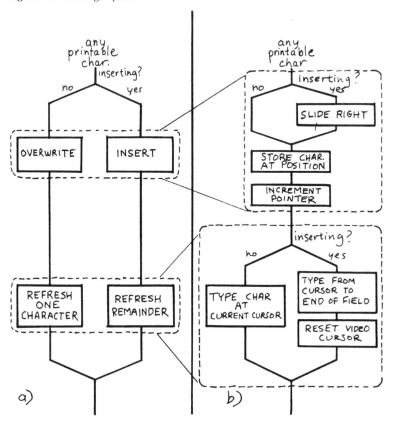

we miss it? By getting preoccupied with control flow structure, a superficial element of program design.

In contrast, in our design by components the correct solution fell out naturally because we "used" the refresh component inside the editing component. Also we used OVERWRITE inside INSERT.

By decomposing our application into components which use one another, we achieved not only *elegance* but a more direct path to *correctness*.

The Interface Component

In computer science terminology, interfacing between modules has two aspects. First, there's the way other modules *invoke* the module; this is the control interface. Second, there's the way other modules pass and receive data to and from the module; this is the data interface.

Because of FORTH's dictionary structure, control is not an issue. Definitions are invoked by being named. In this section, when we use the term "interface" we're referring to data.

When it comes to data interfaces between modules, traditional wisdom says only that "interfaces should be carefully designed, with a minimum of complexity." The reason for the care, of course, is that each module must implement its own end of the interface (Figure 3-8).

This means the presence of redundant code. As we've seen, redundant code brings at least two problems: bulky code and poor maintainability. A change to the interface of one module will affect the interface of the opposite module.

Figure 3-8. *Traditional view of the interface as a junction.*

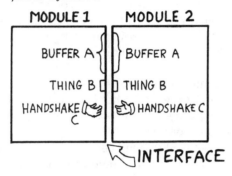

There's more to good interface design than that. Allow me to introduce a design element which I call the "interface component." The purpose an interface component is to implement, and *hide information about,* the data interface between two or more other components (Figure 3-9).

Figure 3-9. *Use of the interface component.*

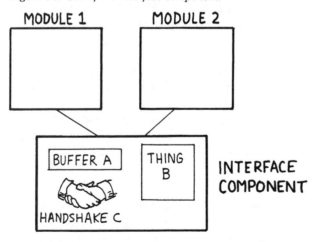

TIP

Both data structures and the commands involved in the communication of data between modules should be localized in an interface component.

Let me give an example from my own recent experience. One of my hobbies is writing text formatter/editors. (I've written two of them, including the one on which I am writing this book.)

In my latest design the formatter portion contains two components. The first component reads the source document and decides where to make line and page breaks, etc. But instead of sending the text directly to the terminal or printer, it saves up a line's worth at a time in a "line buffer."

Similarly, instead of sending printer-control commands—for bold-facing, underlining, etc.—as the text is being formatted, it defers these commands until the text is actually sent. To defer the control commands, I have a second buffer called the "attribute buffer." It corresponds, byte-for-byte, with the line buffer, except that each byte contains a set of flags that indicate whether the corresponding character should be underlined, boldfaced, or whatever.

The second component displays or prints the contents of the line buffer. The component knows whether it is transmitting to the terminal or to the printer, and outputs the text according to the attributes indicated by the attribute buffer.

Here we have two well-defined components—the line-formatter and the output component—each one shouldering part of the function of the formatter as a whole.

The data interface between these two components is fairly complex. The interface consists of two buffers, a variable that indicates the current number of valid characters, and finally a "knowledge" of what all those attribute patterns mean.

In FORTH I've defined these elements together in a single screen. The buffers are defined with **CREATE**, the count is an ordinary **VARIABLE**, and the attribute patterns are defined as **CONSTANT**s, such as:

```
1 CONSTANT UNDERNESS   ( bit mask for underlining)
2 CONSTANT BOLDNESS    ( bit mask for boldface)
```

The formatting component uses phrases like UNDERNESS SET—FLAG to set bits in the attribute buffer. The output component uses phrases like UNDERNESS AND to read the attribute buffer.

A Design Mistake

In designing an interface component, you should ask yourself "What is the set of structures and commands that must be shared by the communicating components?" It's important to determine what elements belong to the interface and what elements should remain within a single component.

In writing my text formatter, I failed to answer this question fully and found myself with a bug. The problem was this:

I allow different type widths to be used: condensed, double widths, etc. This means not only sending different signals to the printer, but changing the number of characters allowed per line.

I keep a variable, called WALL, for the formatter. WALL indicates the right margin: the point beyond which no more text can be set. Changing to a different type width means changing the value of WALL proportionately. (Actually, this turns out to be a mistake in itself. I should be using a finer unit of measurement, the number of which remains constant for the line. Changing type widths would mean changing the number of units per character. But getting back to the mistake at hand . . .)

Alas, I was also using WALL inside the output component to determine how many characters to display. My reasoning was that this value would change depending on what type-width I was using.

I was right—99% of the time. But one day I discovered that, under a certain condition, a line of condensed text was being somehow cut short. The final couple of words were just missing. The reason turned out to be that WALL was getting changed before the output component had a chance to use it.

Originally I had seen nothing wrong with letting the output component blithely use the formatter's WALL as well. Now I realized that the formatter had to leave a separate variable for the output component, to indicate how many valid characters were in the buffers. This would leave any subsequent font commands free to change WALL.

It was important that the two buffers, the attribute commands, and the new variable were the *only* elements that could be shared between the two modules. Reaching into either module from the other one spells trouble.

The moral of this story is that we must distinguish between data structures that are validly used only within a single component and those that may be shared by more than one component.

A related point:

TIP

Express in objective units any data to be shared by components.

For example:

> Module A measures the temperature of the oven.
> Module B controls the burner.
> Module C makes sure the door is locked if the oven is too hot.

The information of global interest is the temperature of the oven, expressed objectively in degrees. While Module A might receive a value representing the voltage from a heat sensor, it should convert this value to degrees before presenting it to the rest of the application.

Decomposition by Sequential Complexity

We've been discussing one way to do decomposition: according to components. The second way is according to sequential complexity.

One of FORTH's rules is that a word must already have been defined to be invoked or referred to. Usually the sequence in which words are defined parallels the order of increasing capabilities which the words must possess. This sequence leads to a natural organization of the source listing. The powerful commands are simply added on top of the elementary application (Figure 3-10a).

Like a textbook, the elementary stuff comes first. A newcomer to the project would be able to read the elementary parts of the code before moving on the advanced stuff.

But in many large applications, the extra capabilities are best

Figure 3-10. *Two ways to add advanced capabilities.*

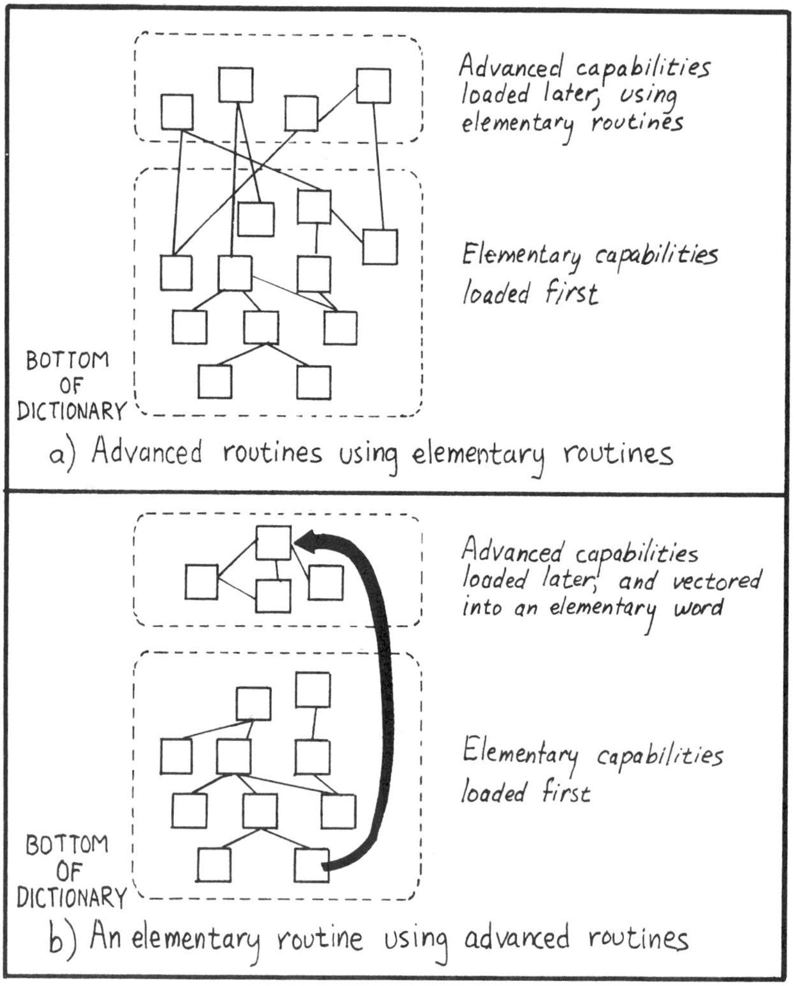

a) Advanced routines using elementary routines

b) An elementary routine using advanced routines

implemented as an enhancement to some private, root function in the elementary part of the application (Figure 3-10b). By being able to change the root's capability, the user can change the capability of all the commands that use the root.

Returning to the word processor for an example, a fairly primitive routine is the one that starts a new page. It's used by the word that starts a new line; when we run out of lines we must start a new page. The word that starts a new line, in turn, is used by the routine that formats words on the line; when the next word won't fit on the current line, we invoke NEWLINE. This "uses" hierarchy demands that we define NEWPAGE early in the application.

The problem? One of the advanced components includes a routine that must be invoked by NEWPAGE. Specifically, if a figure or table appears in the middle of text, but at format time won't fit on what's left of the page, the formatter defers the figure to the next page while continuing with the text. This feature requires somehow "getting inside of" NEWPAGE, so that when NEWPAGE is next executed, it will format the deferred figure at the top of the new page:

```
: NEWPAGE  ... ( terminate page with footer)
    ( start new page with header)  ...  ?HOLDOVER ... ;
```

How can NEWPAGE invoke ?HOLDOVER, if ?HOLDOVER is not defined until much later?

While it's theoretically possible to organize the listing so that the advance capability is defined before the root function, that approach is bad news for two reasons.

First, the natural organization (by degree of capability) is destroyed. Second, the advanced routines often use code that is defined amid the elementary capabilities. If you move the advanced routines to the front of the application, you'll also have to move any routines they use, or duplicate the code. Very messy.

You can organize the listing by degree of complexity using a technique called "vectoring." You can allow the root function to invoke (point to) any of various routines that have been defined after the root function itself. In our example, only the *name* of the routine ?HOLDOVER need be created early; its definition can be given later.

Chapter Seven treats the subject of vectoring in FORTH.

The Limits of Level Thinking

Most of us are guilty of over-emphasizing the difference between "high-level" and "low-level." This notion is an arbitrary one. It limits our ability to think clearly about software problems.

"Level" thinking, in the traditional sense, distorts our efforts in three ways:

1. It implies that the order of development should follow a hierarchical structure
2. It implies that levels should be segregated from each other, prohibiting the benefits of reusability
3. It fosters syntactical differences between levels (e.g., assembler vs. "high-level" languages) and a belief that the nature of programming somehow changes as we move further from machine code.

Let's examine each of these misconceptions one by one.

Where to Begin?

I asked Moore how he would go about developing a particular application, a game for children. As the child presses the digits on the numeric keypad, from zero to nine, that same number of large boxes would appear on the screen.

Moore:

> I don't start at the top and work down. Given that exact problem, I would write a word that draws a box. I'd start at the bottom, and I'd end up with a word called GO, which monitored the keyboard.

How much of that is intuitive?

> Perhaps some degree of it. I know where I'm going so I don't have to start there. But also it's more fun to draw boxes than to program a keyboard. I'll do the thing that's most fun in order to get into the problem. If I have to clean up all those details later, that's the price I pay.

Are you advocating a "fun-down" approach?

> Given that you're doing it in a free-spirit fashion, yes. If we were giving a demonstration to a customer in two days, I'd do it differently. I would start with the most visible thing, not the most fun thing. But still not in that hierarchical sequence, top down. I base my approach on more immediate considerations such as impressing the customer, getting something to work, or showing other people how it's going to work to get them interested.

> If you define a level as "nesting," then yes, it's a good way to decompose a problem. But I've never found the notion of "level" useful. Another aspect of levels is languages, metalanguages, meta-metalanguages. To try and split hairs as to which level you are on—assembler level, first integration level, last integration level—it's just tedious and not helpful. My levels get all mixed up hopelessly.

Designing by components makes where you start less important. You could start with the key interpreter, for instance. Its goal is to receive keystrokes and convert them to numbers, passing these numbers to an internally invoked word. If you substitute the FORTH word . ("dot," which prints a number from the stack), then we can implement the key interpreter, test it, and debug it. without using routines that have anything to do with drawing squares.

On the other hand, if the application required hardware support (such as a graphics package) that we didn't have or couldn't buy, we might want to substitute something available, such as displaying an asterisk, just to get into the problem. Thinking in terms of lexicons is like painting a huge mural that spans several canvases. You work on all the canvases at once, first sketching in the key design elements, then adding splashes of color here and there . . . until the entire wall is complete.

TIP

In deciding where to start designing, look for:

- areas where the most creativity is required (the areas where change is most likely)
- areas that give the most satisfying feedback (get the juices flowing)
- areas in which the approach decided upon will greatly affect other areas, or which will determine whether the stated problem can be solved at all
- things you should show the customer, for mutual understanding
- things you can show the investors, if necessary for the rent.

No Segregation Without Representation

The second way in which levels can interfere with optimal solutions is by encouraging segregation of the levels. A popular design construct called the "object" typifies this dangerous philosophy.

An object is a portion of code that can be invoked by a single name, but that can perform more than one function. To select a particular function you have to invoke the object and pass it a parameter or a group of parameters. You can visualize the parameters as representing a row of buttons you can push to make the object do what you want.

The benefit of designing an application in terms of objects is that, like a component, the object hides information from the rest of the application, making revision easier.

There are several problems, though. First, the object must contain a complicated decision structure to determine which function it must perform. This increases object size and decreases performance. A lexicon, on the other hand, provides all useable functions by name for you to invoke directly.

Second, the object is usually designed to stand alone. It can't take advantage of tools provided by supporting components. As a result, it

"No scrambled?"

tends to duplicate code inside itself that will appear elsewhere in the application. Some objects are even required to parse text in order to interpret their parameters. Each may even use its own syntax. A shameless waste of time and energy!

Finally, because the object is constructed to recognize a finite set of possibilities, it's difficult to make additions to the row of buttons when a new function is needed. The tools inside the object have not been designed for reuse.

The idea of levels pervades the design of my own personal computer, the IBM Personal Computer. Besides the processor itself (with its own machine instruction set, of course), there are these software levels:

- the set of utilities written in assembler and burned into the system's ROM
- the disk operating system, which invokes the utilities
- the high-level language of choice, which invokes the operating system and the utilities
- and finally, any application using the language.

The ROM utilities provide the hardware-dependent routines: those that handle the video screen, disk drives, and keyboard. You invoke them by placing a control code in a certain register and generating the appropriate software interrupt.

For instance, software interrupt 10H causes entry to the video routines. There are 16 of these routines. You load register AH with the number of the video routine you want.

Unfortunately, in all 16 routines there is not one that displays a text string. To do that, you must repeat the process of loading registers and generating a software interrupt, which in turn must make a decision about which routine you want, and do a few other things you don't need—for *every single character.*

Try writing a text editor in which the entire screen may need to be refreshed with each keystroke. Slow as mail! You can't improve the speed because you can't reuse any of the information within the video routines except for what's provided on the outside. The stated reason for this is to "insulate" the programmer from device addresses and other details of the hardware. After all, these could change with future upgrades.

The only way to efficiently implement video I/O on this machine is to move strings directly into video memory. You can do this easily, because the reference manual tells you the address at which video memory starts. But this defeats the intent of the system's designers. Your code may no longer survive a hardware revision.

By supposedly "protecting" the programmer from details, segregation has defeated the purpose of information hiding. Components, in contrast, are not segregated modules but rather cumulative additions to the dictionary. A video lexicon would, at the very least, give a name for the address of video memory.

It's not that anything's wrong with the concept of a bit-switch function interface between components, when it's necessary. The problem here is that this video component was incompletely designed. On the other hand, if the system had been fully integrated—operating system and drivers written in FORTH—the video component would not *have* to be designed to suit all needs. An application programmer could either rewrite the driver or write an extension to the driver using available tools from the video lexicon.

TIP

Don't bury your tools.

The Tower of Babble

The final deception perpetrated by level thinking is that programming languages should become qualitatively different the "higher" you go. We tend to speak of high-level code as something rarified, and low-level code as something grubby and profane.

To some degree these distinctions have validity, but this is only the result of certain arbitrary architectural constraints that we all accept as the norm. We've grown accustomed to assemblers with terse mnemonics and unnatural syntactical rules, because they're "low-level."

The component concept rebels against the polarity of high-level vs. low-level. All code should look and feel the same. A component is simply a set of commands that together transform data structures and algorithms into useful functions. These functions can be used without knowledge of the structures and/or algorithms within.

The distance of these structures from actual machine code is irrelevant. The code written to toggle bits in an output port should, in theory, look no more intimidating than the code to format a report.

Even machine code should be readable. A true FORTH-based engine would enjoy a syntax and dictionary identical and continuous with the "high-level" dictionary we know today.

Summary

In this chapter we've seen two ways that applications can be decomposed: into components, and according to sequential complexity.

Special attention should be paid to those components that serve as interfaces between other components.

Now, if you've done preliminary design correctly, your problem is lying at your feet in a heap of manageable pieces. Each piece represents a problem to solve. Grab your favorite piece and turn to the next chapter.

(Answers appear in Appendix D.)

1. Below are two approaches to defining an editor's keyboard interpreter.
   Which would you prefer? Why?

A)
```
( Define editor keys  )
HEX
72 CONSTANT UPCURSOR
80 CONSTANT DOWNCURSOR
77 CONSTANT RIGHTCURSOR
75 CONSTANT LEFTCURSOR
82 CONSTANT INSERTKEY
83 CONSTANT DELETEKEY
DECIMAL

( Keystroke interpreter)
: EDITOR
   BEGIN  MORE WHILE  KEY   CASE
      UPCURSOR        OF  CURSOR-UP      ENDOF
      DOWNCURSOR      OF  CURSOR-DOWN    ENDOF
      RIGHTCURSOR     OF  CURSOR>        ENDOF
      LEFTCURSOR      OF  CURSOR<        ENDOF
      INSERTKEY       OF  INSERTING      ENDOF
      DELETEKEY       OF  DELETE         ENDOF
   ENDCASE  REPEAT ;
```

B)
```
( Keystroke interpreter)
: EDITOR
   BEGIN  MORE WHILE  KEY    CASE
      72 OF  CURSOR-UP    ENDOF
      80 OF  CURSOR-DOWN  ENDOF
      77 OF  CURSOR>      ENDOF
      75 OF  CURSOR<      ENDOF
      82 OF  INSERTING    ENDOF
      83 OF  DELETE       ENDOF
   ENDCASE  REPEAT ;
```

2. This problem is an exercise in information hiding.

Let's suppose we have a region of memory outside of the FORTH dictionary which we want to allocate for data structures (for whatever reason). The region of memory begins at HEX address C000. We want to define a series of arrays which will reside in that memory.

We might do something like this:

```
HEX
C000 CONSTANT FIRST-ARRAY    ( 8 bytes)
C008 CONSTANT SECOND-ARRAY   ( 6 bytes)
C00C CONSTANT THIRD ARRAY    ( 100 bytes)
```

Each array-name defined above will return the starting address of the appropriate array. But notice we had to compute the correct starting address for each array, based on how many bytes we had already allocated. Let's try to automate this, by keeping an "allocation pointer," called >RAM, showing where the next free byte is. We first set the pointer to the beginning of the RAM space:

```
VARIABLE >RAM
C000 >RAM !
```

Now we can define each array like this:

```
>RAM @   CONSTANT FIRST-ARRAY     8 >RAM +!
>RAM @   CONSTANT SECOND-ARRAY    6 >RAM +!
>RAM @   CONSTANT THIRD-ARRAY   100 >RAM +!
```

Notice that after defining each array, we increment the pointer by the size of the new array to show that we've allocated that much additional RAM.

To make the above more readable, we might add these two definitions:

```
: THERE   ( -- address of next free byte in RAM)
     >RAM @ ;
: RAM-ALLOT  ( #bytes to allocate -- )   >RAM +! ;
```

We can now rewrite the above equivalently as:

```
THERE CONSTANT FIRST-ARRAY     8 RAM-ALLOT
THERE CONSTANT SECOND-ARRAY    6 RAM-ALLOT
THERE CONSTANT THIRD-ARRAY   100 RAM-ALLOT
```

(An advanced FORTH programmer would probably combine these operations into a single defining word, but that whole topic is not germane to what I'm leading up to.)

Finally, suppose we have 20 such array definitions scattered throughout our application.

Now, the problem: Somehow the architecture of our system changes

and we decide that we must allocate this memory such that it *ends* at
HEX address EFFF. In other words, we must start at the end, allocating
arrays backwards. We still want each array name to return its *starting*
address, however.

To do this, we must now write:

```
FOOO >RAM !   ( EFFF, last byte, plus one)
: THERE   ( -- address of next free byte in RAM)
     >RAM @ ;
: RAM-ALLOT   ( #bytes to allocate)   NEGATE >RAM +! ;
    8 RAM-ALLOT   THERE CONSTANT FIRST-ARRAY
    6 RAM-ALLOT   THERE CONSTANT SECOND-ARRAY
  100 RAM-ALLOT   THERE CONSTANT THIRD-ARRAY
```

This time RAM-ALLOT *decrements* the pointer. That's okay, it's easy
to add **NEGATE** to the definition of RAM-ALLOT. Our present concern
is that each time we define an array we must RAM-ALLOT *before* defining it, not after. Twenty places in our code need finding and
correcting.

The words THERE and RAM-ALLOT are nice and friendly, but
they didn't succeed at hiding *how* the region is allocated. If they had, it
wouldn't matter which order we invoked them in.

At long last, our question: What could we have done to THERE and
RAM-ALLOT to minimize the impact of this design change? (Again, the
answer I'm looking for has nothing to do with defining words.)

FOUR

Detailed Design/ Problem Solving

Trivial: I can see how to do this. I just don't know how long it will take.
Non-trivial: I haven't a *clue* how to do this!

—*Operating philosophy developed at the Laboratory
Automation and Instrumentation Design Group,
Chemistry Dept., Virginia Polytechnic Institute and State University*

Once you've decided upon the components in your application, your next step is to design those components. In this chapter we'll apply problem-solving techniques to the detailed design of a FORTH application. This is the time for pure invention, the part that many of us find the most fun. There's a special satisfaction in going to the mat with a non-trivial problem and coming out the victor.

In English it's difficult to separate an idea from the words used to express the idea. In writing a FORTH application it's difficult to separate the detailed design phase from implementation, because we tend to design in FORTH. For this reason, we'll get a bit ahead of ourselves in this chapter by not only presenting a problem but also designing a solution to it, right on through to the coded implementation.

Problem-Solving Techniques

Even neophytes can solve programming problems without devoting any conscious thought to problem solving techniques. So what's the point in studying techniques of problem solving? To quicken the process. By thinking about the *ways* in which we solve problems, apart from the problems themselves, we enrich our subconscious storehouse of techniques.

G. Polya has written several books on problem solving, especially of the mathematical problem. The most accessible of these is *How to Solve It* [1]. Although solving a mathematical problem isn't quite the same as solving a software problem, you'll find some valuable suggestions there.

The following series of tips summarize several techniques recommended by the science of problem solving:

TIP

Determine your goal.

Know what you're trying to accomplish. As we saw in Chapter Two, this step can be detailed further:

Determine the data interfaces: Know what data will be required to accomplish the goal, and make sure those data are available (input). Know what data the function is expected to produce (output). For a single definition, this means writing the stack-effect comment.

Determine the rules; review all the facts that you know. In Chapter Two we described the rates for computing the cost of a phone call along with the rules for applying the rates.

TIP

Picture the problem as a whole.

In the *analysis* phase we separated the problem into its parts, to clarify our understanding of each piece. We are now entering the *synthesis* phase. We must visualize the problem as a whole.

Try to retain as much information about the problem in your mind as possible. Use words, phrases, figures and tables, or any kind of graphic representation of the data and/or rules to help you see the maximum information at a glance. Fill your mind to bursting with the requirements of the problem you need to solve, the way you might fill your lungs with air.

Now hold that mental image, the way you might hold your breath. One of two things will happen:

You may see the solution in a flash of insight. Great! Exhale a sigh of relief and proceed directly to implementation. Or . . . , the problem is too complex or too unfamiliar to be solved so easily. In this case, you'll have to turn your attention to analogies and partial solutions. As you do so, it's important that you have already concentrated on the problem's requirements all at once, engraving these requirements on your mental retina.

TIP

Develop a plan.

If the solution didn't come at a glance, the next step is to determine the approach that you will take to solve it. Set a course for action and avoid the trap of fumbling about aimlessly.

The following tips suggest several approaches you might consider.

Does this problem sound familiar? Have you written a definition like it before? Figure out what parts of the problem are familiar, and in what ways this problem might differ. Try to remember how you solved it before, or how you solved something like it.

The normal, obvious way to attack a problem is by begining with the known, and proceeding to the unknown. In deciding which horse to bet on, you'd begin with their recent histories, their current health, and so on, apply weights to these various factors and arrive at a favorite.

More complicated problems present many possible ways to go with the incoming data. How do you know which route will take you closer to the solution? You don't. This class of problem is best solved by working backward (Figure 4-1).

Figure 4-1. *A problem that is easier to solve backward than forward.*

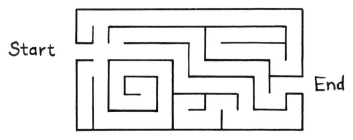

Belief is a necessary ingredient for successfully working backward. We'll illustrate with a famous mathematical problem. Suppose we have two containers. The containers have no graduation marks, but one holds nine gallons and the other holds four gallons. Our task is to measure out exact-

Figure 4-2. *Two containers.*

ly six gallons of water from the nearby stream in one of the containers (Figure 4-2).

Try to solve this on your own before reading further.

How can we get a "six" out of a "nine" and a "four"? We can start out working forward, by mentally transferring water from one container to the other. For example, if we fill the large container twice from the small container, we'll get eight gallons. If we fill the nine-gallon container to the brim, then empty enough water to fill the four-gallon container, we'll have exactly five gallons in the large container.

These ideas are interesting, but they haven't gotten us six gallons. And it's not clear how they will get us six gallons.

Let's try working backward. We assume we've measured six gallons of water, and it's sitting in the large container (it won't fit in the small one!). Now, how did we get it there? What was the state of our containers one step previously?

There are only two possibilities (Figure 4-3):

1. The four-gallon container was full, and we just added it to the large container. This implies that we already had two gallons in the large container. Or . . .
2. The nine gallon container was full, and we just poured off three gallons into the small container.

Which choice? Let's make a guess. The first choice requires a two-gallon measurement, the second requires a three-gallon measurement. In our initial playing around, we never saw a unit like two. But we did see a difference of one, and one from four is three. Let's go with version b.

Now comes the real trick. We must make ourselves *believe* without doubt that we have arrived at the situation described. We have just poured off three gallons into the small container. Suspending all disbelief, we concentrate on how we did it.

How can we pour off three gallons into the small container? If there had already been one gallon in the small container! Suddenly we're over the hump. The simple question now is, how do we get one gallon in the small container? We must have started with a full nine-gallon container,

Figure 4-3. *Achieving the end result.*

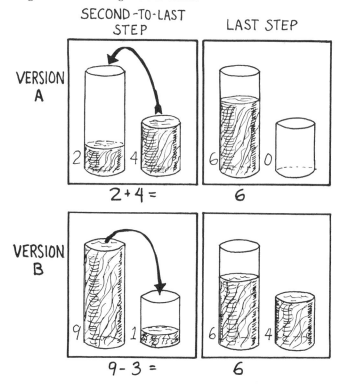

poured off four gallons twice, leaving one gallon. Then we transferred the one gallon to the small container.

Our final step should be to check our logic by running the problem forwards again.

Here's another benefit of working backward: If the problem is unsolvable, working backward helps you quickly prove that it has no solution.

TIP

Recognize the auxiliary problem.

Before we've solved a problem, we have only a hazy notion of what steps—or even how many steps—may be required. As we become more familiar with the problem, we begin to recognize that our problem includes one or more subproblems that somehow seem different from the main outline of the proposed procedure.

In the problem we just solved, we recognized two subproblems: filling the small container with one gallon and then filling the large container with six gallons.

Intent on a complicated problem.

Recognizing these smaller problems, sometimes called "auxiliary problems," is an important problem-solving technique. By identifying the subproblem, we can assume it has a straightforward solution. Without stopping to determine what that solution might be, we forge ahead with our main problem.

(FORTH is ideally suited to this technique, as we'll see.)

TIP

Step back from the problem.

It's easy to get so emotionally attached to one particular solution that we forget to keep an open mind.

The literature of problem solving often employs the example of the nine dots. It stumped me, so I'll pass it along. We have nine dots arranged as shown in Figure 4-4. The object is to draw straight lines that touch or pass through all nine dots, without lifting the pen off the paper. The constraint is that you must touch all nine dots with only four lines.

Figure 4-4. *The nine dots problem.*

> • • •
>
> • • •
>
> • • •

You can sit a good while and do no better than the almost-right Figure 4-5. If you concentrate really hard, you may eventually conclude that the problem is a trick—there's no solution.

Figure 4-5. *Not quite right.*

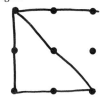

But if you sit back and ask yourself,

"Am I cheating myself out a useful tack by being narrow-minded? Am I assuming any constraints not specified in the problem? What constraints might they be?"

then you might think of extending some of the lines beyond the perimeter of the nine dots.

TIP

Use whole-brain thinking.

When a problem has you stumped and you seem to be getting nowhere, relax, stop worrying about it, perhaps even forget about it for a while.

Creative people have always noted that their best ideas seem to come out of the blue, in bed or in the shower. Many books on problem solving suggest relying on the subconscious for the really difficult problems.

Contemporary theories on brain functions explore the differences between rational, conscious thought (which relies on the manipulation of symbols) and subconscious thought (which correlates perceptions to previously stored information, recombining and relinking knowledge in new and useful ways).

Leslie Hart [2] explains the difficulty of solving a large problem by means of logic:

> A huge load is placed on that one small function of the brain that can be brought into the attention zone for a period. The feat is possible, like the circus act, but it seems more sensible to . . . use the full resources of our glorious neocortex . . . the multibillion-neuron capacity of the brain.
>
> . . . The work aspect lies in providing the brain with raw input, as in observing, reading, collecting data, and reviewing what others have achieved. Once in, [subconscious] procedures take over, simultaneously, automatically, outside of the attention zone.
>
> . . . It seems apparent . . . that a search is going on during the interval, though not necessarily continuously, much as in a large computer. I would hazard the guess that the search ramifies, starts and stops, reaches dead ends and begins afresh, and eventually assembles an answer that is evaluated and then popped into conscious attention—often in astonishingly full-blown detail.

TIP

Evaluate your solution. Look for other solutions.

You may have found one way of skinning the cat. There may be other ways, and some of them may be better.

Don't invest too much effort in your first solution without asking yourself for a second opinion.

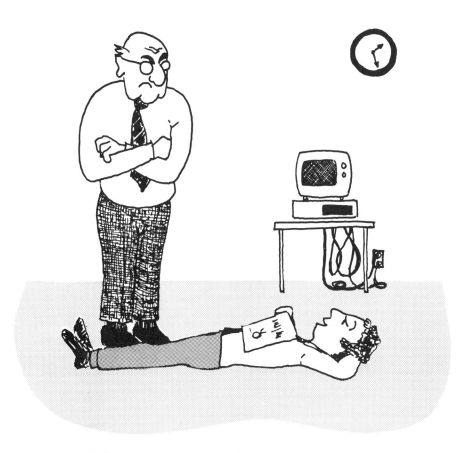

"I'm not just sleeping. I'm using my neocortex."

Donald A. Burgess, owner and president of Scientek Instrumentation, Inc.:

I have a few techniques I've found useful over the years in designing anything, to keep myself flexible. My first rule is, "Nothing is impossible." My second rule is, "Don't forget, the object is to make a buck."

First examine the problem, laying out two or three approaches on paper. Then try the most appealing one, to see if it works. Carry it through. Then deliberately go all the way back to the beginning, and start over.

Starting over has two values. First, it gives you a fresh approach. You either gravitate back to the way you started, or the way you started gravitates toward the new way.

Second, the new approach may show all kinds of powerful possibilities. Now you have a benchmark. You can look at both approaches and compare the advantages of both. You're in a better position to judge.

Getting stuck comes from trying too hard to follow a single approach. Remember to say, "I want this kumquat crusher to be different. Let's reject the traditional design as not interesting. Let's try some crazy ideas."

The best thing is to start drawing pictures. I draw little men. That keeps it from looking like "data" and interfering with my thinking process. The human mind works exceptionally well with analogies. Putting things in context keeps you from getting stuck within the confines of any language, even FORTH.

When I want to focus my concentration, I draw on little pieces of paper. When I want to think in broad strokes, to capture the overall flow, I draw on great big pieces of paper. These are some of the crazy tricks I use to keep from getting stagnant.

When I program in FORTH, I spend a day just dreaming, kicking around ideas. Usually before I start typing, I sketch it out in general terms. No code, just talk. Notes to myself.

Then I start with the last line of code first. I describe what I would like to do, as close to English as I can. Then I use the editor to slide this definition towards the bottom of the screen, and begin coding the internal words. Then I realize that's a lousy way to do it. Maybe I split my top word into two and transfer one of them to an earlier block so I can use it earlier. I run the hardware if I have it; otherwise I simulate it.

FORTH requires self-discipline. You have to stop diddling with the keyboard. FORTH is so willing to do what I tell it to, I'll tell it to do all kinds of ridiculous things that have nothing to do with where I'm trying to go. At those times I have to get away from the keyboard.

FORTH lets you play. That's fine, chances are you'll get some ideas. As long as you keep yourself from playing as a habit. Your head is a whole lot better than the computer for inventing things.

Detailed Design

We're now at the point in the development cycle at which we've decided we need a component (or a particular word). The component will consist of a number of words, some of which (those that comprise the lexicon) will be used by other components and some of which (the internal words) will be only used within this component.

Create as many words as necessary to obey the following tip:

TIP

Each definition should perform a simple, well-defined task.

Here are the steps generally involved in designing a component:

1. Based on the required functions, decide on the names and syntax for the external definitions (define the interfaces).
2. Refine the conceptual model by describing the algorithm(s) and data structure(s).
3. Recognize auxiliary definitions.
4. Determine what auxiliary definitions and techniques are already available.
5. Describe the algorithm with pseudocode,
6. Implement it by working backwards from existing definitions to the inputs,
7. Implement any missing auxiliary definitions.
8. If the lexicon contains many names with strong elements in common, design and code the commonalities as internal definitions, then implement the external definitions.

We'll discuss the first two steps in depth. Then we'll engage in an extended example of designing a lexicon.

FORTH Syntax

At this point in the development cycle you must decide how the words in your new lexicon will be used in context. In doing so, keep in mind how the lexicon will be used by subsequent components.

TIP

In designing a component, the goal is to create a lexicon that will make your later code readable and easy to maintain.

Each component should be designed with components that use it in mind. You must design the syntax of the lexicon so that the words make sense when they appear in context. Hiding interrelated information within the component will ensure maintainability, as we've seen.

At the same time, observe FORTH's own syntax. Rather than insisting on a certain syntax because it seems familiar, you may save yourself from writing a lot of unnecessary code by choosing a syntax that FORTH can support without any special effort on your part.

Here are some elementary rules of FORTH's natural syntax:

TIP

Let numbers precede names.

Words that require a numeric argument will naturally expect to find that number on the stack. Syntactically speaking, then, the number should precede the name. For instance, the syntax of the word **SPACES**, which emits "n" number of spaces, is

    20 SPACES

Sometimes this rule violates the order that our ear is accustomed to hearing. For instance, the FORTH word + expects to be preceded by both arguments, as in

    3 4 +

This ordering, in which values precede operators, is called "postfix."

FORTH, in its magnanimity, won't *insist* upon postfix notation. You could redefine + to expect one number in the input stream, like this:

    3 + 4

by defining it so:

    : +   BL WORD   NUMBER DROP   + ;

(where **WORD** is 79/83 Standard, returning an address, and **NUMBER** returns a double-length value as in the 83 Standard Uncontrolled Reference Words).

Fine. But you wouldn't be able to use this definition inside other colon definitions or pass it arguments, thereby defeating one of FORTH's major advantages.

Frequently, "noun" type words pass their addresses (or any type of pointer) as a stack argument to "verb" type words. The FORTH-like syntax of

    "noun" "verb"

will generally prove easiest to implement because of the stack.

In some cases this word order sounds unnatural. For instance, suppose we have a file named INVENTORY. One thing we can do with that file is SHOW it; that is, format the information in pretty columns. If IN-

LAWN MOW

FENCE PAINT

POST FIX

VENTORY passes a pointer to SHOW, which acts upon it, the syntax becomes

```
INVENTORY SHOW
```

If your spec demands the English word-order, FORTH offers ways to achieve it. But most involve new levels of complexity. Sometimes the best thing to do is to choose a better name. How about

```
INVENTORY REPORT
```

(We've made the "pointer" an adjective, and the "actor" a noun.)

If the requirements insist on the syntax

```
SHOW INVENTORY
```

we have several options. SHOW might set a flag and INVENTORY would act according to the flag. Such an approach has certain disadvantages, especially that INVENTORY must be "smart" enough to know all the possible actions that might be taken on it. (We'll treat these problems in Chapters Seven and Eight.)

Or, SHOW might look ahead at the next word in the input stream. We'll discuss this approach in a tip, "Avoid expectations," later in this chapter.

Or, the recommended approach, SHOW might set an "execution variable" that INVENTORY will then execute. (We'll discuss vectored execution in Chapter Seven.)

TIP

Let text follow names.

If the FORTH interpreter finds a string of text that is neither a number nor a predefined word, it will abort with an error message. For this reason, an undefined string must be preceded by a defined word.

An example is ." (dot-quote), which precedes the text it will later print. Another example is **CREATE** (as well as all defining words), which precedes the name that is, at the moment, still undefined.

The rule also applies to defined words that you want to refer to, but not execute in the usual way. An example is **FORGET**, as in

```
FORGET TASK
```

Syntactically, **FORGET** must precede TASK so that TASK doesn't execute.

Let definitions consume their arguments.

This syntax rule is more a convention of good FORTH programming than a preference of FORTH.

Suppose you're writing the word LAUNCH, which requires the number of a launch pad and fires the appropriate rocket. You want the definition to look roughly like this:

```
: LAUNCH   ( pad#)   LOAD   AIM   FIRE ;
```

Each of the three internal definitions will require the same argument, the launch pad number. You'll need two **DUP**s somewhere. The question is where? If you put them inside LOAD and AIM, then you can keep them out of LAUNCH, as in the definition above. If you leave them out of LOAD and AIM, you'll have to define:

```
: LAUNCH   ( pad#)   DUP LOAD   DUP AIM   FIRE ;
```

By convention, the latter version is preferable, because LOAD and AIM are cleaner. They do what you expect them to do. Should you have to define READY, you can do it so:

```
: READY   ( pad#)   DUP LOAD   AIM ;
```

and not

```
: READY   ( pad#)   LOAD   AIM   DROP ;
```

Use zero-relative numbering.

By habit we humans number things starting with one: "first, second, third," etc. Mathematical models, on the other hand, work more naturally when starting with zero. Since computers are numeric processors, software becomes easier to write when we use zero-relative numbering.

To illustrate, suppose we have a table of eight-byte records. The first record occupies the first eight bytes of the table. To compute its starting address, we add "0" to TABLE. To compute the starting address of the "second" record, we add "8" to TABLE.

Figure 4-6. *A table of 8-byte records.*

It's easy to derive a formula to achieve these results:

```
first record starts at:      0 × 8 =  0
second record starts at:     1 × 8 =  8
third record starts at:      2 × 8 = 16
```

We can easily write a word which converts a record# into the address where that record begins:

```
: RECORD  ( record# -- adr )
   8 *  TABLE + ;
```

Thus in computer terms it makes sense to call the "first record" the 0th record.

If your requirements demand that numbering start at one, that's fine. Use zero-relative numbering throughout your design and then, only in the "user lexicons" (the set of words that the end-user will use) include the conversion from zero-to one-relative numbering:

```
: ITEM  ( n -- adr)  1- RECORD ;
```

TIP

Let addresses precede counts.

Again, this is a convention, not a requirement of FORTH, but such conventions are essential for readable code. You'll find examples of this rule in the words **TYPE**, **ERASE**, and **BLANK**.

TIP

Let sources precede destinations.

Another convention for readability. For instance, in some systems, the phrase

```
22 37 COPY
```

copies Screen 22 to Screen 37. The syntax of CMOVE incorporates both this convention and the previous convention:

```
source destination count CMOVE
```

TIP

Avoid expectations (in the input stream).

Generally try to avoid creating words that presume there will be other words in the input stream.

Suppose your color computer represents blue with the value 1, and light-blue with 9. You want to define two words: BLUE will return 1; LIGHT may precede BLUE to produce 9.

In FORTH, it would be possible to define BLUE as a constant, so that when executed it always returns 1.

```
1 CONSTANT BLUE
```

And then define LIGHT such that it looks for the next word in the input stream, executes it, and "ors" it with 8 (the logic of this will become apparent when we visit this example again, later in the book):

```
: LIGHT   ( precedes a color)   ( -- color value)
      ' EXECUTE   8 OR ;
```

(in fig-FORTH:

```
: LIGHT    [COMPILE] '   CFA EXECUTE   8 OR ;)
```

(For novices: The apostrophe in the definition of LIGHT is a FORTH word called "tick." Tick is a dictionary-search word; it takes a name and looks it up in the dictionary, returning the address where the definition resides. Used in this definition, it will find the address of the word following LIGHT—for instance, BLUE—and pass this address to the word **EXECUTE**, which will execute BLUE, pushing a one onto the stack. Having "sucked up" the operation of BLUE, LIGHT now "or"s an 8 into the 1, producing a 9.)

This definition will work when invoked in the input stream, but special handling is required if we want to let LIGHT be invoked within a colon definition, as in:

```
: EDITING   LIGHT BLUE BORDER ;
```

Even in the input stream, the use of **EXECUTE** here will cause a crash if LIGHT is accidentally followed by something other than a defined word.

The preferred technique, if you're forced to use this particular syntax, is to have LIGHT set a flag, and have BLUE determine whether that flag was set, as we'll see later on.

There will be times when looking ahead in the input stream is desirable, even necessary. (The proposed TO solution is often implemented this way [3].)

But generally, avoid expectations. You're setting yourself up for disappointment.

TIP

Let commands perform themselves.

This rule is a corollary to "Avoid expectations." It's one of FORTH's philosophical quirks to let words do their own work. Witness the FORTH compiler (the function that compiles colon definitions), caricatured in Figure 4-7. It has very few rules:

Figure 4-7. *The traditional compiler vs. the FORTH compiler.*

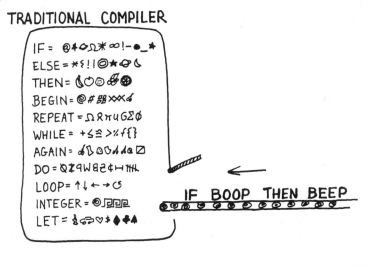

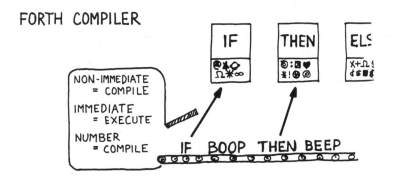

Scan for the next word in the input stream and look it up in the dictionary.

If it's an ordinary word, *compile* its address.

If it's an "immediate" word, *execute* it.

If it's not a defined word, try to convert it to a number and compile it as a literal.

If it's not a number, abort with an error message.

Nothing is mentioned about compiling-words such as **IF, ELSE, THEN,** etc. The colon compiler doesn't know about these words. It merely recognizes certain words as "immediate" and executes them, letting them do their own work. (See *Starting FORTH*, Chapter Eleven, "How to Control the Colon Compiler.")

The compiler doesn't even "look for" semicolon to know when to stop compiling. Instead it *executes* semicolon, allowing it to do the work of ending the definition and shutting off the compiler.

There are two tremendous advantages to this approach. First, the compiler is so simple it can be written in a few lines of code. Second, there's no limit on the number of compiling words you can add at any time, simply by making them immediate. Thus, even FORTH's colon compiler is extensible!

FORTH's text interpreter and FORTH's address interpreter also adhere to this same rule.

The following tip is perhaps the most important in this chapter:

TIP

Don't write your own interpreter/compiler when you can use FORTH's.

One class of applications answers a need for a special purpose language—a self-contained set of commands for doing one particular thing. An example is a machine-code assembler. Here you have a large group of commands, the mnemonics, with which you can describe the instructions you want assembled. Here again, FORTH takes a radical departure from mainstream philosophy.

Traditional assemblers are special-purpose interpreters—that is, they are complicated programs that scan the assembly-language listing looking for recognized mnemonics such as ADD, SUB, JMP, etc., and assemble machine instructions correspondingly. The FORTH assembler, however, is merely a lexicon of FORTH words that themselves assemble machine instructions.

There are many more examples of the special purpose language, each specific to individual applications. For instance:

1. If you're building an Adventure-type game, you'd want to write a language that lets you create and describe monsters and rooms, etc. You might create a defining word called ROOM to be used like this:

```
ROOM DUNGEON
```

Then create a set of words to describe the room's attributes by building unseen data structures associated with the room:

```
EAST-OF DRAGON-LAIR
WEST-OF BRIDGE
CONTAINING POT-O-GOLD
etc.
```

The commands of this game-building language can simply be FORTH WORDS, with FORTH as the interpreter.

2. If you're working with Programmable Array Logic (PAL) devices, you'd like a form of notation that lets you describe the behavior of the output pins in logical terms, based on the states of the input pins. A PAL programmer was written with wonderful simplicity in FORTH by Michael Stolowitz [4].

3. If you must create a series of user menus to drive your application, you might want to first develop a menu-compiling language. The words of this new language allow an application programmer to quickly program the needed menus—while hiding information about how to draw borders, move the cursor, etc.

All of these examples can be coded in FORTH as lexicons, using the normal FORTH interpreter, without having to write a special-purpose interpreter or compiler.

Moore:

A simple solution is one that does not obscure the problem with irrelevancies. It's conceivable that something about the problem requires a unique interpreter. But every time you see a unique interpreter, it implies that there is something particularly awkward about the problem. And that is almost never the case.

If you write your own interpreter, the interpreter is almost certainly the most complex, elaborate part of your entire application. You have switched from solving a problem to writing an interpreter.

I think that programmers like to write interpreters. They like to do these elaborate difficult things. But there comes a time when the world is going to have to quit programming keypads and converting numbers to binary, and start solving problems.

Algorithms and Data Structures

In Chapter Two we learned how to describe a problem's requirements in terms of interfaces and rules. In this section we'll refine the conceptual model for each component into clearly defined algorithms and data structures.

An algorithm is a procedure, described as a finite number of rules, for accomplishing a certain task. The rules must be unambiguous and guaranteed to terminate after a finite number of applications. (The word is named for the ninth century Persian mathematician al-Khowarizimi.)

An algorithm lies halfway between the imprecise directives of human speech, such as "Please sort these letters chronologically," and the precise directives of computer language, such as "BEGIN 2DUP < IF ..." etc. The algorithm for sorting letters chronologically might be this:

1. Take an unsorted letter and note its date.
2. Find the correspondence folder for that month and year.
3. Flip through the letters in the folder, starting from the front, until you find the first letter dated later than your current letter.
4. Insert your current letter just in front of the letter dated later. (If the folder is empty, just insert the letter.)

There may be several possible algorithms for the same job. The algorithm given above would work fine for folders containing ten or fewer letters, but for folders with a hundred letters, you'd probably resort to a more efficient algorithm, such as this:

1. (same)
2. (same)
3. If the date falls within the first half of the month, open the folder a third of the way in. If the letter you find there is dated later than your current letter, search forward until you find a letter dated the same or before your current letter. Insert your letter at that point. If the letter you find is dated earlier than your current letter, search backward ...

... You get the point. This second algorithm is more complicated than the first. But in execution it will require fewer steps on the average (because you don't have to search clear from the beginning of the folder every time) and therefore can be performed faster.

A data structure is an arrangement of data or locations for data, organized especially to match the problem. In the last example, the file cabinet containing folders and the folders containing individual letters can be thought of as data structures.

The new conceptual model includes the filing cabinets and folders (data structures) plus the steps for doing the filing (algorithms).

Calculations vs. Data Structures vs. Logic

We've stated before that the best solution to a problem is the simplest adequate one; for any problem we should strive for the simplest approach.

Suppose we must write code to fulfill this specification:

if the input argument is 1, the output is 10

if the input argument is 2, the output is 12
if the input argument is 3, the output is 14

There are three approaches we could take:

Calculation
```
( n)   1-   2*   10 +
```

Data Structure
```
CREATE TABLE   10 C,   12 C,   14 C,
( n)   1- TABLE + C@
```

Logic
```
( n)   CASE
           1 OF 10 ENDOF
           2 OF 12 ENDOF
           3 OF 14 ENDOF   ENDCASE
```

In this problem, calculation is simplest. Assuming it is also adequate (speed is not critical), calculation is best.

The problem of converting angles to sines and cosines can be implemented more simply (at least in terms of lines of code and object size) by calculating the answers than by using a data structure. But for many applications requiring trig, it's faster to look up the answer in a table stored in memory. In this case, the simplest *adequate* solution is using the data structure.

In Chapter Two we introduced the telephone rate problem. In that problem the rates appeared to be arbitrary, so we designed a data structure:

	Full Rate	Lower Rate	Lowest Rate
First Min.	.30	.22	.12
Add'l Mins.	.12	.10	.06

Using a data structure was simpler than trying to invent a formula by which these values could be calculated. And the formula might prove wrong later. In this case, table-driven code is easier to maintain.

In Chapter Three we designed a keystroke interpreter for our Tiny Editor using a decision table:

Key	*Not-Inserting*	*Inserting*
Cntrl-D	DELETE	INSERT-OFF
Cntrl-I	INSERT-ON	INSERT-OFF
backspace	BACKWARD	INSERT<
etc.		

We could have achieved this same result with logic:

```
CASE
    CNTRL-D    OF    'INSERTING @   IF
        INSERT-OFF  ELSE   DELETE      THEN    ENDOF
    CNTRL-I    OF    'INSERTING @   IF
        INSERT-OFF  ELSE   INSERT-ON  THEN    ENDOF
    BACKSPACE OF    'INSERTING @   IF
        INSERT<     ELSE   BACKWARD   THEN    ENDOF
ENDCASE
```

but the logic is more confusing. And the use of logic to express such a multi-condition algorithm gets even more convoluted when a table was not used in the original design.

The use of logic becomes advisable when the result is not calculable, or when the decision is not complicated enough to warrent a decision table. Chapter Eight is devoted to the issue of minimizing the use of logic in your programs.

TIP

In choosing which approach to apply towards solving a problem, give preference in the following order:
  1. calculation (except when speed counts)
  2. data structures
  3. logic

Of course, one nice feature of modular languages such as FORTH is that the actual implementation of a component—whether it uses calculation, data structures, or logic—doesn't have to be visible to the rest of the application.

Solving a Problem: Computing Roman Numerals

In this section we'll attempt to demonstrate the process of designing a lexicon. Rather than merely present the problem and its solution, I'm hoping we can crack this problem together. (I kept a record of my thought processes as I solved this problem originally.) You'll see elements of the problem-solving guidelines previously given, but you'll also see them being applied in a seemingly haphazard order—just as they would be in reality.

Here goes: The problem is to write a definition that consumes a number on the stack and displays it as a Roman numeral.

This problem most likely represents a component of a larger system. We'll probably end up defining several words in the course of solving this problem, including data structures. But this particular lexicon will include only one name, ROMAN, and it will take its argument from the stack. (Other words will be internal to the component.)

Having thus decided on the external syntax, we can now proceed to devise the algorithms and data structures.

We'll follow the scientific method—we'll observe reality, model a solution, test it against reality, modify the solution, and so on. We'll begin by recalling what we know about Roman numerals.

Actually, we don't remember any formal rules about Roman numerals. But if you give us a number, we can make a Roman numeral out of it. We know how to do it—but we can't yet state the procedure as an algorithm.

So, let's look at the first ten Roman numerals:

```
   I
  II
 III
 IV
  V
 VI
VII
VIII
 IX
  X
```

We make a few observations. First, there's the idea of a tally, where we represent a number by making that many marks (3 = III). On the other hand, special symbols are used to represent groups (5 = V). In fact, it seems we can't have more than three I's in a row before we use a larger symbol.

Second, there's a symmetry around five. There's a symbol for five (V), and a symbol for ten (X). The pattern I, II, III repeats in the second half, but with a preceding V.

One-less-than-five is written IV, and one-less-than-ten is written IX. It seems that putting an "I" in front of a larger-value symbol is like saying "one-less-than . . ."

These are vague, hazy observations. But that's alright. We don't have the whole picture yet.

Let's study what happens above ten:

```
 XI
 XII
XIII
XIV
 XV
XVI
```

XVII
XVIII
XIX
XX

This is exactly the pattern as before, with an extra "X" in front. So there's a repeating cycle of ten, as well.

If we look at the twenties, they're the same, with two "X"s; the thirties with three "X"s. In fact, the number of "X" is the same as the number in the tens column of the original decimal number.

This seems like an important observation: we can decompose our decimal number into decimal digits, and treat each digit separately. For instance, 37 can be written as

XXX   (thirty)

followed by

VII   (seven)

It may be premature, but we can already see a method by which FORTH will let us decompose a number into decimal digits—with modulo divison by ten. For instance, if we say

    37 10 /MOD

we'll get a 7 and a 3 on the stack (the three—being the quotient—is on top.)

But these observations raise a question: What about below ten, where there is no decimal digit? Is this a special case? Well, if we consider that each "X" represents ten, then the absence of "X" represents zero. So it's *not* a special case. Our algorithm works, even for numbers less than ten.

Let's continue our observations, paying special attention to the cycles of ten. We notice that forty is "XL." This is analogous to 4 being "IV," only shifted by the value of ten. The "X" before the "L" says "ten-less-than-fifty." Similarly,

L	(50)	is analogous to	V	(5)
LX	(60)	"	VI	(6)
LXX	(70)	"	VII	(7)
LXXX	(80)	"	VIII	(8)
XC	(90)	"	IX	(9)
C	(100)	"	X	(10)

Apparently the same patterns apply for any decimal digit—only the symbols themselves change. Anyway, it's clear now that we're dealing with an essentially decimal system.

If pressed to do so, we could even build a model for a system to display Roman numerals from 1 to 99, using a combination of algorithm and data structure.

Data Structure

Ones' Table		Tens' Table	
0		0	
1	I	1	X
2	II	2	XX
3	III	3	XXX
4	IV	4	XL
5	V	5	L
6	VI	6	LX
7	VII	7	LXX
8	VIII	8	LXXX
9	IX	9	XC

Algorithm

Divide n by 10. The quotient is the tens' column digit; the remainder is the ones' column digit. Look up the ten's digit in the tens' table and print the corresponding symbol pattern. Look up the ones' digit in the one's table and print that corresponding symbol pattern.

For example, if the number is 72, the quotient is 7, the remainder is 2. 7 in the tens' table corresponds to "LXX," so print that. 2 in the ones' column corresponds to "II," so print that. The result:

LXXII

We've just constructed a model that works for numbers from one to 99. Any higher number would require a hundreds' table as well, along with an initial division by 100.

The logical model just described might be satisfactory, as long as it does the job. But somehow it doesn't seem we've fully solved the problem. We avoided figuring out how to produce the basic pattern by storing all possible combinations in a series of tables. Earlier in this chapter we observed that calculating an answer, if it's possible, can be easier than using a data structure.

Since this section deals with devising algorithms, let's go all the way. Let's look for a general algorithm for producing any digit, using only the elementary set of symbols. Our data structure should contain only this much information:

```
I    V
X    L
C    D
M
```

In listing the symbols, we've also *organized* them in a way that seems right. The symbols in the left column are all multiples of ten; the symbols in the right column are multiples of five. Furthermore, the symbols in each row have ten times the value of the symbols directly above them.

Another difference, the symbols in the first column can all be combined in multiples, as "XXXIII." But you can't have multiples of any of the right-column symbols, such as VVV. Is this observation useful? Who knows?

Let's call the symbols in the left column ONERS and in the right column FIVERS. The ONERS represent the values 1, 10, 100, and 1,000; that is, the value of one in every possible decimal place. The FIVERS represent 5, 50, and 500; that is, the value of five in every possible decimal place.

Using these terms, instead of the symbols themselves, we should be able to express the algorithm for producing any digit. (We've factored out the actual symbols from the *kind* of symbols.) For instance, we can state the following preliminary algorithm:

For any digit, print as many ONERS as necessary to add up to the value.

Thus, for 300 we get "CCC," for 20 we get "XX" for one we get "I." And for 321 we get "CCCXXI."

This algorithm works until the digit is 4. Now we'll have to expand our algorithm to cover this exception:

Print as many ONERS as necessary to add up to the value, but if the digit is 4, print a ONER then a FIVER.

Hence, 40 is "XL"; 4 is "IV."

This new rule works until the digit is 5. As we noticed before, digits of five and above begin with a FIVER symbol. So we expand our rule again:

If the digit is 5 or more, begin with a FIVER and subtract five from the value; otherwise do nothing. Then print as many ONERS as necessary to add up to the value. But if the digit is 4, print only a ONER and a FIVER.

This rule works until the digit is 9. In this case, we must print a ONER preceding a—what? A ONER from the next higher decimal place (the next row below). Let's call this a TENER. Our complete model, then is:

If the digit is 5 or more, begin with a FIVER and subtract five from the value; otherwise do nothing. Then, print as many ONERS as necessary to add up to the value. But if the digit is 4, print only a ONER and a FIVER, or if it's 9, print only a ONER and a TENER.

We now have an English-language version of our algorithm. But we still have some steps to go before we can run it on our computer.

In particular, we have to be more specific about the exceptions. We can't just say,

Do a, b, and c. *But* in such and such a case, do something different.

because the computer will do a, b, and c before it knows any better.

Instead, we have to check whether the exceptions apply *before* we do anything else.

TIP

In devising an algorithm, consider exceptions last. In writing code, handle exceptions first.

This tells us something about the general structure of our digit-producing word. It will have to begin with a test for the 4/9 exceptions. In either of those cases, it will respond accordingly. If neither exception applies, it will follow the "normal" algorithm. Using pseudocode, then:

```
: DIGIT  ( n )  4-OR-9? IF  special cases
    ELSE  normal case  THEN ;
```

An experienced FORTH programmer would not actually write out this pseudocode, but would more likely form a mental image of the structure for eliminating the special cases. A less experienced programmer might find it helpful to capture the structure in a diagram, or in code as we've done here.

In FORTH we try to minimize our dependence on logic. But in this case we need the conditional **IF** because we have an exception we need to eliminate. Still, we've minimized the complexity of the control structure by limiting the number of **IF THEN**s in this definition to one.

Yes, we still have to distinguish between the 4-case and the 9-case, but we've deferred that structural dimension to lower-level definitions—the test for 4-or-9 and the "special case" code.

What our structure really says is that *either* the 4-exception or the 9-exception must prohibit execution of the normal case. It's not enough merely to test for each exception, as in this version:

```
: DIGIT  ( n )  4-CASE? IF  ONER FIVER  THEN
                9-CASE? IF  ONER TENER  THEN
                normal case... ;
```

because the normal case is never excluded. (There's no way to put an

ELSE just before the normal case, because **ELSE** must appear between **IF** and **THEN**.)

If we insist on handling the 4-exception and the 9-exception separately, we could arrange for each exception to pass an additional flag, indicating that the exception occurred. If either of these flags is true, then we can exclude the normal case:

```
: DIGIT  ( n )  4-CASE? DUP IF  ONER FIVER  THEN
                9-CASE? DUP IF  ONER TENER  THEN
                OR  NOT IF normal case THEN ;
```

But this approach needlessly complicates the definition by adding new control structures. We'll leave it like it was.

Now we have a general idea of the structure of our main definition.

We stated, "If the digit is 5 or more, begin with a FIVER and subtract five from the value; otherwise do nothing. Then, print as many ONERS as necessary to add up to the value."

A direct translation of these rules into FORTH would look like this:

```
( n)  DUP  4 > IF  FIVER  5 -  THEN  ONERS
```

This is technically correct, but if we're familiar with the technique of modulo divison, we'll see this as a natural situation for modulo division by 5. If we divide the number by five, the quotient will be zero (false) when the number is less than five, and one (true) when it's between 5 and 9. We can use it as the boolean flag to tell whether we want the leading FIVER:

```
( n )  5 / IF FIVER THEN ...
```

The quotient/flag becomes the argument to IF.

Furthermore, the remainder of modulo 5 division is always a number between 0 and 4, which means that (except for our exception) we can use the remainder directly as the argument to ONERS. We revise our phrase to

```
( n )  5 /MOD IF FIVER THEN  ONERS
```

Getting back to that exception, we now see that we can test for both 4 and 9 with a single test—namely, if the remainder is 4. This suggests that we can do our 5 /MOD first, then test for the exception. Something like this:

```
: DIGIT  ( n )
    5 /MOD  OVER 4 =  IF  special case  ELSE
    IF FIVER THEN  ONERS  THEN ;
```

(Notice that we **OVER**ed the remainder so that we could compare it with 4 without consuming it.)

So it turns out we *do* have a doubly-nested **IF THEN** construct after all. But it seems justified because the **IF THEN** is handling the special case. The other is such a short phrase, "IF FIVER THEN", it's hardly worth making into a separate definition. You could though. (But we won't.)

Let's focus on the code for the special case. To state its algorithm: "If the digit is four, print a ONER and a FIVER. If the digit is nine, print a ONER and a TENER."

We can assume that the digit will be one or the other, or else we'd never be executing this definition. The question is, how do we tell which one?

Again, we can use the quotient of division by five. If the quotient is zero, the digit must have been four; otherwise it was nine. So we'll play the same trick and use the quotient as a boolean flag. We'll write:

```
: ALMOST   ( quotient )
     IF  ONER TENER  ELSE  ONER FIVER   THEN ;
```

In retrospect, we notice that we're printing a ONER either way. We can simplify the definition to:

```
: ALMOST   ( quotient )
     ONER   IF TENER ELSE FIVER THEN ;
```

We've assumed that we have a quotient on the stack to use. Let's go back to our definition of DIGIT and make sure that we do, in fact:

```
: DIGIT  ( n )
     5 /MOD  OVER 4 =  IF  ALMOST  ELSE
     IF FIVER THEN  ONERS  THEN ;
```

It turns out that we have not only a quotient, but a remainder underneath as well. We're keeping both on the stack in the event we execute the **ELSE** clause. The word **ALMOST**, however, only needs the quotient. So, for symmetry, we must **DROP** the remainder like this:

```
: DIGIT  ( n )
     5 /MOD  OVER 4 =  IF  ALMOST  DROP  ELSE
     IF FIVER THEN  ONERS  THEN ;
```

There we have the complete, coded definition for producing a single digit of a Roman numeral. If we were desperate to try it out before writing the needed auxiliary definitions, we could very quickly define a lexicon of words to print one group of symbols, say the ONES row:

```
: ONER      ." I " ;
: FIVER     ." V" ;
: TENER     ." X";
: ONERS   ( # of oners -- )
        ?DUP IF  0 DO  ONER  LOOP   THEN ;
```

before loading our definitions of ALMOST and DIGIT.

But we're not that desperate. No, we're anxious to move on to the problem of defining the words ONER, FIVER, and TENER so that their symbols depend on which decimal digit we're formatting.

Let's go back to the symbol table we drew earlier:

	ONERs	FIVERs
ones	I	V
tens	X	L
hundreds	C	D
thousands	M	

We've observed that we also need a "TENER"—which is the ONER in the next row below. It's as if the table should really be written:

	ONERs	FIVERs	TENERs
ones	I	V	(X)
tens	(X)	L	(C)
hundreds	(C)	D	(M)
thousands	(M)		

But that seems redundant. Can we avoid it? Perhaps if we try a different model, perhaps a linear table, like this:

ones	I
	V
tens	X
	L
hundreds	C
	D
thousands	M

Now we can imagine that each column name ("ones," "tens," etc.) points to the ONER of that column. From there we can also get each column's FIVER by reaching down one slot below the current ONER, and the TENER by reaching down two slots.

It's like building an arm with three hands. We can attach it to the ONES column, as in Figure 4-8 a, or we can attach it to the tens' column, as in Figure 4-8 b, or to any power of ten.

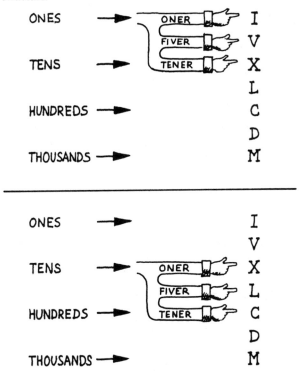

Figure 4-8. *A mechanical representation: accessing the data structure.*

An experienced FORTH programmer is not likely to imagine arms, hands, or things like that. But there must be a strong mental image—the stuff of right-brain thinking—before there's any attempt to construct the model with code.

Beginners who are learning to think in this right-brain way might find the following tip helpful:

TIP

If you have trouble thinking about a conceptual model, visualize it—or draw it—as a mechanical device.

Our table is simply an array of characters. Since a character requires only a byte, let's make each "slot" one byte. We'll call the table ROMANS:

```
CREATE ROMANS      ( ones)    ASCII I  C,    ASCII V  C,
                   ( tens)    ASCII X  C,    ASCII L  C,
               ( hundreds)    ASCII C  C,    ASCII D  C,
              ( thousands)    ASCII M  C,
```

Note: This use of **ASCII** requires that **ASCII** be "STATE-dependent" (see Appendix C). If you don't have **ASCII**, or if it is not state-dependent, use:

```
CREATE ROMANS  73 C,  86 C,  88 C,  76 C,
     67 C,  68 C,  77 C,
```

We can select a particular symbol from the table by applying two different offsets at the same time. One dimension represents the decimal place: ones, tens, hundreds, etc. This dimension is made "current," that is, its state stays the same until we change it.

The other dimension represents the kind of symbol we want—ONER, FIVER, TENER—within the current decimal column. This dimension is incidental, that is, we'll specify which symbol we want each time.

Let's start by implementing the "current" dimension. We need some way to point to the current decimal column. Let's create a variable called COLUMN# (pronounced "column-number") and have it contain an offset into the table:

```
VARIABLE COLUMN#   ( current offset)
: ONES        0 COLUMN# ! ;
: TENS        2 COLUMN# ! ;
: HUNDREDS    4 COLUMN# ! ;
: THOUSANDS   6 COLUMN# ! ;
```

Now we can find our way to any "arm position" by adding the contents of COLUMN# to the beginning address of the table, given by ROMANS:

```
: COLUMN  ( -- adr of column)  ROMANS  COLUMN# @  + ;
```

Let's see if we can implement one of the words to display a symbol. We'll start with ONER.

The thing we want to do in ONER is **EMIT** a character.

```
: ONER                EMIT ;
```

Working backward, **EMIT** requires the ASCII character on the stack. How do we get it there? With C@.

```
: ONER                C@ EMIT ;
```

C@ requires the *address* of the slot that contains the symbol we want. How do we get that address?

The ONER is the first "hand" on the movable arm—the position that COLUMN is already pointing to. So, the address we want is simply the address returned by COLUMN:

```
: ONER    COLUMN        C@ EMIT ;
```

Now let's write FIVER. It computes the same slot address, then adds one to get the next slot, before fetching the symbol and emitting it:

```
: FIVER   COLUMN 1+     C@ EMIT ;
```

And TENER is:

```
: TENER   COLUMN 2+     C@ EMIT ;
```

These three definitions are redundant. Since the only difference between them is the incidental offset, we can factor the incidental offset out from the rest of the definitions:

```
: .SYMBOL   ( offset)   COLUMN +   C@ EMIT ;
```

Now we can define:

```
: ONER    0 .SYMBOL ;
: FIVER   1 .SYMBOL ;
: TENER   2 .SYMBOL ;
```

All that remains for us to do now is to decompose our complete decimal number into a series of decimal digits. Based on the observations we've already made, this should be easy. Figure 4-9 shows our completed listing.

Voila! From problem, to conceptual model, to code.

Note: this solution is not optimal. The present volume does not address the optimization phase.

One more thought: Depending on who uses this application, we may want to add error-checking. Fact is, the highest symbol we know is M; the highest value we can represent is 3,999, or MMMCMXCIX.

We might redefine ROMAN as follows:

```
: ROMAN   ( n)
     DUP  3999 > ABORT" Too large"   ROMAN ;
```

Moore:

> There's a definite sense of rightness when you've done it right. It may be that feeling that distinguishes FORTH from other languages, where you never feel you've really done well. In FORTH, it's the "Aha!" reaction. You want to run off and tell somebody.
>
> Of course, nobody will appreciate it like you do.

Figure 4-9. *Roman numerals, solved.*

```
Screen # 20
 0 \ Roman numerals                                              8/18/83
 1 CREATE ROMANS      ( ones)     ASCII I   C,     ASCII V   C,
 2                    ( tens)     ASCII X   C,     ASCII L   C,
 3                ( hundreds)     ASCII C   C,     ASCII D   C,
 4               ( thousands)     ASCII M   C,
 5 VARIABLE COLUMN#   ( current offset)
 6 : ONES         0 COLUMN# ! ;
 7 : TENS         2 COLUMN# ! ;
 8 : HUNDREDS     4 COLUMN# ! ;
 9 : THOUSANDS    6 COLUMN# ! ;
10
11 : COLUMN   ( -- address of column)  ROMANS  COLUMN# @  + ;
12
```

```
Screen # 21
 0 \ Roman numerals cont'd                                       8/18/83
 1 : .SYMBOL  ( offset -- )   COLUMN +  C@ EMIT ;
 2 : ONER     0 .SYMBOL ;
 3 : FIVER    1 .SYMBOL ;
 4 : TENER    2 .SYMBOL ;
 5
 6 : ONERS   ( # of oners -- )
 7    ?DUP  IF  0 DO  ONER  LOOP  THEN ;
 8 : ALMOST  ( quotient of 5 / -- )
 9    ONER  IF  TENER  ELSE  FIVER  THEN ;
10 : DIGIT   ( digit -- )
11    5 /MOD  OVER  4 = IF  ALMOST  DROP  ELSE  IF FIVER THEN
12    ONERS   THEN ;
13
```

```
Screen # 22
 0 \ Roman numerals cont'd                                       8/18/83
 1 : ROMAN   ( number --)   1000 /MOD   THOUSANDS DIGIT
 2                           100 /MOD   HUNDREDS DIGIT
 3                            10 /MOD        TENS DIGIT
 4                                           ONES DIGIT  ;
 5
```

Summary

In this chapter we've learned to develop a single component, starting first with deciding on its syntax, then proceeding with determining its algorithm(s) and data structure(s), and concluding with an implementation in FORTH.

With this chapter we complete our discussion of design. The remainder of the book will discuss style and programming techniques.

References

1. G. Polya, *How To Solve It: A New Aspect of Mathematical Method,* (Princeton, New Jersey, Princeton University Press).
2. Leslie A. Hart, *How the Brain Works,* © 1975 by Leslie A. Hart, (New York, Basic Books, Inc., 1975).
3. Evan Rosen, "High Speed, Low Memory Consumption Structures," *1982 FORML Conference Proceedings,* p. 191.
4. Michael Stolowitz, "A Compiler for Programmable Logic in FORTH," *1982 FORML Conference Proceedings,* p. 257.

For Further Thinking

Design the components and describe the algorithm(s) necessary to simulate shuffling a deck of cards. Your algorithm will produce an array of numbers, 0-51, arranged in random order.

The special constraint of this problem, of course, is that no one card may appear twice in the array.

You may assume you have a random-number generator called CHOOSE. It's stack argument is "n"; it produces a random number between zero and n-1 inclusive. (See the Handy Hint, Chapter Ten, *Starting FORTH.*)

Can you design the card-shuffling algorithm so that it avoids the time-consuming burden of checking some undetermined number of slots on each pass of the loop? Can you do so using only the one array?

FIVE

Implementation: Elements of FORTH Style

Badly written FORTH has been accused of looking like "code that went through a trash compactor." It's true, FORTH affords more freedom in the way we write applications. But that freedom also gives us a chance to write exquisitely readable and easily maintainable code, provided we consciously employ the elements of good FORTH style.

In this chapter we'll delve into FORTH coding convention including:

> listing organization
> screen layout, spacing and indentation
> commenting
> choosing names.

I wish I could recommend a list of hard-and-fast conventions for everyone. Unfortunately, such a list may be inappropriate in many situations. This chapter merges many widely-adopted conventions with personal preferences, commented with alternate ideas and the reasons for the preferences. In other words:

> : TIP   VALUE JUDGEMENT ;

I'd especially like to thank Kim Harris, who proposed many of the conventions described in this chapter, for his continuing efforts at unifying divergent views on good FORTH style.

Listing Organization

A well-organized book has clearly defined chapters, with clearly defined sections, and a table of contents to help you see the organization at a glance. A well-organized book is easy to read. A badly organized book makes comprehension more difficult, and makes finding information later on nearly impossible.

I still don't see how these programming conventions enhance readability.

The necessity for good organization applies to an application listing as well. Good organization has three aspects:

1. Decomposition
2. Composition
3. Disk partitioning

Decomposition

As we've already seen, the organization of a listing should follow the decomposition of the application into lexicons. Generally these lexicons should be sequenced in "uses" order. Lexicons being *used* should precede the lexicons which *use* them.

On a larger scale, elements in a listing should be organized by degree of complexity, with the most complex variations appearing towards the end. It's best to arrange things so that you can leave off the lattermost screens (i.e., not load them) and still have a self-sufficient, running application, working properly except for the lack of the more advanced features.

We discussed the art of decomposition extensively in Chapter Three.

Composition

Composition is the putting together of pieces to create a whole. Good composition requires as much artistry as good decomposition.

One of FORTH's present conventions is that source code resides in "screens," which are 1K units of mass storage. (The term "screen" refers to a block used specifically for source code.) It's possible in FORTH to chain every screen of code to the next, linking the entire listing together linearly like a lengthy parchment scroll. This is not a useful approach. Instead:

TIP

Structure your application listing like a book: hierarchically.

An application may consist of:

Screens: the smallest unit of FORTH source
Lexicons: one to three screens, enough to implement a component
Chapters: a series of related lexicons, and
Load screens: analogous to a table of contents, a screen that loads the chapters in the proper sequence.

Figure 5-1. *Example of an application-load screen.*

```
Screen # 1
   0 \ QTF+ Load Screen                                    07/09/83
   1 : RELEASE#    ." 2.01" ;
   2    9 LOAD   \ compiler tools, language primitives
   3   12 LOAD   \ video primitives
   4   21 LOAD   \ editor
   5   39 LOAD   \ line display
   6   48 LOAD   \ formatter
   7   69 LOAD   \ boxes
   8   81 LOAD   \ deferring
   9   90 LOAD   \ framing
  10   96 LOAD   \ labels, figures, tables
  11  102 LOAD   \ table of contents generator
  12
  13
  14
  15
```

Application-load Screen

Figure 5-1 is an example of an application-load screen. Since it resides in Screen 1, you can load this entire application by entering

    1 LOAD

The individual load commands within this screen load the chapters of the application. For instance, Screen 12 is the load screen for the video primitives chapter.

   As a reference tool, the application-load screen tells you where to find all of the chapters. For instance, if you want to look at the routines that do framing, you can see that the section starts at Screen 90.

   Each chapter-load screen in turn, loads all of the screens comprising the chapter. We'll study some formats for chapter-load screens shortly.

   The primary benefit of this hierarchical scheme is that you can load any section, or any screen by itself, without having to load the entire application. Modularity of the source code is one of the reasons for FORTH's quick turnaround time for editing, loading, and testing (necessary for the iterative approach). Like pages of a book, each screen can be accessed individually and quickly. It's a "random access" approach to source-code maintenance.

   You can also replace any passage of code with a new, trial version by simply changing the screen numbers in the load screen. You don't have to move large passages of source code around within a file.

   In small applications, there may not be such things as chapters. The application-load screen will directly load all the lexicons. In larger applications, however, the extra level of hierarchy can improve maintainability.

A screen should either be a load-screen or a code-screen, not a mixture. Avoid embedding a **LOAD** or **THRU** command in the middle of a screen containing definitions just because you "need something" or because you "ran out of room."

Skip Commands

Two commands make it easy to control what gets loaded in each screen and what gets ignored. They are:

```
\
\S also called EXIT
```

\ is pronounced "skip-line." It causes the FORTH interpreter to ignore everything to the right of it on the same line. (Since \ is a FORTH word, it must be followed by a space.) It does not require a delimiter.

In Figure 5-1, you see \ used in two ways: to begin the screen-comment line (Line 0), and to begin comments on individual lines which have no more code to the right of the comment.

During testing, \ also serves to temporarily "paren out" lines that already contain a right parenthesis in a name or comment. For instance, these two "skip-line"'s keep the definition of NUTATE from being compiled without causing problems in encountering either right parenthesis:

```
\ : NUTATE   ( x y z )
\    SWAP ROT   (NUTATE) ;
```

\S is pronounced "skip-screen." It causes the FORTH interpreter to stop interpreting the screen entirely, as though there were nothing else in the screen beyond \S.

In many FORTH systems, this function is the same as **EXIT**, which is the run-time routine for semicolon. In these systems the use of **EXIT** is acceptable. Some FORTH systems, however, require for internal reasons a different routine for the "skip-screen" function.

Definitions for \ and \S can be found in Appendix C.

Chapter-load Screens

Figure 5-2 illustrates a typical chapter-load screen. The screens loaded by this screen are referred to relatively, not absolutely as they were in the application-load screen.

This is because the chapter-load screen is the first screen of the contiguous range of screens in the chapter. You can move an entire chapter forward or backward within the listing; the relative pointers in the chapter-load screen are position-independent. All you have to change is

Figure 5-2. *Example of a chapter-load screen.*

```
Screen # 100
  0 \ GRAPHICS              Chapter load               07/11/83
  1
  2  1 FH LOAD              \ dot-drawing primitive
  3  2 FH 3 FH THRU         \ line-drawing primitives
  4  4 FH 7 FH THRU         \ scaling, rotation
  5  8 FH LOAD              \ box
  6  9 FH 11 FH THRU        \ circle
  7
  8
  9
 10 CORNER  \ initialize relative position to low-left corner
 11
 12
 13
 14
 15
```

the single number in the application-load screen that points to the beginning of the chapter.

TIP

Use absolute screen numbers in the application-load screen. Use relative screen numbers in the chapter- or section-load screens.

There are two ways to implement relative loading. The most common is to define:

```
: +LOAD  ( offset -- )  BLK @ +  LOAD ;
```

and

```
: +THRU  ( lo-offset hi-offset -- )
      1+ SWAP DO  I +LOAD  LOOP ;
```

My own way, which I submit as a more useful factoring, requires a single word, **FH** (see Appendix C for its definition).

The phrase

```
1 FH LOAD
```

is read "1 from here LOAD," and is equivalent to 1 + LOAD.

Similarly,

```
2 FH  5 FH THRU
```

is read "2 from here, 5 from here THRU."

Some programmers begin each chapter with a dummy word; e.g.,

```
: VIDEO-IO ;
```

and list its name in the comment on the line where the chapter is loaded in the application-load screen. This permits selectively **FORGET**ting any chapter and reloading from that point on without having to look at the chapter itself.

Within a chapter the first group of screens will usually define those variables, constants, and other data structures needed globally within the chapter. Following that will come the lexicons, loaded in "uses" order. The final lines of the chapter-load screen normally invoke any needed initialization commands.

Some of the more style-conscious FORTHwrights begin each chapter with a "preamble" that discusses in general terms the theory of operation for the components described in the chapter. Figure 5-3 is a sample preamble screen which demonstrates the format required at Moore Products Co.

Charles Moore (no relation to Moore Products Co.) places less importance on the well-organized hierarchical listing than I do. Moore:

Figure 5-3. *Moore Products Co.'s format for chapter preambles.*

```
 0    CHAPTER 5   -   ORIGIN/DESTINATION - MULTILOOP BIT ROUTINES
 1
 2    DOCUMENTS - CONSOLE STRUCTURE CONFIGURATION
 3           DESIGN SPECIFICATION
 4           SECTIONS - 3.2.7.5.4.1.2.8
 5                      3.2.7.5.4.1.2.10
 6
 7    ABSTRACT   -   File control types E M T Q and R can all
 8                   originate from a Regional Satellite or a
 9                   Data Survey Satellite.  These routines allow
10                   the operator to determine whether the control
11                   originated from a Regional Satellite or not.
12
13
14
15


 0    CHAPTER NOTES   - Whether or not a point originates from
 1                      a Regional Satellite is determined by
 2                      the Regional bit in BITS, as follows:
 3
 4                      1 = Regional Satellite
 5                      2 = Data Survey Satellite
 6
 7                      For the location of the Regional bit
 8                      in BITS, see the Design Specification
 9                      Section - 3.2.7.5.4.1.2.10
10
11    HISTORY   -
12
13
14
15
```

I structure *applications* hierarchically, but not necessarily *listings*. My listings are organized in a fairly sloppy way, not at all hierarchically in the sense of primitives first.

I use **LOCATE** [also known as **VIEW**; see the Handy Hint in *Starting FORTH*, Chapter Nine]. As a result, the listing is much less carefully organized because I have **LOCATE** to find things for me. I never look at listings.

-- > vs. THRU

On the subject of relative loading, one popular way to load a series of adjacent screens is with the word -- > (pronounced "next block"). This word causes the interpreter to immediately cease interpreting the current screen and begin interpreting the next (higher-numbered) screen.

If your system provides -- >, you must choose between using the **THRU** command in your chapter-load screen to load each series of screens, or linking each series together with the arrows and **LOAD**ing only the first in the series. (You can't do both; you'd end up loading most of the screens more than once.)

The nice thing about the arrows is this: suppose you change a screen in the middle of a series, then reload the screen. The rest of the series will automatically get loaded. You don't have to know what the last screen is.

That's also the nasty thing about the arrows: There's no way to stop the loading process once it starts. You may compile a lot more screens than you need to test this one screen.

To get analytical about it, there are three things you might want to do after making the change just described:

1. load the one screen only, to test the change,
2. load the entire section in which the screen appears,
   or
3. load the entire remainder of the application.

The use of **THRU** seems to give you the greatest control.

Some people consider the arrow to be useful for letting definitions cross screen boundaries. In fact -- > is the only way to compile a high-level (colon) definition that occupies more than one screen, because -- > is "immediate." But it's NEVER good style to let a colon definition cross screen boundaries. (They should never be that long!)

On the other hand, an extremely complicated and time-critical piece of assembler coding might occupy several sequential screens. In this case, though, normal **LOAD**ing will do just as well, since the assembler does not use compilation mode, and therefore does not require immediacy.

Finally, the arrow wastes an extra line of each source screen. We don't recommend it.

An Alternative to Screens: Source in Named Files

Some FORTH practitioners advocate storing source code in variable-length, named text files, deliberately emulating the approach used by traditional compilers and editors. This approach may become more and more common, but its usefulness is still controversial.

Sure, it's nice not to have to worry about running out of room in a screen, but the hassle of writing in a restricted area is compensated for by retaining control of discrete chunks of code. In developing an application, you spend a lot more time loading and reloading screens than you do rearranging their contents.

"Infinite-length" files allow sloppy, disorganized thinking and bad factoring. Definitions become longer without the discipline imposed by the 1K block boundaries. The tendency becomes to write a 20K file, or worse: a 20K definition.

Perhaps a nice compromise would be a file-based system that allows nested loading, and encourages the use of very small named files. Most likely, though, the more experienced FORTH programmers would not use named files longer than 5K to 10K. So what's the benefit?

Some might answer that rhetorical question: "It's easier to remember names than numbers." If that's so, then predefine those block numbers as constants, e.g.:

```
90 CONSTANT FRAMING
```

Then to load the "framing" section, enter

```
FRAMING LOAD
```

Or, to list the section's load block, enter

```
FRAMING LIST
```

(It's a convention that names of sections end in "ING.")

Of course, to minimize the hassle of the screen-based approach you need good tools, including editor commands that move lines of source from one screen to another, and words that slide a series of screens forward or back within the listing.

Disk Partitioning

The final aspect of the well-organized listing involves standardizing an arrangement for what goes where on the disk. These standards must be set by each shop, or department, or individual programmer, depending on the nature of the work.

```
Screen 0 is the title screen, showing the name of the
    application, the current release number, and primary
    author

Screen 1 is the application-load block

Screen 2 is reserved for possible continuation from
    Screen 1

Screen 4 and 5 contain system messages

Screens 9 thru 29 incorporate general utilities needed
    in, but not restricted to, this application

Screen 30 begins the application screens
```

Figure 5-4 shows a typical department's partitioning scheme.

In many FORTH shops it's considered desirable to begin sections of code on screen numbers that are evenly divisible by three. Major divisions on a disk should be made on boundaries evenly divisible by thirty.

The reason? By convention, FORTH screens are printed three to a page, with the top screen always evenly divisible by three. Such a page is called a "triad"; most FORTH systems include the word TRIAD to produce it, given as an argument the number of any of the three screens in the triad. For instance, if you type

```
77 TRIAD
```

you'll get a page that includes 75, 76, and 77.

The main benefit of this convention is that if you change a single screen, you can slip the new triad right into your binder containing the current listing, replacing exactly one page with no overlapping screens.

Similarly, the word **INDEX** lists the first line of each screen, 60 per page, on boundaries evenly divisible by 60.

TIP

Begin sections or lexicons on screen numbers evenly divisible by three. Begin applications or chapters on screen numbers evenly divisible by thirty.

Electives

Vendors of FORTH systems have a problem. If they want to include every command that the customer might expect—words to control graphics, printers, and other niceties—they often find that the system has swollen to more than half the memory capacity of the computer, leaving less room for serious programmers to compile their applications.

The solution is for the vendor to provide the bare bones as a precompiled nucleus, with the extra goodies provided in *source* form. This approach allows the programmer to pick and choose the special routines actually needed.

These user-loadable routines are called "electives." Double-length arithmetic, date and time support, CASE statements and the DOER/MAKE construct (described later) are some of the features that FORTH systems should offer as electives.

Screen Layout

In this section we'll discuss the layout of each source screen.

TIP

Reserve Line 0 as a "comment line."

The comment line serves both as a heading for the screen, and also as a line in the disk INDEX. It should describe the purpose of the screen (not list the words defined therein).

The comment line minimally contains the name of the screen. In larger applications, you may also include both the chapter name and screen name. If the screen is one of a series of screens implementing a lexicon, you should include a "page number" as well.

The upper right hand corner is reserved for the "stamp." The stamp includes the date of latest revision and, when authorship is important, the programmer's initials (three characters to the left of the date); e.g.:

```
( Chapter name       Screen Name -- pg #        JPJ 06/10
```

Some FORTH editors will enter the stamp for you at the press of a key.

A common form for representing dates is

```
mm-dd-yy
```

that is, February 6, 1984 would be expressed

```
02—06—84
```

An increasingly popular alternative uses

```
ddMmmyy
```

where "Mmm" is a three-letter abbreviation of the month. For instance:

```
22Oct84
```

This form requires fewer characters than

    10—22—84

and eliminates possible confusion between dates and months.

If your system has / ("skip-line"—see Appendix C), you can write the comment line like this:

```
\ Chapter name       Screen Name -- pg.#       JPJ 06/10/83
```

As with all comments, use lower-case or a mixture of lower- and upper-case text in the comment line.

One way to make the index of an application reveal more about the organization of the screens is to indent the comment line by three spaces in screens that continue a lexicon. Figure 5-5 shows a portion of a list produced by **INDEX** in which the comment lines for the continuing screens are indented.

TIP

Begin all definitions at the left edge of the screen, and define only one word per lines.

Bad:

```
: ARRIVING    ." HELLO" ;   : DEPARTING    ." GOODBYE" ;
```

Good:

```
: ARRIVING    ." HELLO" ;
: DEPARTING    ." GOODBYE" ;
```

This rule makes it easier to find a definition in the listing. (When definitions continue for more than one line, the subsequent lines should always be indented.)

Figure 5-5. *The output of INDEX showing indented comment lines.*

```
 90 \ Graphics            Chapter load      JPJ 06/10/83
 91     \ Dot-drawing primitives            JPJ 06/10/83
 92 \ Line-drawing primitives               JPJ 06/11/83
 93     \ Line-drawing primitives           JPJ 06/10/83
 94     \ Line-drawing primitives           JPJ 09/02/83
 95 \ Scaling, rotation                     JPJ 06/10/83
 96     \ Scaling, rotation                 JPJ 02/19/84
 97     \ Scaling, rotation                 JPJ 02/19/84
 98     \ Scaling, rotation                 JPJ 02/19/84
 99 \ Boxes                                 JPJ 06/10/83
100 \ Circles                               JPJ 06/10/83
101     \ Circles                           JPJ 06/10/83
102     \ Circles                           JPJ 06/10/83
```

VARIABLES and **CONSTANTS** should also be defined one per line. (See "Samples of Good Commenting Style" in Appendix E.) This leaves room for an explanatory comment on the same line. The exception is a large "family" of words (defined by a common defining-word) which do not need unique comments:

```
0 HUE BLACK      1 HUE BLUE      2 HUE GREEN
3 HUE CYAN       4 HUE RED       5 HUE MAGENTA
```

TIP

Leave lots of room at the bottom of the screen for later additions.

On your first pass, fill each screen no more than half with code. The iterative approach demands that you sketch out the components of your application first, then iteratively flesh them out until all the requirements are satisfied. Usually this means adding new commands, or adding special-case handling, to existing screens. (Not *always,* though. A new iteration may see a simplification of the code. Or a new complexity may really belong in another component and should be factored out, into another screen.)

Leaving plenty of room at the outset makes later additions more pleasant. One writer recommends that on the initial pass, the screen should contain about 20–40 percent code and 80–60 percent whitespace [1].

Don't skip a line between each definition. You may, however, skip a line between *groups* of definitions.

TIP

All screens must leave **BASE** set to **DECIMAL**.

Even if you have three screens in a row in which the code is written in **HEX** (three screens of assembler code, for instance), each screen must set **BASE** to **HEX** at the top, and restore base to **DECIMAL** at the bottom. This rule ensures that each screen could be loaded separately, for purposes of testing, without mucking up the state of affairs. Also, in reading the listing you know that values are in decimal unless the screen explicitly says **HEX**.

Some shops take this rule even further. Rather than brashly resetting base to **DECIMAL** at the end, they reset base to *whatever it was at the beginning.* This extra bit of insurance can be accomplished in this fashion:

```
BASE @        HEX      \ save original BASE on stack
0A2 CONSTANT BELLS
0A4 CONSTANT WHISTLES
... etc. ...
BASE !                 \ restore it
```

Sometimes an argument is passed on the stack from screen to screen, such as the value returned by **BEGIN** or **IF** in a multiscreen assembler definition, or the base address passed from one defining word to another—see "Compile-Time Factoring" in Chapter Six. In these cases, it's best to save the value of BASE on the return stack like this:

```
BASE @ >R       HEX
... etc. ...
R> BASE !
```

Some folks make it a policy to use this approach on any screen that changes **BASE**, so they don't have to worry about it.

Moore prefers to define **LOAD** to invoke **DECIMAL** after loading. This approach simplifies the screen's contents because you don't have to worry about resetting.

Spacing and Indentation

TIP

Spacing and indentation are essential for readability.

The examples in this book use widely accepted conventions of spacing and indenting style. Whitespace, appropriately used, lends readability. There's no penalty for leaving space in source screens except disk memory, which is cheap.

For those who like their conventions in black and white, Table 5-1 is a list of guidelines. (But remember, FORTH's interpreter couldn't care less about spacing or indentation.)

Table 5-1 Indentation and spacing guidelines

---

1 space between the colon and the name

2 spaces between the name and the comment*

2 spaces, or a carriage return, after the comment and before the definition*

3 spaces between the name and definition if no comment is used

3 spaces indentation on each subsequent line (or multiples of 3 for nested indentation)

1 space between words/numbers within a phrase

2 or 3 spaces between phrases

1 space between the last word and the semicolon

1 space between semicolon and **IMMEDIATE** (if invoked)

No blank lines between definitions, except to separate distinct groups of definitions

An often-seen alternative calls for 1 space between the name and comment and 3 between the comment and the definition. A more liberal technique uses 3 spaces before and after the comment. Whatever you choose, be consistent.

The last position of each line should be blank except for:

    a)   quoted strings that continue onto the next line, or
    b)   the end of a comment.

A comment that begins with \ may continue right to the end of the line. Also, a comment that begins with (may have its delimiting right parenthesis in the last column.

Here are some common errors of spacing and indentation:

Bad (name not separated from the body of the definition):

```
: PUSH HEAVE HO ;
```

Good:

```
: PUSH    HEAVE HO ;
```

Bad (subsequent lines not indented three spaces):

```
: RIDDANCE   ( thing-never-to-darken-again -- )
DARKEN   NEVER AGAIN ;
```

Good:

```
: RIDDANCE   ( thing-never-to-darken-again -- )
   DARKEN   NEVER AGAIN ;
```

Bad (lack of phrasing):

```
: GETTYSBURG    4 SCORE 7 YEARS + AGO ;
```

Good:

```
: GETTYSBURG    4 SCORE   7 YEARS +   AGO ;
```

Phrasing is a subjective art; I've yet to see a useful set of formal rules. Simply strive for readability.

Comment Conventions

Appropriate commenting is essential. There are five types of comments: stack-effect comments, data-structure comments, input-stream comments, purpose comments and narrative comments.

A *stack-effect comment* shows the arguments that the definition consumes from the stack, and the arguments it returns to the stack, if any.

A *data-structure comment* indicates the position and meaning of elements in a data structure. For instance, a text buffer might contain a count in the first byte, and 63 free bytes for text.

An *input-stream comment* indicates what strings the word expects to see in the input stream. For example, the FORTH word FORGET scans for the name of a dictionary entry in the input stream.

A *purpose comment* describes, in as few words possible, what the definition does. How the definition works is not the concern of the purpose comment.

A *narrative comment* appears amidst a definition to explain what is going on, usually line-by-line. Narrative comments are used only in the "vertical format," which we'll describe in a later section.

Comments are usually typed in lower-case letters to distinguish them from source code. (Most FORTH words are spelled with upper-case letters, but lower-case spellings are sometimes used in special cases.)

In the following sections we'll summarize the standardized formats for these types of comments and give examples for each type.

Stack Notation

TIP

Every colon or code definition that consumes and/or returns any arguments on the stack must include a stack-effect comment.

"Stack notation" refers to conventions for representing what's on the stack. Forms of stack notation include "stack pictures," "stack effects," and "stack-effect comments."

Stack Picture

A stack picture depicts items understood to be on the stack at a given time. Items are listed from left to right, with the leftmost item representing the bottom of the stack and the rightmost item representing the top.

For instance, the stack picture

    n1 n2

indicates two numbers on the stack, with n2 on the top (the most accessible position).

This is the same order that you would use to type these values in; i.e., if n1 is 100 and n2 is 5000, then you would type

    100 5000

to place these values correctly on the stack.

A stack picture can include either abbreviations, such as "n1," or fully spelled-out words. Usually abbreviations are used. Some standard abbreviations appear in Table 5-2. Whether abbreviations or fully spelled-out words are used, each stack item should be separated by a space.

If a stack item is described with a phrase (such as "address-of-latest-link"), the words in the phrase should be joined by hyphens. For example, the stack picture:

```
address current-count max-count
```

shows three elements on the stack.

Stack Effect

A "stack effect" shows two stack pictures: one picture of any items that may be *consumed* by a definition, and another picture of any items *returned* by the definition. The "before" picture comes first, followed by two hyphens, then the "after" picture.

For instance, the stack effect for FORTH's addition operator, + is

```
n n -- sum
```

where + consumes two numbers and returns their sum.

Remember that the stack effect describes only the *net result* of the operation on the stack. Other values that happen to reside on the stack beneath the arguments of interest don't need to be shown. Nor do values that may appear or dissappear while the operation is executing.

If the word returns any input arguments unchanged, they should be repeated in the output picture; e.g.,

```
3rd 2nd top-input -- 3rd 2nd top-output
```

Conversely, if the word changes any arguments, the stack comment must use a different descriptor:

```
n1 -- n2
n -- n'
```

A stack effect might appear in a formatted glossary.

Stack Effect Comment

A "stack-effect comment" is a stack effect that appears in source code surrounded by parentheses. Here's the stack-effect comment for the word COUNT:

```
( address-of-counted-string -- address-of-text count )
```

or:

```
( 'counted-string -- 'text count)
```

(The "count" is on top of the stack after the word has executed.)

If a definition has no effect on the stack (that is, no effect the user is aware of, despite what gyrations occur within the definition), it needs no stack-effect comment:

```
: BAKE    COOKIES OVEN ! ;
```

On the other hand, you may want to use an empty stack comment—i.e.,

```
: BAKE  ( -- )  COOKIES OVEN ! ;
```

to emphasize that the word has no effect on the stack.

If a definition consumes arguments but returns none, the double-hyphen is optional. For instance,

```
( address count -- )
```

can be shortened to

```
( address count )
```

The assumption behind this convention is this: There are many more colon definitions that consume arguments and return nothing than definitions that consume nothing and return arguments.

Stack Abbreviation Standards

Abbreviations used in stack notation should be consistent. Table 5-2 lists most of the commonly used abbreviations. (This table reappears in Appendix E.) The terms "single-length," "double-length," etc. refer to the size of a "cell" in the particular FORTH system. (If the system uses a 16-bit cell, "n" represents a 16-bit number; if the system uses a 32-bit cell, "n" represents a 32-bit number.)

Notation of Flags

Table 5-2 shows three ways to represent a boolean flag. To illustrate, here are three versions of the same stack comment for the word —TEXT:

```
( a1 u a2 -- ?)
( a1 u a2 -- t=no-match)
( a1 u a2 -- f=match)
```

Table 5-2. Stack_comment abbreviations.

n	single-length signed number
d	double-length signed number
u	single-length unsigned number
ud	double-length unsigned number
t	triple-length
q	quadruple-length
c	7-bit character value
b	8-bit byte
?	boolean flag; or;
t=	true
f=	false
a or adr	address
acf	address of code field
apf	address of parameter field
'	(as prefix) address of
s d	(as a pair) source destination
lo hi	lower-limit upper-limit (inclusive)
#	count
o	offset
i	index
m	mask
x	don't care (data structure notation)

An "offset" is a difference expressed in absolute units, such as bytes.
An "index" is a difference expressed in logical units, such as elements or records.

The equal sign after the symbols "t" and "f" equates the flag outcome with its meaning. The result-side of the second version would be read "true means no match."

Notation of Variable Possibilities

Some definitions yield a different stack effect under different circumstances.

If the number of items on the stack remains the same under all conditions, but the items themselves change, you can use the vertical bar (|) to mean "or." The following stack-effect comment describes a word that returns either the address of a file or, if the requested file is not found, zero:

```
( -- address!0=undefined-file)
```

If the number of items in a stack picture can very—in either the "before" or "after" picture—you must write out both versions of the entire stack picture, along with the double-hypen, separated by the "or" symbol. For instance:

```
-FIND    ( -- apf len t=found ¦ -- f=not-found )
```

This comment indicates that if the word is found, three arguments are returned (with the flag on top); otherwise only a false flag is returned.

Note the importance of the second "--". Its omission would indicate that the definition always returned three arguments, the top one being a flag.

If you prefer, you can write the entire stack effect twice, either on the same line, separated by three spaces:

```
?DUP    \ if zero:( n -- n)    if non-zero:( n -- n n)
```

or listed vertically:

```
-FIND  \      found:( -- apf len t )
       \ not-found:( -- f )
```

Data-Structure Comments

A "data-structure comment" depicts the elements in a data structure. For example, here's the definition of an insert buffer called |INSERT :

```
CREATE ¦INSERT  64 ALLOT  \   { 1# ¦ 63text }
```

The "faces" (curly-brackets) begin and end the structure comment; the bars separate the various elements in the structure; the numbers represent bytes per element. In the comment above, the first byte contains the count, and the remaining 63 bytes contain the text.

A "bit comment" uses the same format as a data-structure comment to depict the meaning of bits in a byte or cell. For instance, the bit comment

```
{ 1busy? ¦ 1acknowledge? ¦ 2x ¦ 6input-device ¦
    6output-device }
```

describes the format of a 16-bit status register of a communications channel. The first two bits are flags, the second two bits are unused, and the final pair of six-bit fields indicate the input and output devices which this channel is connected to.

If more than one data structure employs the same pattern of elements, write out the comment only once (possibly in the preamble), and give a name to the pattern for reference in subsequent screens. For instance, if the preamble gives the above bit-pattern the name "status," then "status" can be used in stack comments to indicate values with that pattern:

```
: STATUS?   ( -- status) ... ;
```

If a **2VARIABLE** contains one double-length value, the comment should be a stack picture that indicates the contents:

```
2VARIABLE PRICE   \ price in cents
```

If a **2VARIABLE** contains two single-length data elements, it's given a stack picture showing what would be on the stack after a 2@. Thus:

```
2VARIABLE MEASUREMENTS   ( height weight )
```

This is different from the comment that would be used if MEASUREMENTS were defined by **CREATE**.

```
CREATE MEASUREMENTS   4 ALLOT   \ { 2weight | 2height
```

(While both statements produce the same result in the dictionary, the use of **2VARIABLE** implies that the values will normally be "2-fetched" and "2-stored" together—thus we use a *stack* comment. The high-order part, appearing on top of the stack, is listed to the right. The use of **CREATE** implies that the values will normally be fetched and stored separately—thus we use a data structure comment. The item in the 0th position is listed to the left.)

Input-stream Comments

The input-stream comment indicates what words and/or strings are presumed to be in the input stream. Table 5-3 lists the designations used for input stream arguments.

Table 5-3. Input-stream comment designations.

c	single character, blank-delimited
name	sequence of characters, blank delimited
text	sequence of characters, delimited by non-blank

Follow "text" with the actual delimiter required; e.g.: text" or text)

The input-stream comment appears *before* the stack comment, and is *not* encapsulated between its own pair of parentheses, but simply surrounded by three spaces on each side. For instance, here's one way to comment the definition of ' (tick) showing first the input-stream comment, then the stack comment:

```
:  '    \   name    ( -- a)
```

If you prefer to use (, the comment would look like this:

```
:  '    (   name    ( -- a)
```

Incidentally, there are three distinct ways to receive string input. To avoid confusion, here are the terms:

- *Scanning-for* means looking ahead in the input stream, either for a word or number as in the case of tick, or for a delimiter as in the case of ." and (.
- *Expecting* means waiting for. **EXPECT** and **KEY**, and definitions that invoke them, are ones that "expect" input.
- *Presuming* indicates that in normal usage something will follow. The word : "scans-for" the name to be defined, and "presumes" that a definition will follow.

The input-stream comment is only appropriate for input being scanned-for.

Purpose Comments

TIP

Every definition should bear a purpose comment unless:
  a. its purpose is clear from its name or its stack-effect comment, or
  b. if it consists of three or fewer words.

The purpose comment should be kept to a minimum—never more than a full line. For example:

```
: COLD    \ restore system to start condition
    ... ;
```

use the imperative mood: "set Foreground color," not "sets Foreground color."

On the other hand, a word's purpose can often be described in terms of its stack-effect comment. You rarely need both a stack comment and a purpose comment. For instance:

```
: SPACES   ( #)
```

or

```
: SPACES   ( #spaces-to-type -- )   ...   ;
```

This definition takes as its incoming argument a number that represents the number of spaces to type.

```
: ELEMENT   ( element# -- 'element)   2*   TABLE + ;
```

This definition converts an index, which it consumes, into an address within a table of 2-byte elements corresponding to the indexed element.

```
: PAD   ( -- 'scratch-pad)   HERE   80 + ;
```

This definition returns an address of a scratch region of memory.

Occasionally, readability is best served by including both types of comment. In this case, the purpose comment should appear last. For instance:

```
: BLOCK   ( n -- a)   \   ensure block n in buffer at a
```

TIP

Indicate the type of comment by ordering: input-stream comments first, stack-effect comments second, purpose comments last.

For example:

```
: GET   \   name   ( -- a)   get first match
```

If you prefer to use (, then write:

```
: GET   (   name   ( -- a)   ( get first match)
```

If necessary, you can put the purpose comment on a second line:

```
: WORD   \   name   ( c -- a)
    \ scan for string delimt'd by "c"; leave at a
    ...   ;
```

Comments for Defining Words

The definition of a defining word involves two behaviors:

> that of the defining word as it defines its "child" (compile-time behavior), and
> that of the child itself (run-time behavior).

These two behaviors must be commented separately.

TIP

Comment a defining word's compile-time behavior in the usual way; comment its run-time behavior separately, following the word **DOES>** (or **;CODE**).

For instance,

```
: CONSTANT  ( n )
    DOES>  ( -- n)  @ ;
```

The stack-effect comment for the run-time (child's) behavior represents the net stack effect for the child word. Therefore it does not include the address returned by **DOES>**, even though this address is on the stack when the run-time code begins.

Bad (run-time comment includes apf):

```
: ARRAY    \ name  ( #cells)
    CREATE 2* ALLOT
    DOES>   ( i apf -- 'cell)  SWAP  2* + ;
```

Good:

```
: ARRAY    \ name  ( #cells)
    CREATE 2* ALLOT
    DOES>   ( i -- 'cell)  SWAP  2* + ;
```

Words defined by this word ARRAY will exhibit the stack effect:

```
( i -- 'cell )
```

If the defining word does not specify the run-time behavior, there still exists a run-time behavior, and it may be commented:

```
: VARIABLE  ( name  ( -- )   CREATE  2 ALLOT ;
    \ does>  ( -- adr )
```

Comments for Compiling Words

As with defining words, most compiling words involve two behaviors:

1. That of the compiling word as the definition in which it appears is compiled
2. That of the run-time routine which will execute when we invoke the word being defined. Again we must comment each behavior separately.

Comment a compiling word's run-time behavior in the usual way; comment its compile-time behavior separately, beginning with the label "Compile:".

For instance:

```
: IF   ( ? -- ) ...
\ Compile:   ( -- address-of-unresolved-branch)
     ... ; IMMEDIATE
```

In the case of compiling words, the first comment describes the run-time behavior, which is usually the *syntax for using* the word. The second comment describes what the word *actually does* in compiling (which is of less importance to the user).

Other examples:

```
: ABORT"   ( ? -- )
\ Compile:   text"   ( -- )
```

Occasionally a compiling word may exhibit a different behavior when it is invoked *outside* a colon definition. Such words (to be fastidious about it) require three comments. For instance:

```
: ASCII   ( -- c)
\ Compile:   c   ( -- )
\ Interpret:   c   ( -- c)
     ... ; IMMEDIATE
```

Appendix E includes two screens showing good commenting style.

Vertical Format vs. Horizontal Format

The purpose of commenting is to allow a reader of your code to easily determine what's going on. But how much commenting is necessary? To determine the level of commenting appropriate for your circumstances, you must ask yourself two questions:

Who will be reading my code?
How readable are my definitions?

There are two basic styles of commenting to choose from. The first style, often called the "vertical format," includes a step-by-step description of the process, in the manner of a well-commented assembly language listing. These line-by-line comments are called "narrative comments."

```
\ CRC Checksum
: ACCUMULATE    ( oldcrc char -- newcrc)
    256 *                    \ shift char to hi-order byte
    XOR                      \ & xor into previous crc
    8 0 DO                   \ Then for eight repetitions,
        DUP 0< IF            \ if hi-order bit is "1"
            16386 XOR        \ xor it with mask and
            DUP +            \ shift it left one place
            1+               \ set lo-order bit to "1"
                ELSE         \ otherwise, i.e. hi-order bit is "0"
            DUP +            \ shift it left one place
                THEN
        LOOP ;               \ complete the loop
```

The other approach does not intersperse narrative comments between code phrases. This is called the "horizontal format."

```
: ACCUMULATE    ( oldcrc char -- newcrc)
    256 *  XOR  8 0 DO  DUP 0< IF
        16386 XOR  DUP +  1+  ELSE  DUP +  THEN  LOOP ;
```

The vertical format is preferred when a large team of programmers are coding and maintaining the application. Typically, such a team will include several junior-level programmers responsible for minor corrections. In such an environment, diligent commenting can save a lot of time and upset. As Johnson of Moore Products Co. says: "When maintaining code you are usually interested in just one small section, and the more information written there the better your chances for a speedy fix."

Here are several pertinent rules required of the FORTH programmers at Moore Products Co. (I'm paraphrasing):

1. A vertical format will be used. Comments will appear to the right of the source code, but may continue to engulf the next line totally if needed.
2. There should be more comment characters than source characters. (The company encourages long descriptive names, greater than ten characters, and allows the names to be counted as comment characters.)
3. Any conditional structure or application word should appear on a separate line. "Noise words" can be grouped together. Indentation is used to show nested conditionals.

There are some difficulties with this format, however. For one thing, line-by-line commenting is time-consuming, even with a good screen editor. Productivity can be stifled, especially when stopping to write the comments breaks your chain of thought.

Also, you must also carefully ensure that the comments are up-to-date. Very often code is corrected, the revision is tested, the change works—and the programmer forgets to change the comments. The more comments there are, the more likely they are to be wrong. If they're wrong, they're worse than useless.

This problem can be alleviated if the project supervisor carefully reviews code and ensures the accuracy of comments.

Finally, line-by-line commenting can allow a false sense of security. Don't assume that because each *line* has a comment, the *application* is well-commented. Line-by-line commenting doesn't address the significant aspects of a definition's operation. What, for instance, is the thinking behind the checksum algorithm used? Who knows, from the narrative comments?

To properly describe, in prose, the implications of a given procedure usually requires many paragraphs, not a single phrase. Such descriptions properly belong in auxiliary documentation or in the chapter preamble.

Despite these cautions, many companies find the vertical format necessary. Certainly a team that is newly exposed to FORTH should adopt it, as should any very large team.

What about the horizontal format? Perhaps it's an issue of art vs. practicality, but I feel compelled to defend the horizontal format as equally valid and in some ways superior.

If FORTH code is really well-written, there should be nothing ambiguous about it. This means that:

- supporting lexicons have a well-designed syntax
- stack inputs and outputs are commented
- the purpose is commented (if it's not clear from the name or stack comment)
- definitions are not too long
- not too many arguments are passed to a single definition via the stack (see "The Stylish Stack" in Chapter Seven).

FORTH is simply not like other languages, in which line-by-line commenting is one of the few things you can do to make programs more readable.

Skillfully written FORTH code is like poetry, containing precise meaning that both programmer and machine can easily read. Your *goal* should be to write code that does not need commenting, even if you choose to comment it. Design your application so that the code, not the comments, conveys the meaning.

If you succeed, then you can eliminate the clutter of excessive commenting, achieving a purity of expression without redundant explanations.

TIP

The most-accurate, least-expensive documentation is self-documenting code.

The quick	(set up for fox; fast-moving...)
brown	(and of same color as chocolate.)
fox	(do fox)
jumped over	(give fox's action)
the lazy	(set up for dog)
dog.	(what the fox jumped over)

Wiggins, proud of his commenting technique.

Unfortunately, even the best programmers, given the pressure of a deadline, may write working code that is not easily readable without comments. If you are writing for yourself, or for a small group with whom you can verbally communicate, the horizontal format is ideal. Otherwise, consider the vertical format.

Choosing Names: The Art

> Besides a mathematical inclination, an exceptionally good mastery of one's native tongue is the most vital asset of a competent programmer (*Prof. Edsger W. Dijkstra* [3]).

We've talked about the significance of using names to symbolize ideas and objects in the application. The choosing of names turns out to be an important part of the design process.

Newcomers tend to overlook the important of names. "After all," they think, "the computer doesn't care what names I choose."

But good names are essential for readability. Moreover, the mental exercise of summoning a one-word description bears a synergistic effect on your perceptions of what the entity should or should not do.

Here are some rules for choosing good names:

TIP

Choose names according to "what," not "how."

A definition should hide the complexities of implementation from other definitions which invoke it. The name, too, should hide the details of the procedure, and instead should describe the outward appearance or net effect.

For instance, the FORTH word **ALLOT** simply increments the dictionary pointer (called **DP** or **H** in most systems). But the name **ALLOT** is better than DP+! because the user is thinking of reserving space, not incrementing a pointer.

The '83 Standard adopted the name CMOVE> instead of the previous name for the same function, <CMOVE. The operation makes it possible to copy a region of memory *forward* into overlapping memory. It accomplishes this by starting with the last byte and working *backward*. In the new name, the forwardness of the "what" supercedes the backwardness of the "how."

TIP

Find the most expressive word.

A powerful agent is the right word. Whenever we come upon one of those intensely right words in a book or a newspaper the resulting effect is physical as well as spiritual, and electrically prompt (*Mark Twain*).

The difference between the right word and the almost-right word is like the difference between lightning and the lightning bug (*Mark Twain*).

Suit the action to the word, the word to the action (*Shakespeare, Hamlet, Act III*).

Henry Laxen, a FORTH consultant and author, suggests that the most important FORTH development tool is a good thesaurus [4].

Sometimes you'll think of an adequate word for a definition, but it doesn't feel quite right. It may be months later before you realize that you fell short of the mark. In the Roman numeral example in Chapter Four, there's a word that handles the exception case: numbers that are one-less-than the next symbol's value. My first choice was 4-OR-9. That's awkward, but it was much later that I thought of ALMOST.

Most fig-FORTH systems include the word VLIST, which lists the names of all the words in the current vocabulary. After many years someone realized that a nicer name is WORDS. Not only does WORDS sound more pleasant by itself, it also works nicely with vocabulary names. For instance:

```
EDITOR WORDS
```

or

```
ASSEMBLER WORDS
```

On the other hand, Moore points out that inappropriate names can become a simple technique for encryption. If you need to provide security when you're forced to distribute source, you can make your code very unreadable by deliberately choosing misleading names. Of course, maintenance becomes impossible.

TIP

Choose names that work in phrases.

Faced with a definition you don't know what to call, think about how the word will be used in context. For instance:

```
SHUTTER OPEN
    OPEN is the appropriate name for a word that sets a
    bit in an I/O address identified with the name
    SHUTTER.
```

3 BUTTON DOES IGNITION

> DOES is a good choice for a word that vectors the
> address of the function IGNITION into a table of
> functions, so that IGNITION will be executed when
> Button 3 is pushed.

SAY HELLO

> SAY is the perfect choice for vectoring HELLO into an
> execution variable. (When I first wrote this example
> for Starting FORTH, I called it VERSION. Moore
> reviewed the manuscript and suggested SAY, which is
> clearly much better.)

I'M HARRY

> The word I'M seems more natural than LOGON HARRY,
> LOGIN HARRY or SESSION HARRY, as often seen.

The choice of I'M is another invention of Moore, who says:

> I detest the word LOGON. There is no such word in English. I was looking
> for a word that said, "I'm . . . ." It was a natural. I just stumbled across it.
> Even though it's clumsy with that apostrophe, it has that sense of
> rightness.
>
> All these little words are the nicest way of getting the "Aha!" reaction. If
> you think of the right word, it is *obviously* the right word.
>
> If you have a wide recall vocabulary, you're in a better position to come up
> with the right word.

Another of Moore's favorite words is **TH**, which he uses as an array in-
dexing word. For instance, the phrase

    5 TH

returns the address of the "fifth" element of the array.

TIP

Spell names in full.

I once saw some FORTH code published in a magazine in which the
author seemed hell-bent on purging all vowels from his names, inventing
such eyesores as DSPL-BFR for "display buffer." Other writers seem to
think that three characters magically says it all, coining LEN for
"length." Such practices reflect thinking from a bygone age.

FORTH words should be fully spelled out. Feel proud to type every
letter of INITIALIZE or TERMINAL or BUFFER. These are the words
you mean.

The worst problem with abbreviating a word is that you forget just how you abbreviated it. Was that DSPL or DSPLY?

Another problem is that abbreviations hinder readability. Any programming language is hard enough to read without compounding the difficulty.

Still, there are exceptions. Here are a few:

1. Words that you use extremely frequently in code. FORTH employs a handful of commands that get used over and over, but have little or no intrinsic meaning:

   ```
   :   ;   @   !   .   ,
   ```

   But there are so few of them, and they're used so often, they become old friends. I would never want to type, on a regular basis,

   ```
   DEFINE   END-DEFINITION   FETCH   STORE
        PRINT   COMPILE#
   ```

   (Interestingly, most of these symbols don't have English counterparts. We use the phrase "*colon* definition" because there's no other term; we say "*comma* a number into the dictionary" because it's not exactly compiling, and there's no other term.)
2. Words that a terminal operator might use frequently to control an operation. These words should be spelled as single letters, as are line editor commands.
3. Words in which familiar usage implies that they be abbreviated. FORTH assembler mnemonics are typically patterned after the manufacturer's suggested mnemonics, which are abbreviations (such as JMP and MOV).

Your names should be pronounceable; otherwise you may regret it when you try to discuss the program with other people. If the name is symbolic, invent a pronunciation (e.g., $>$R is called "to-r"; R$>$ is called "r-from").

TIP

Favor short words.

Given the choice between a three-syllable word and a one-syllable word that means the same thing, choose the shorter. BRIGHT is a better name than INTENSE. ENABLE is a better name than ACTIVATE; GO, RUN, or ON may be better still.

Shorter names are easier to type. They save space in the source screen. Most important, they make your code crisp and clean.

TIP

Hyphenated names may be a sign of bad factoring.

Moore:

> There are diverging programming styles in the FORTH community. One uses hyphenated words that express in English what the word is doing. You string these big long words together and you get something that is quite readable.
>
> But I immediately suspect that the programmer didn't think out the words carefully enough, that the hyphen should be broken and the words defined separately. That isn't always possible, and it isn't always advantageous. But I suspect a hyphenated word of mixing two concepts.

Compare the following two strategies for saying the same thing:

```
ENABLE-LEFT-MOTOR          LEFT MOTOR ON
ENABLE-RIGHT-MOTOR         RIGHT MOTOR ON
DISABLE-LEFT-MOTOR         LEFT MOTOR OFF
DISABLE-RIGHT-MOTOR        RIGHT MOTOR OFF
ENABLE-LEFT-SOLENOID       LEFT SOLENOID ON
ENABLE-RIGHT-SOLENOID      RIGHT SOLENOID ON
DISABLE-LEFT-SOLENOID      LEFT SOLENOID OFF
DISABLE-RIGHT-SOLENOID     RIGHT SOLENOID OFF
```

The syntax on the left requires eight dictionary entries; the syntax on the right requires only six—and some of the words are likely to be reused in other parts of the application. If you had a MIDDLE motor and solenoid as well, you'd need only seven words to describe sixteen combinations.

TIP

Don't bundle numbers into names.

Watch out for a series of names beginning or ending with numbers, such as 1CHANNEL, 2CHANNEL, 3CHANNEL, etc.

This bundling of names and numbers may be an indication of bad factoring. The crime is similar to hyphenation, except that what should be factored out is a number, not a word. A better factoring of the above would be

```
1 CHANNEL
2 CHANNEL
3 CHANNEL
```

In this case, the three words were reduced to one.

Often the bundling of names and numbers indicates fuzzy naming.

In the above case, more descriptive names might indicate the purpose of the channels, as in

```
VOICE , TELEMETRY , GUITAR
```

We'll amplify on these ideas in the next chapter on "Factoring."

Naming Standards: The Science

TIP

Learn and adopt FORTH's naming conventions.

In the quest for short, yet meaningful names, FORTH programmers have adopted certain naming conventions. Appendix E includes a list of the most useful conventions developed over the years.

An example of the power of naming conventions is the use of "dot" to mean "print" or "display." FORTH itself uses

```
.    D.    U.R
```

for displaying various types of numbers in various formats. The convention extends to application words as well. If you have a variable called DATE, and you want a word that displays the date, use the name

```
.DATE
```

A caution: The overuse of prefixes and suffixes makes words uglier and ultimately less readable. Don't try to describe everything a word does by its name alone. After all, a name is a symbol, not a shorthand for code. Which is more readable and natural sounding?:

Oedipus complex

(which bears no intrinsic meaning), or

subconscious-attachment-to-parent-of-opposite-sex complex

Probably the former, even though it assumes you know the play.

TIP

Use prefixes and suffices to differentiate between like words rather than to cram details of meaning into the name itself.

For instance, the phrase

```
... DONE IF CLOSE THEN ...
```

is just as readable as

```
... DONE? IF CLOSE THEN ...
```

and cleaner as well. It is therefore preferable, unless we need an additional word called DONE (as a flag, for instance).

A final tip on naming:

TIP

Begin all hex numbers with "0" (zero) to avoid potential collisions with names.

For example, write 0ADD, not ADD.

By the way, don't expect your FORTH system to necessarily conform to the above conventions. The conventions are meant to be used in new applications.

FORTH was created and refined over many years by people who used it as a means to an end. At that time, it was neither reasonable nor possible to impose naming standards on a tool that was still growing and evolving.

Had FORTH been designed by committee, we would not love it so.

More Tips for Readability

Here are some final suggestions to make your code more readable. (Definitions appear in Appendix C.)

One constant that pays for itself in most applications is BL (the ASCII value for "blank-space").

The word **ASCII** is used primarily within colon definitions to free you from having to know the literal value of an ASCII character. For instance, instead of writing:

```
: (    41 WORD   DROP ;   IMMEDIATE
```

where 41 is the ASCII representation for right-parenthesis, you can write

```
: (    ASCII ) WORD   DROP ;   IMMEDIATE
```

A pair of words that can make dealing with booleans more readable are **TRUE** and **FALSE**. With these additions you can write phrases such as

```
TRUE 'STAMP? !
```

to set a flag or

```
FALSE 'STAMP? !
```

to clear it.

(I once used **T** and **F**, but the words are needed so rarely I now heed the injunction against abbreviations.)

As part of your application (not necessarily part of your FORTH system), you can take this idea a step further and define:

```
: ON   ( a)   TRUE SWAP ! ;
: OFF  ( a)   FALSE SWAP ! ;
```

These words allow you to write:

```
'STAMP? ON
```

or

```
'STAMP? OFF
```

Other names for these definitions include SET and RESET, although SET and RESET most commonly use bit masks to manipulate individual bits.

An often-used word is **WITHIN**, which determines whether a given value lies within two other values. The syntax is:

```
n  lo hi WITHIN
```

where "n" is the value to be tested and "lo" and "hi" represent the range. **WITHIN** returns true if "n" is greater-than *or equal-to* "lo" and *less-than* "hi." This use of the non-inclusive upper limit parallels the syntax of **DO LOOP**s.

Moore recommends the word **UNDER+**. It's useful for adding a value to the number just under the top stack item, instead of to the top stack item. It could be implemented in high level as:

```
: UNDER+  ( a b c -- a+c b )  ROT + SWAP ;
```

Summary

Maintainability requires readability. In this chapter we've enumerated various ways to make a source listing more readable. We've assumed a policy of making our code as self-documenting as possible. Techniques include listing organization, spacing and indenting, commenting, name choices, and special words that enhance clarity.

We've mentioned only briefly auxiliary documentation, which includes all documentation apart from the listing itself. We won't discuss auxiliary documentation further in this volume, but it remains an integral part of the software development process.

References

1. Gregory Stevenson, "Documentation Priorities," *1981 FORML Conference Proceedings,* p. 401.
2. Joanne Lee, "Quality Assurance in a FORTH Environment," (Appendix A), *1981 FORML Proceedings,* p. 363.
3. Edsger W. Dijkstra, *Selected Writings on Computing: A Personal Perspective,* New York, Springer Verlag, Inc., 1982.
4. Henry Laxen, "Choosing Names," *FORTH Dimensions,* vol. 4, no. 4, FORTH Interest Group.

SIX

Factoring

In this chapter we'll continue our study of the implementation phase, this time focusing on factoring.

Decomposition and factoring are chips off the same block. Both involve dividing and organizing. Decomposition occurs during preliminary design; factoring occurs during detailed design and implementation.

Since every colon definition reflects decisions of factoring, an understanding of good factoring technique is perhaps the most important skill for a FORTH programmer.

What is factoring? Factoring means organizing code into useful fragments. To make a fragment useful, you often must separate reusable parts from non-reusable parts. The reusable parts become new definitions. The non-reusable parts become arguments or parameters to the definitions.

Making this separation is usually referred to as "factoring out." The first part of this chapter will discuss various "factoring-out" techniques.

Deciding how much should go into, or stay out of, a definition is another aspect of factoring. The second section will outline the criteria for useful factoring.

Factoring Techniques

> If a module seems almost, but not quite, useful from a second place in the system, try to identify and isolate the useful subfunction. The remainder of the module might be incorporated in its original caller (from "*Structured Design* [1]).

The "useful subfunction" of course becomes the newly factored definition. What about the part that "isn't quite useful"? That depends on what it is.

Factoring Out Data

The simplest thing to factor out is data, thanks to FORTH's data stack. For instance, to compute two-thirds of 1,000, we write

```
1000 2 3 */
```

To define a word that computes two-thirds of *any* number, we factor out the argument from the definition:

```
: TWO-THIRDS  ( n1 -- n2)  2 3 */ ;
```

When the datum comes in the *middle* of the useful phrase, we have to use stack manipulation. For instance, to center a piece of text ten characters long on an 80-column screen, we would write:

```
80  10 -  2/ SPACES
```

But text isn't always 10 characters long. To make the phrase useful for any string, you'd factor out the length by writing:

```
: CENTER  ( length -- )  80  SWAP -  2/ SPACES ;
```

The data stack can also be used to pass addresses. Therefore what's factored out may be a *pointer* to data rather than the data themselves. The data can be numbers or even strings, and still be factored out through use of the stack.

Sometimes the difference appears to be a function, but you can factor it out simply as a number on the stack. For instance:

```
Segment 1:  WILLY NILLY  PUDDIN' PIE AND
Segment 2:  WILLY NILLY  8 *  PUDDING PIE AND
```

How can you factor out the "8 *" operation? By including "*" in the factoring and passing it a one or eight:

```
: NEW  ( n )  WILLY NILLY  *  PUDDIN' PIE AND ;
Segment 1:    1 NEW
Segment 2:    8 NEW
```

(Of course if WILLY NILLY changes the stack, you'll need to add appropriate stack-manipulation operators.)

If the operation involves addition, you can nullify it by passing a zero.

TIP

For simplicity, try to express the difference between similar fragments as a numeric difference (values or addresses), rather than as a procedural difference.

Factoring Out Functions

On the other hand, the difference sometimes *is* a function. Witness:

```
Segment 1:   BLETCH-A  BLETCH-B   BLETCH-C
             BLETCH-D  BLETCH-E  BLETCH-F
Segment 2:   BLETCH-A  BLETCH-B  PERVERSITY
             BLETCH-D  BLETCH-E  BLETCH-F
```

Wrong approach:

```
: BLETCHES   ( t=do-BLETCH-C : f=do-PERVERSITY -- )
   BLETCH-A   BLETCH-B   IF BLETCH-C  ELSE  PERVERSITY
      THEN   BLETCH-D BLETCH-E   BLETCH-F ;

Segment 1:    TRUE BLETCHES
Segment 2:    FALSE BLETCHES
```

A better approach:

```
: BLETCH-AB    BLETCH-A   BLETCH-B ;
: BLETCH-DEF    BLETCH-D   BLETCH-E   BLETCH-F ;

Segment 1:    BLETCH-AB  BLETCH-C  BLETCH-DEF
Segment 2:    BLETCH-AB  PERVERSITY  BLETCH-DEF
```

TIP

Don't pass control flags downward.

Why not? First, you are asking your running application to make a pointless decision—one which you knew the answer to while programming—thereby reducing efficiency. Second, the terminology doesn't match the conceptual model. What are TRUE BLETCHES as opposed to FALSE BLETCHES?

Factoring Out Code from Within Control Structures

Be alert to repetitions on either side of an **IF ELSE THEN** statement. For instance:

```
... ( c)  DUP  BL 127 WITHIN
       IF  EMIT  ELSE
       DROP  ASCII . EMIT   THEN ...
```

This fragment normally emits an ASCII character, but if the character is a control code, it emits a dot. Either way, an **EMIT** is performed. Factor **EMIT** out of the conditional structure, like this:

```
...  ( c)   DUP  BL 127 WITHIN NOT
      IF   DROP   ASCII .  THEN  EMIT  ...
```

The messiest situation occurs when the difference between two definitions is a function within a structure that makes it impossible to factor
out the half-fragments. In this case, use stack arguments, variables, or
even vectoring. We'll see how vectoring can be used in a section of
Chapter Seven called "Using DOER/MAKE."

Here's a reminder about factoring code from out of a **DO LOOP**:

TIP

In factoring out the contents of a **DO LOOP** into a new definition, rework
the code so that **I** (the index) is not referenced within the new definition, but
rather passed as a stack argument to it.

Factoring Out Control Structures Themselves

Here are two definitions whose difference lies within an **IF THEN**
construct:

```
: ACTIVE    A B OR  C AND   IF  TUMBLE JUGGLE JUMP    THEN ;
: LAZY      A B OR  C AND   IF   SIT  EAT  SLEEP      THEN ;
```

The condition and control structure remain the same; only the event
changes. Since you can't factor the **IF** into one word and the **THEN** into
another, the simplest thing is to factor the condition:

```
: CONDITIONS?   ( -- ?)   A B OR  C AND ;
: ACTIVE    CONDITIONS? IF  TUMBLE JUGGLE JUMP   THEN
: LAZY      CONDITIONS? IF   SIT  EAT  SLEEP     THEN ;
```

Depending on the number of repetitions of the same condition and control structure, you may even want to factor out both. Watch this:

```
: CONDITIONALLY   A B OR  C AND NOT IF  R> DROP   THEN ;
: ACTIVE    CONDITIONALLY    TUMBLE JUGGLE JUMP ;
: LAZY      CONDITIONALLY SIT  EAT   SLEEP ;
```

The word **CONDITIONALLY** may—depending on the condition—alter
the control flow so that the remaining words in each definition will be
skipped. This approach has certain disadvantages as well. We'll discuss
this technique—pros and cons—in Chapter Eight.

More benign examples of factoring-out control structures include
case statements, which eliminate nested **IF ELSE THEN**s, and multiple
exit loops (the **BEGIN WHILE WHILE WHILE . . . REPEAT** construct). We'll also discuss these topics in Chapter Eight.

Factoring Out Names

It's even good to factor out names, when the names seem almost, but not quite, the same. Examine the following terrible example of code, which is meant to initialize three variables associated with each of eight channels:

```
VARIABLE OSTS          VARIABLE 1STS          VARIABLE 2!
VARIABLE 3STS          VARIABLE 4STS          VARIABLE 5!
VARIABLE 6STS          VARIABLE 7STS          VARIABLE O`
VARIABLE 1TNR          VARIABLE 2TNR          VARIABLE 3`
VARIABLE 4TNR          VARIABLE 5TNR          VARIABLE 6`
VARIABLE 7TNR          VARIABLE OUPS          VARIABLE 1U
VARIABLE 2UPS          VARIABLE 3UPS          VARIABLE 4U
VARIABLE 5UPS          VARIABLE 6UPS          VARIABLE 7U
```

```
: INIT-CHO    O OSTS !   1000 OTNR !   -1 OUPS ! ;
: INIT-CH1    O 1STS !   1000 1TNR !   -1 1UPS ! ;
: INIT-CH2    O 2STS !   1000 2TNR !   -1 2UPS ! ;
: INIT-CH3    O 3STS !   1000 3TNR !   -1 3UPS ! ;
: INIT-CH4    O 4STS !   1000 4TNR !   -1 4UPS ! ;
: INIT-CH5    O 5STS !   1000 5TNR !   -1 5UPS ! ;
: INIT-CH6    O 6STS !   1000 6TNR !   -1 6UPS ! ;
: INIT-CH7    O 7STS !   1000 7TNR !   -1 7UPS ! ;

: INIT-ALL-CHS    INIT-CHO   INIT-CH1   INIT-CH2   INIT-CH3
    INIT-CH4   INIT-CH5   INIT-CH6   INIT-CH7 ;
```

First there's a similarity among the names of the variables; then there's a similarity in the code used in all the INIT—CH words.

Here's an improved rendition. The similar variable names have been factored into three data structures, and the lengthy recital of INIT—CH words has been factored into a **DO LOOP**:

```
: ARRAY   ( #cells -- )   CREATE  2* ALLOT
    DOES> ( i -- 'cell)   SWAP  2* + ;
8 ARRAY STATUS   ( channel# -- adr)
8 ARRAY TENOR    (      "       )
8 ARRAY UPSHOT   (      "       )
: STABLE    8 0 DO   O I STATUS !   1000 I TENOR !
    -1 I UPSHOT !  LOOP ;
```

That's all the code we need.

Even in the most innocent cases, a little data structure can eliminate extra names. By convention FORTH handles text in "counted strings" (i.e., with the count in the first byte). Any word that returns the "address of a string" actually returns this beginning address, where the count is. Not only does use of this two-element data structure eliminate the need for separate names for string and count, it also makes it easier to move a string in memory, because you can copy the string *and* the count with a single **CMOVE**.

When you start finding the same awkwardnesses here and there, you can combine things and make the awkwardness go away.

Factoring Out Functions into Defining Words

TIP

If a series of definitions contains identical functions, with variation only in data, use a defining word.

Examine the structure of this code (without worrying about its purpose—you'll see the same example later on):

```
: HUE   ( color -- color')
    'LIGHT? @   OR   0 'LIGHT? ! ;
: BLACK    0 HUE ;
: BLUE     1 HUE ;
: GREEN    2 HUE ;
: CYAN     3 HUE ;
: RED    4 HUE ;
: MAGENTA    5 HUE ;
: BROWN    6 HUE ;
: GRAY    7 HUE ;
```

The above approach is technically correct, but less memory-efficient than the following approach using defining words:

```
: HUE    ( color -- )   CREATE ,
    DOES>  ( -- color )   @  'LIGHT? @   OR   0 'LIGHT? ! ;
  0 HUE BLACK           1 HUE BLUE            2 HUE GREEN
  3 HUE CYAN            4 HUE RED             5 HUE MAGENTA
  6 HUE BROWN           7 HUE GRAY
```

(Defining words are explained in *Starting FORTH*, Chapter Eleven).

By using a defining word, we save memory because each compiled colon definition needs the address of **EXIT** to conclude the definition. (In defining eight words, the use of a defining word saves 14 bytes on a 16-bit FORTH.) Also, in a colon definition each reference to a numeric literal requires the compilation of **LIT** (or **literal**), another 2 bytes per definition. (If 1 and 2 are predefined constants, this costs another 10 bytes—24 total.)

In terms of readability, the defining word makes it absolutely clear that all the colors it defines belong to the same family of words.

The greatest strength of defining words, however, arises when a series of definitions share the same *compile-time* behavior. This topic is the subject of a later section, "Compile-Time Factoring."

Factoring Criteria

Armed with an understanding of factoring techniques, let's now discuss several of the criteria for factoring FORTH definitions. They include:

1. Limiting the size of definitions
2. Limiting repetition of code
3. Nameability
4. Information hiding
5. Simplifying the command interface

TIP

Keep definitions short.

We asked Moore, "How long should a FORTH definition be?"

A word should be a line long. That's the target.

When you have a whole lot of words that are all useful in their own right—perhaps in debugging or exploring, but inevitably there's a reason for their existence—you feel you've extracted the essence of the problem and that those words have expressed it.

Short words give you a good feeling.

An informal examination of one of Moore's applications shows that he averages seven references, including both words and numbers, per definition. These are remarkably short definitions. (Actually his code was divided about 50-50 between one-line and two-line definitions.)

Psychological tests have shown that the human mind can only focus its conscious attention on seven things, plus or minus two, at a time [2]. Yet all the while, day and night, the vast resources of the mind are subconsciously storing immense amounts of data, making connections and associations and solving problems.

Even if our subconscious mind knows each part of an application inside out, our narrow-viewed conscious mind can only correlate seven elements of it at once. Beyond that, our grasp wavers. Short definitions match our mental capabilities.

Something that tempts many FORTH programmers to write overly long definitions is the knowledge that headers take space in the dictionary. The coarser the factoring, the fewer the names, and the less memory that will be wasted.

It's true that more memory will be used, but it's hard to say that anything that helps you test, debug and interact with your code is a "waste." If your application is large, try using a default width of three, with the ability to switch to a full-length name to avoid a specific collision. ("Width" refers to a limit on the number of characters stored in the name field of each dictionary header.)

If the application is still too big, switch to a FORTH with multiple dictionaries on a machine with extended memory, or better yet, a 32-bit FORTH on a machine with 32-bit addressing.

A related fear is that over-factoring will decrease performance due to the overhead of FORTH's inner interpreter. Again, it's true that there is some penalty for each level of nesting. But ordinarily the penalty for extra nesting due to proper factoring will not be noticeable. If your timings are that tight, the real solution is to translate something into assembler.

TIP

Factor at the point where you feel unsure about your code (where complexity approaches the conscious limit).

Don't let your ego take over with an "I can lick this!" attitude. FORTH code should never feel uncomfortably complex. Factor!

Moore:

Feeling like you might have introduced a bug is one reason for factoring. Any time you see a doubly-nested **DO LOOP**, that's a sign that something's wrong because it will be hard to debug. Almost always take the inner **DO LOOP** and make it a word.

And having factored out a word for testing, there's no reason for putting it back. You found it useful in the first place. There's no guarantee you won't need it again.

Here's another facet of the same principle:

TIP

Factor at the point where a comment seems necessary.

Particularly if you feel a need to remind yourself what's on the stack, this may be a good time to "make a break."

Suppose you have

```
... BALANCE  DUP xxx xxx xxx xxx xxx xxx xxx xxx xxx
    xxx xxx xxx xxx xxx xxx    ( balance) SHOW  ...
```

which begins by computing the balance and ends by displaying it. In the meantime, several lines of code use the balance for purposes of their own. Since it's difficult to see that the balance is still on the stack when SHOW executes, the programmer has interjected a stack picture.

This solution is generally a sign of bad factoring. Better to write:

```
: REVISE   ( balance -- )  xxx xxx xxx xxx xxx xxx xxx
     xxx xxx xxx xxx xxx xxx xxx ;
... BALANCE  DUP REVISE  SHOW  ...
```

No narrative stack pictures are needed. Furthermore, the programmer now has a reusable, testable subset of the definition.

TIP

Limit repetition of code.

The second reason for factoring, to eliminate repeated fragments of code, is even more important than reducing the size of definitions.

Moore:

> When a word is just a piece of something, it's useful for clarity or debugging, but not nearly as good as a word that is used multiple times. Any time a word is used only once you want to question its value.
>
> Many times when a program has gotten too big I will go back through it looking for phrases that strike my eye as candidates for factoring. The computer can't do this; there are too many variables.

In looking over your work, you often find identical phrases or short passages duplicated several times. In writing an editor I found this phrase repeated several times:

```
FRAME   CURSOR @ +
```

Because it appeared several times I factored it into a new word called AT. It's up to you to recognize fragments that are coded differently but functionally equivalent, such as:

```
FRAME   CURSOR @ 1-   +
```

The −1 appears to make this phrase different from the one defined as AT. But in fact, it can be written

```
AT  1-
```

On the other hand:

TIP

When factoring out duplicate code, make sure the factored code serves a single purpose.

Don't blindly seize upon duplications that may not be useful. For instance, in several places in one application I used this phrase:

```
BLK @ BLOCK  >IN @ +  C@
```

I turned it into a new word and called it LETTER, since it returned the letter being pointed to by the interpreter.

In a later revision, I unexpectedly had to write:

```
BLK @ BLOCK  >IN @ +  C!
```

I could have used the existing LETTER were it not for its C@ at the end. Rather than duplicate the bulk of the phrase in the new section, I chose to refactor LETTER to a finer resolution, taking out the C@. The usage was then either LETTER C@ or LETTER C!. This change required me to search through the listing changing all instances of LETTER to LETTER C@. But I should have done that in the first place, separating the computation of the letter's address from the operation to be performed on the address.

Similar to our injunction against repetition of code:

TIP

Look for repetition of patterns.

If you find yourself referring back in the program to copy the pattern of previously-used words, then you may have mixed in a general idea with a specific application. The part of the pattern you are copying perhaps can be factored out as an independent definition that can be used in all the similar cases.

TIP

Be sure you can name what you factor.

Moore:

If you have a concept that you can't assign a single name to, not a hyphenated name, but a name, it's not a well-formed concept. The ability to assign a name is a necessary part of decomposition. Certainly you get more confidence in the idea.

Compare this view with the criteria for decomposing a module espoused by structured design in Chapter One. According to that method, a module should exhibit "functional binding," which can be verified by describing its function in a single, non-compound, *sentence*. FORTH's "atom," a *name*, is an order of magnitude more refined.

TIP

Factor definitions to hide details that may change.

We've seen the value of information hiding in earlier chapters, especially with regard to preliminary design. It's useful to remember this criterion during the implementation stage as well.

Here's a very short definition that does little except hide information:

```
: >BODY   ( acf -- apf )   2+ ;
```

This definition allows you to convert an acf (address of code field) to an apf (address of parameter field) without depending on the actual structure of a dictionary definition. If you were to use 2+ instead of the word **>BODY**, you would lose transportability if you ever converted to a FORTH system in which the heads were separated from the bodies. (This is one of a set of words suggested by Kim Harris, and included as an Experimental Proposal in the FORTH–83 Standard [3].)

Here's a group of definitions that might be used in writing an editor:

```
: FRAME  ( -- a)   SCR @ BLOCK ;
: CURSOR ( -- a)   R# ;
: AT ( -- a)   FRAME  CURSOR @ + ;
```

These three definitions can form the basis for all calculations of addresses necessary for moving text around. Use of these three definitions completely separates your editing algorithms from a reliance on FORTH blocks.

What good is that? If you should decide, during development, to create an editing buffer to protect the user from making errors that destroy a block, you merely have to redefine two of these words, perhaps like this:

```
CREATE FRAME   1024 ALLOT
VARIABLE CURSOR
```

The rest of your code can remain intact.

Factor calculation algorithms out of definitions that display results.

This is really a question of decomposition.

Here's an example. The word defined below, pronounced "people-to-paths," computes how many paths of communication there are between a given number of people in a group. (This is a good thing for managers of programmer teams to know—the number of communication paths increases drastically with each new addition to the team.)

```
: PEOPLE>PATHS  ( #people -- #paths )  DUP 1-  *  2/ ;
```

This definition does the calculation only. Here's the "user definition" that invokes **PEOPLE>PATHS** to perform the calculation, and then displays the result:

```
: PEOPLE  ( #people)
     ." = "  PEOPLE>PATHS  .  ." PATHS " ;
```

This produces:

```
2 PEOPLE = 1 PATHS
3 PEOPLE = 3 PATHS
5 PEOPLE = 10 PATHS
10 PEOPLE = 45 PATHS
```

Even if you think you're going to perform a particular calculation only once, to display it in a certain way, believe me, you're wrong. You will have to come back later and factor out the calculating part. Perhaps you'll need to display the information in a right-justified column, or perhaps you'll want to record the results in a data base—you never know. But you'll always have to factor it, so you might as well do it right the first time. (The few times you might get away with it aren't worth the trouble.)

The word . (dot) is a prime example. Dot is great 99% of the time, but occasionally it does too much. Here's what it does, in fact (in FORTH—83):

```
: .  ( n )  DUP ABS 0 <# #S  ROT SIGN  #> TYPE SPACE ;
```

But suppose you want to convert a number on the stack into an ASCII string and store it in a buffer for typing later. Dot converts it, but also types it. Or suppose you want to format playing cards in the form 10C (for "ten of clubs"). You can't use dot to display the 10 because it prints a final space.

Here's a better factoring found in some FORTH systems:

```
: (.)   ( n -- a #)   DUP ABS 0   <# #S   ROT SIGN   #> ;
: .   ( n)   (.) TYPE SPACE ;
```

We find another example of failing to factor the output function from the calculation function in our own Roman numeral example in Chapter Four. Given our solution, we can't store a Roman numeral in a buffer or even center it in a field. (A better approach would have been to use **HOLD** instead of **EMIT**.)

Information hiding can also be a reason *not* to factor. For instance, if you factor the phrase

```
SCR @ BLOCK
```

into the definition

```
: FRAME   SCR @ BLOCK ;
```

remember you are doing so only because you may want to change the location of the editing frame. Don't blindly replace all occurrences of the phrase with the new word FRAME, because you may change the definition of FRAME and there will certainly be times when you really want **SCR @ BLOCK**.

TIP

If a repeated code fragment is likely to change in some cases but not others, factor out only those instances that might change. If the fragment is likely to change in more than one way, factor it into more than one definition.

Knowing when to hide information requires intuition and experience. Having made many design changes in your career, you'll learn the hard way which things will be most likely to change in the future.

You can never predict everything, though. It would be useless to try, as we'll see in the upcoming section called "The Iterative Approach in Implementation."

TIP

Simplify the command interface by reducing the number of commands.

It may seem paradoxical, but good factoring can often yield *fewer* names. In Chapter 5 we saw how six simple names (LEFT, RIGHT, MOTOR, SOLENOID, ON, and OFF) could do the work of eight badly-factored, hyphenated names.

As another example, I found two definitions circulating in one department in which FORTH had recently been introduced. Their purpose was purely instructional, to remind the programmer which vocabulary was CURRENT, and which was CONTEXT:

```
: .CONTEXT    CONTEXT ə  8 - NFA ID. ;
: .CURRENT    CURRENT ə  8 - NFA ID. ;
```

If you typed

```
.CONTEXT
```

the system would respond

```
.CONTEXT_FORTH
```

(They worked—at least on the system used there—by backing up to the name field of the vocabulary definition, and displaying it.)

The obvious repetition of code struck my eye as a sign of bad factoring. It would have been possible to consolidate the repeated passage into a third definition:

```
: .VOCABULARY    ( pointer )  ə  8 -  NFA  ID. ;
```

shortening the original definitions to:

```
: .CONTEXT    CONTEXT .VOCABULARY ;
: .CURRENT    CURRENT .VOCABULARY ;
```

But in this approach, the only difference between the two definitions was the pointer to be displayed. Since part of good factoring is to make fewer, not more definitions, it seemed logical to have only one definition, and let it take as an argument either the word CONTEXT or the word CURRENT.

Applying the principles of good naming, I suggested:

```
: IS ( adr)   ə  8 -  NFA  ID. ;
```

allowing the syntax

```
CONTEXT IS_ASSEMBLER_ok
```

or

```
CURRENT IS_FORTH_ok
```

The initial clue was repetition of code, but the final result came from attempting to simplify the command interface.

Here's another example. The IBM PC has four modes for displaying text only:

```
40 column monochrome
40 column color
80 column monochrome
80 column color
```

The word MODE is available in the FORTH system I use. MODE takes an argument between 0 and 3 and changes the mode accordingly. Of course, the phrase 0 MODE or 1 MODE doesn't help me remember which mode is which.

Since I need to switch between these modes in doing presentations, I need to have a convenient set of words to effect the change. These words must also set a variable that contains the current number of columns—40 or 80.

Here's the most straightforward way to fulfill the requirements:

```
: 40-B&W      40 #COLUMNS !   0 MODE ;
: 40-COLOR    40 #COLUMNS !   1 MODE ;
: 80-B&W      80 #COLUMNS !   2 MODE ;
: 80-COLOR    80 #COLUMNS !   3 MODE ;
```

By factoring to eliminate the repetition, we come up with this version:

```
: COL-MODE!   ( #columns mode )   MODE   #COLUMNS ! ;
: 40-B&W      40 0 COL-MODE! ;
: 40-COLOR    40 1 COL-MODE! ;
: 80-B&W      80 2 COL-MODE! ;
: 80-COLOR    80 3 COL-MODE! ;
```

But by attempting to reduce the number of commands, and also by following the injunctions against numerically-prefixed and hyphenated names, we realize that we can use the number of columns as a stack argument, and *calculate* the mode:

```
: B&W     ( #cols -- )   DUP #COLUMNS !   20 / 2-      MODE
: COLOR   ( #cols -- )   DUP #COLUMNS !   20 / 2- 1+   MODE
```

This gives us this syntax:

```
40 B&W
80 B&W
40 COLOR
80 COLOR
```

We've reduced the number of commands from four to two.

Once again, though, we have some duplicate code. If we factor out this code we get:

```
: COL-MODE!   ( #columns chroma?)
    SWAP DUP #COLUMNS !  20 / 2-  +  MODE ;
: B&W     ( #columns -- )  0 COL-MODE! ;
: COLOR   ( #columns -- )  1 COL-MODE! ;
```

Now we've achieved a nicer syntax, and at the same time greatly reduced the size of the object code. With only two commands, as in this example, the benefits may be marginal. But with larger sets of commands the benefits increase geometrically.

Our final example is a set of words to represent colors on a particular system. Names like BLUE and RED are nicer to use than numbers. One solution might be to define:

```
 0 CONSTANT BLACK            1 CONSTANT BLUE
 2 CONSTANT GREEN            3 CONSTANT CYAN
 4 CONSTANT RED              5 CONSTANT MAGENTA
 6 CONSTANT BROWN            7 CONSTANT GRAY
 8 CONSTANT DARK-GREY        9 CONSTANT LIGHT-BLUE
10 CONSTANT LIGHT-GREEN     11 CONSTANT LIGHT-CYAN
12 CONSTANT LIGHT-RED       13 CONSTANT LIGHT-MAGENTA
14 CONSTANT YELLOW          15 CONSTANT WHITE
```

These colors can be used with words such as BACKGROUND, FOREGROUND, and BORDER:

```
WHITE BACKGROUND   RED FOREGROUND   BLUE BORDER
```

But this solution requires 16 names, and many of them are hyphenated. Is there a way to simplify this?

We notice that the colors between 8 and 15 are all "lighter" versions of the colors between 0 and 7. (In the hardware, the only difference between these two sets is the setting of the "intensity bit.") If we factor out the "lightness," we might come up with this solution:

```
VARIABLE 'LIGHT?  ( intensity bit?)
: HUE   ( color)  CREATE ,
    DOES> ( -- color )  @  'LIGHT? @  OR  0 'LIGHT? ! ;
 0 HUE BLACK           1 HUE BLUE           2 HUE GREEN
 3 HUE CYAN            4 HUE RED            5 HUE MAGENTA
 6 HUE BROWN           7 HUE GRAY
: LIGHT    8 'LIGHT? ! ;
```

With this syntax, the word

    BLUE

by itself will return a "1" on the stack, but the phrase

    LIGHT BLUE

will return a "9." (The adjective LIGHT sets flag which is used by the hues, then cleared.)

If necessary for readability, we still might want to define:

    8 HUE DARK-GRAY
    14 HUE YELLOW

Again, through this approach we've achieved a more pleasant syntax and shorter object code.

TIP

Don't factor for the sake of factoring. Use cliches.

The phrase

    OVER + SWAP

may be seen commonly in certain applications. (It converts an address and count into an ending address and starting address appropriate for a **DO LOOP**.)

Another commonly seen phrase is

    1+ SWAP

(It rearranges a first-number and last-number into the last-number-plus-one and first-number order required by **DO**.)

It's a little tempting to seize upon these phrases and turn them into words, such as (for the first phrase) RANGE.

Moore:

> That particular phrase [**OVER + SWAP**] is one that's right on the margin of being a useful word. Often, though, if you define something as a word, it turns out you use it only once. If you name such a phrase, you have trouble knowing exactly what RANGE does. You can't see the manipulation in your mind. **OVER + SWAP** has greater mnemonic value than RANGE.

I call these phrases "clichés." They stick together as meaningful functions. You don't have to remember how the phrase works, just what it does. And you don't have to remember an extra name.

Compile-Time Factoring

In the last section we looked at many techniques for organizing code and data to reduce redundance.

We can also apply limited redundance during compilation, by letting FORTH do some of our dirty work.

TIP

For maximum maintainability, limit redundancy even at compile time.

Suppose in our application we must draw nine boxes as shown in Figure 6-1.

Figure 6-1. *What we're supposed to display.*

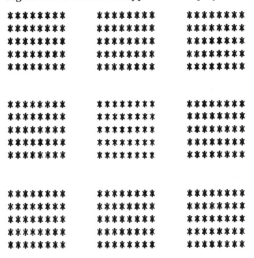

In our design we need to have constants that represent values such as the size of each box, the size of the gap between boxes, and the left-most and top-most coordinates of the first box.

Naturally we can define:

```
8 CONSTANT WIDE
5 CONSTANT HIGH
4 CONSTANT AVE
2 CONSTANT STREET
```

(Streets run east and west; avenues run north and south.)

Now, to define the left margin, we might compute it mentally, We want to center all these boxes on a screen 80 columns wide. To center something, we subtract its width from 80 and divide by two to determine the left margin. To figure the total width of all the boxes, we add

$$8 + 4 + 8 + 4 + 8 = 32$$

(three widths and two avenues). $(80 - 31) / 2 = 24$.

So we could, crudely, define:

```
24 CONSTANT LEFTMARGIN
```

and use the same approach for TOPMARGIN.

But what if we should later redesign the pattern, so that the width changed, or perhaps the gap between the boxes? We'd have to recompute the left margin ourselves.

In the FORTH environment, we can use the full power of FORTH even when we're compiling. Why not let FORTH do the figuring?

```
WIDE 3 *   AVE 2 *  +  80 SWAP -  2/ CONSTANT LEFTMARGIN
HIGH 3 *   STREET 2 * +  24 SWAP - 2/ CONSTANT TOPMARGIN
```

TIP

If a constant's value depends on the value of an earlier constant, use FORTH to calculate the value of the second.

None of these computations are performed when the application is running, so run-time speed in not affected.

Here's another example. Figure 6-2 shows the code for a word that draws shapes. The word DRAW emits a star at every x—y coordinate listed in the table called POINTS. (Note: the word XY positions the cursor to the (x y) coordinate on the stack.)

Notice the line immediately following the list of points:

```
HERE POINTS -   ( /table)   2/   CONSTANT #POINTS
```

Figure 6-2. *Another example of limiting compile-time redundancy.*

```
: P  ( x y -- )  C, C, ;
CREATE POINTS
    10 10 P      10 11 P      10 12 P      10 13 P      10 14 P
    11 10 P      12 10 P      13 10 P      14 10 P
    11 12 P      12 12 P      13 12 P      14 12 P
HERE POINTS -   ( /table)  2/   CONSTANT #POINTS
: @POINTS  ( i -- x y)  2* POINTS +   DUP 1+ C@  SWAP C@ ;
: DRAW    #POINTS 0 DO  I @POINTS  XY   ASCII * EMIT   LOOP ;
```

The phrase "HERE POINTS —" computes the number of bytes consumed by the table. Dividing this value by two computes the number of x—y coordinates in the table; this value becomes the constant #POINTS, used as the limit in DRAW's **DO LOOP**.

This construct lets you add or subtract points from the table without worrying about the number of points there are. FORTH computes this for you.

Compile-Time Factoring through Defining Words

Let's examine a series of approaches to the same problem—defining a group of related addresses. Here's the first try:

```
HEX 01A0 CONSTANT BASE.PORT.ADDRESS
BASE.PORT.ADDRESS CONSTANT SPEAKER
BASE.PORT.ADDRESS 2+ CONSTANT FLIPPER-A
BASE.PORT.ADDRESS 4 + CONSTANT FLIPPER-B
BASE.PORT.ADDRESS 6 + CONSTANT WIN-LIGHT
DECIMAL
```

The idea is right, but the implementation is ugly. The only elements that change from port to port are the numeric offset and the name of the port being defined; everything else repeats. This repetition suggests the use of a defining word.

The following approach, which is more readable, combines all the repeated code into the "does" part of a defining word:

```
: PORT  ( offset -- )   CREATE ,
    DOES>  ( -- 'port)  @  BASE.PORT.ADDRESS + ;
0 PORT SPEAKER
2 PORT FLIPPER-A
4 PORT FLIPPER-B
6 PORT WIN-LIGHT
```

In this solution we're performing the offset calculation at *run*-time, every time we invoke one of these names. It would be more efficient to perform the calculation at compile time, like this:

```
: PORT  ( offset -- )   BASE.PORT.ADDRESS + CONSTANT ;
    \ does>  ( -- 'port)
0 PORT SPEAKER
2 PORT FLIPPER-A
4 PORT FLIPPER-B
6 PORT WIN-LIGHT
```

Here we've created a defining word, PORT, that has a unique *compile-time* behavior, namely adding the offset to BASE.PORT.ADDRESS and defining a CONSTANT.

We might even go one step further. Suppose that all port addresses are two bytes apart. In this case there's no reason we should have to specify these offsets. The numeric sequence

        0 2 4 6

is itself redundant.

In the following version, we begin with the BASE.PORT.ADDRESS on the stack. The defining word PORT duplicates this address, makes a constant out of it, then adds 2 to the address still on the stack, for the next invocation of PORT.

```
: PORT    ( 'port -- 'next-port)   DUP CREATE ,   2+ ;
     \ does>  ( -- 'port)
BASE.PORT.ADDRESS
   PORT SPEAKER
   PORT FLIPPER-A
   PORT FLIPPER-B
   PORT WIN-LIGHT
DROP ( port.address)
```

Notice we must supply the initial port address on the stack before defining the first port, then invoke **DROP** when we've finished defining all the ports to get rid of the port address that's still on the stack.

One final comment. The base-port address is very likely to change, and therefore should be defined in only one place. This does *not* mean it has to be defined as a constant. Provided that the base-port address won't be used outside of this lexicon of port names, it's just as well to refer to it by number here.

```
HEX 01A0   ( base port adr)
   PORT SPEAKER
   PORT FLIPPER-A
   PORT FLIPPER-B
   PORT WIN-LIGHT
DROP
```

The Iterative Approach in Implementation

Earlier in the book we discussed the iterative approach, paying particular attention to its impact on the design phase. Now that we're talking about implementation, let's see how the approach is actually used in writing code.

TIP

Work on only one aspect of a problem at a time.

Suppose we're entrusted with the job of coding a word to draw or erase a box at a given x—y coordinate. (This is the same problem we introduced in the section called "Compile-Time Factoring.)

At first we focus our attention on the problem of drawing a box— never mind erasing it. We might come up with this:

```
: LAYER   WIDE  0 DO  ASCII * EMIT  LOOP ;
: BOX    ( upper-left-x  upper-left-y -- )
    HIGH  0 DO  2DUP  I +  XY LAYER  LOOP  2DROP ;
```

Having tested this to make sure it works correctly, we turn now to the problem of using the same code to *un*draw a box. The solution is simple: instead of hard-coding the **ASCII** * we'd like to change the emitted character from an asterisk to a blank. This requires the addition of a variable, and some readable words for setting the contents of the variable. So:

```
VARIABLE INK
: DRAW    ASCII * INK ! ;
: UNDRAW   BL INK ! ;
: LAYER   WIDTH  0 DO  INK @  EMIT  LOOP ;
```

The definition of BOX, along with the remainder of the application, remains the same.

This approach allows the syntax

```
( x y ) DRAW BOX
```

or

```
( x y ) UNDRAW BOX
```

By switching from an explicit value to a variable that contains a value, we've added a level of indirection. In this case, we've added indirection "backwards," adding a new level of complexity to the definition of LAYER without substantially lengthening the definition.

By concentrating on one dimension of the problem at a time, you can solve each dimension more efficiently. If there's an error in your thinking, the problem will be easier to see if it's not obscured by yet another untried, untested aspect of your code.

While you're editing your application—adding a new feature or fixing something—it's often tempting to go and fix several other things at the same time. Our advice: Don't.

Make as few changes as you can each time you edit-compile. Be sure to test the results of each revision before going on. You'd be amazed how often you can make three innocent modifications, only to recompile and have nothing work!

Making changes one at a time ensures that when it stops working, you know why.

Some people wonder why most FORTH systems don't include the defining word ARRAY. This rule is the reason.

Moore:

> I often have a class of things called arrays. The simplest array merely adds a subscript to an address and gives you back an address. You can define an array by saying

```
CREATE X    100 ALLOT
```

> then saying

```
X +
```

> Or you can say

```
: X    X + ;
```

> One of the problems that's most frustrating for me is knowing whether it's worth creating a defining word for a particular data structure. Will I have enough instances to justify it?

> I rarely know in advance if I'm going to have more than one array. So I don't define the word ARRAY.

> After I discover I need two arrays, the question is marginal.

> If I need three then it's clear. Unless they're different. And odds are they will be different. You may want it to fetch for you. You may want a byte ar-

ray, or a bit array. You may want to do bounds checking, or store its current length so you can add things to the end.

I grit my teeth and say, "Should I make the byte array into a cell array, just to fit the data structure into the word I already have available?"

The more complex the problem, the less likely it will be that you'll find a universally applicable data structure. The number of instances in which a truly complex data structure has found universal use is very small. One example of a successful complex data structure is the FORTH dictionary. Very firm structure, great versatility. It's used everywhere in FORTH. But that's rare.

If you choose to define the word ARRAY, you've done a decomposition step. You've factored out the concept of an array from all the words you'll later put back in. And you've gone to another level of abstraction.

Building levels of abstraction is a dynamic process, not one you can predict.

TIP

Today, make it work. Tomorrow, optimize it.

Again Moore. On the day of this interview, Moore had been completing work on the design of a board-level FORTH computer, using commercially available ICs. As part of his toolkit for designing the board, he created a simulator in FORTH, to test the board's logic:

> This morning I realized I've been mixing the descriptions of the chips with the placement of the chips on the board. This is perfectly convenient for my purposes at the moment, but when I come up with another board that I want to use the same chips for, I have arranged things very badly.
>
> I should have factored it with the descriptions here and the uses there. I would then have had a chip description language. Okay. At the time I was doing this I was not interested in that level of optimization.
>
> Even if the thought had occurred to me then, I probably would have said, "All right, I'll do that later," then gone right ahead with what I was doing. Optimization wasn't the most important thing to me at the time.
>
> Of course I try to factor things well. But if there doesn't seem to be a good way to do something, I say, "Let's just make it work."
>
> My motivation isn't laziness, it's knowing that there are other things coming down the pike that are going to affect this decision in ways I can't predict. Trying to optimize this now is foolish. Until I get the whole picture in front of me, I can't know what the optimimum is.

The observations in this section shouldn't contradict what's been said before about information hiding and about anticipating elements that may change. A good programmer continually tries to balance the expense of building-in changeability against the expense of changing things later if necessary.

These decisions take experience. But as a general rule:

TIP

Anticipate things-that-may-change by organizing information, not by adding complexity. Add complexity only as necessary to make the current iteration work.

Summary

In this chapter we've discussed various techniques and criteria for factoring. We also examined how the iterative approach applies to the implementation phase.

References

1. W.P. Stevens, G.J. Myers, and L.L. Constantine, *IBM Systems Journal,* vol. 13, no. 2, 1974, Copyright 1974 by International Business Machines Corporation.
2. G.A. Miller, "The Magical Number Seven, Plus or Minus Two: Some Limits on Our Capacity for Processing Information," *Psychol. Rev.,* vol. 63, pp. 81-97, Mar. 1956.
3. Kim R. Harris, "Definition Field Address Conversion Operators," *FORTH—83 Standard,* FORTH Standards Team.

SEVEN

Handling Data: Stacks and States

FORTH handles data in one of two ways: either on the stack or in data structures. When to use which approach and how to manage both the stack and data structures are the topics of this chapter.

The Stylish Stack

The simplest way for FORTH words to pass arguments to each other is via the stack. The process is "simple" because all the work of pushing and popping values to and from the stack is implicit.

Moore:

> The data stack uses this idea of "hidden information." The arguments being passed between subroutines are not explicit in the calling sequence. The same argument might ripple through a whole lot of words quite invisibly, even below the level of awareness of the programmer, simply because it doesn't have to be referred to explicitly.

One important result of this approach: Arguments are unnamed. They reside on the stack, not in named variables. This effect is one of the reasons for FORTH's elegance. At the same time it's one of the reasons badly written FORTH code can be unreadable. Let's explore this paradox.

The invention of the stack is analogous to that of pronouns in English. Consider the passage:

> Take this gift, wrap it in tissue paper and put it in a box.

Notice the word "gift" is mentioned only once. The gift is referred to henceforth as "it."

The informality of the "it" construct makes English more readable (provided the reference is unambiguous). So with the stack, the implicit passing of arguments makes code more readable. We emphasize the *processes*, not the *passing of arguments* to the processes.

Our analogy to pronouns suggests why bad FORTH can be so un-readable. The spoken language gets confusing when too many things are referred to with pronouns.

> Take off the wrapping and open the box. Remove the gift and throw it away.

The problem with this passage is that we're using "it" to refer to too many things at once. There are two solutions to this error. The easiest solution is to supply a real name instead of "it":

> Remove the wrapping and open the box. Take out the gift and throw *the box* away.

Or we can introduce the words "former" and "latter." But the best solution is to redesign the passage:

> Remove the wrapping and open the present. Throw away the box.

So in FORTH we have analogous observations:

TIP

Simplify code by using the stack. But don't stack too deeply within any single definition. Redesign, or, as a last resort, use a named variable.

Some newcomers to FORTH view the stack the way a gymnast views a trampoline: as a fun place to bounce around on. But the stack is meant for data-passing, not acrobatics.

So how deep is "too deep"? Generally, three elements on the stack is the most you can manage within a single definition. (In double-length arithmetic, each "element" occupies two stack positions but is logically treated as a single element by operators such as **2DUP**, **2OVER**, etc.)

In your ordinary lexicon of stack operators, **ROT** is the only one that gives you access to the third stack item. Aside from **PICK** and **ROLL** (which we'll comment on soon), there's no easy way to get at anything below that.

To stretch our analogy to the limit, perhaps three elements on the stack corresponds to the three English pronouns "this," "that," and "th'other."

Redesign

Let's witness a case where a wrong-headed approach leads to a messy stack problem. Suppose we're trying to write the definition of +THRU (see Chapter Five, "Listing Organization" section, "Relative Loading" subsection). We've decided that our loop body will be

```
...   DO   I LOAD   LOOP ;
```

that is, we'll put **LOAD** in a loop, then arrange for the index and limit to correspond to the absolute screens being loaded.

On the stack initially we have:

```
lo hi
```

where "lo" and "hi" are the *offsets* from **BLK**.

We need to permute them for **DO**, like this:

```
hi+1+blk lo+blk
```

Our biggest problem is adding the value of **BLK** to both offsets.

We've already taken a wrong turn but we don't know it yet. So let's proceed. We try:

```
lo hi
                    BLK @
lo hi blk
                    SWAP
lo blk hi
                    OVER
lo blk hi blk
                    +
lo blk hi+blk
                    1+
lo blk hi+blk+1
                    ROT ROT
hi+blk+1 lo blk
                    +
hi+blk+1 lo+blk
```

We made it, but what a mess!

If we're gluttons for punishment, we might make two more stabs at it arriving at:

```
BLK @  DUP ROT + 1+  ROT ROT +
```

and

```
BLK @  ROT OVER +  ROT ROT + 1+  SWAP
```

All three sequences do the same thing, but the code seems to be getting blurrier, not better.

With experience we learn to recognize the combination ROT ROT as a danger sign: the stack is too crowded. Without having to work out the alternates, we recognize the problem: once we make two copies of "blk." we have four elements on the stack.

At this point, the first resort is usually the return stack:

```
BLK @  DUP >R  + 1+  SWAP R> + +
```

(See "The Stylish Return Stack," coming up next.) Here we've DUPed "blk," saving one copy on the return stack and adding the other copy to "hi."

Admittedly an improvement. But readable?

Next we think, "Maybe we need a named variable." Of course, we have one already: **BLK**. So we try:

```
BLK @  + 1+  SWAP  BLK @ +
```

Now it's more readable, but it's still rather long, and redundant too. **BLK** @ + appears twice.

"**BLK** @ +"? That sounds famililar. Finally our neurons connect. We look back at the source for +LOAD just defined:

```
: +LOAD  ( offset -- )  BLK @ +  LOAD ;
```

This word, +LOAD, should be doing the work. All we have to write is:

```
: +THRU  ( lo hi )  1+ SWAP  DO  I +LOAD  LOOP ;
```

We haven't created a more efficient version here, because the work of **BLK** @ + will be done on every pass of the loop. But we have created a cleaner, conceptually simpler, and more readable piece of code. In this case, the inefficiency is unnoticeable because it only occurs as each block is loaded.

Redesigning, or rethinking the problem, was the path we should have taken as soon as things got ugly.

Local Variables

Most of the time problems can be arranged so that only a few arguments are needed on the stack at any one time. Occasionally, however, there's nothing you can do.

Here's an example of a worst case. Assume you have a word called LINE which draws a line between any two points, specified as coordinates in this order:

```
( x1 y1 x2 y2)
```

where x1,y1 represent the x,y coordinates for the one end-point, and x2,y2 represent the opposite end-point.

Now you have to write a box-drawing word called [BOX] which takes four arguments in this order:

```
( x1 y1 x2 y2)
```

where x1 y1 represent the x,y coordinates for the upper left-hand corner of the box, and x2 y2 represent the lower right-hand corner coordinates.

Not only do you have four elements on the stack, they each have to be referred to more than once as you draw lines from point to point. Although we're using the stack to get the four arguments, the algorithm for drawing a box doesn't lend itself to the nature of the stack. If you're in a hurry, it would probably be best to take the easy way out:

```
VARIABLE TOP         ( y coordinate: top of box)
VARIABLE LEFT        ( x       "         left side)
VARIABLE BOTTOM      ( y       "         bottom)
VARIABLE RIGHT       ( x       "         right side)
: [BOX]   ( x1 y1 x2 y2)  BOTTOM !  RIGHT !  TOP !  LEFT
    LEFT @ TOP @  RIGHT @ TOP @  LINE
    RIGHT @ TOP @  RIGHT @ BOTTOM @  LINE
    RIGHT @ BOTTOM @  LEFT @ BOTTOM @  LINE
    LEFT @ BOTTOM @  LEFT @ TOP @  LINE    ;
```

What we've done is create four named variables, one for each coordinate. The first thing [BOX] does is fill these variables with the arguments from the stack. Then the four lines are drawn, referencing the variables. Variables such as these that are used only within a definition (or in some cases, within a lexicon) are called "local variables."

I've been guilty many times of playing hotshot, trying to do as much as possible on the stack rather than define a local variable. There are three reasons to avoid this cockiness.

First, it's a pain to code that way. Second, the result is unreadable. Third, all your work becomes useless when a design change becomes necessary, and the order of two arguments changes on the stack. The **DUPs**, **OVERs** and **ROTs** weren't really solving the problem, just jockeying things into position.

With this third reason in mind, I recommend the following:

TIP

Especially in the design phase, keep on the stack only the arguments you're using immediately. Create local variables for any others. (If necessary, eliminate the variables during the optimization phase.)

Fourth, if the definition is extremely time-critical, those tricky stack manipulators, (e.g., **ROT ROT**) can really eat up clock cycles. Direct access to variables is faster.

If it's *really* time-critical, you may need to convert to assembler anyway. In this case, all your stack problems fly out the door, because all your data will be referenced either in registers or indirectly through registers. Luckily, the definitions with the messiest stack arguments are often the ones written in code. Our [BOX] primitive is a case in point. **CMOVE**> is another.

The approach we took with [BOX] certainly beats spending half an hour juggling items on the stack, but it is by no means the best solution. What's nasty about it is the expense of creating four named variables, headers and all, solely for use within this one routine.

(If you're target compiling an application that will not require headers in the dictionary, the only loss will be the 8 bytes in RAM for the variables. In FORTH systems of the future, headers may be separated into other pages of memory anyway; again the loss will be only 8 bytes.)

Let me repeat: This example represents a worst-case situation, and occurs rarely in most FORTH applications. If words are well-factored, then each word is designed to do very little. Words that do little generally require few arguments.

In this case, though, we are dealing with two points each represented by two coordinates.

Can we change the design? First, LINE may be *too* primitive a primitive. It requires four arguments because it can draw lines between any two points, diagonally, if necessary.

In drawing our box, we may only need perfectly vertical and horizontal lines. In this case we can write the more powerful, but less specific, words VERTICAL and HORIZONTAL to draw these lines. Each requires only *three* arguments: the starting position's x and y and the length. This factoring of function simplifies the definition of [BOX].

Or we might discover that this syntax feels more natural to the user:

```
10 10 ORIGIN!   30 30 BOX
```

where ORIGIN! sets a two-element pointer to the "origin," the place where the box will start (the upper left-hand corner). Then "30 30 BOX" draws a box 30 units high and 30 units wide, relative to the origin.

This approach reduces the number of stack arguments to BOX as part of the design.

TIP

When determining which arguments to handle via data structures rather than via the stack, choose the arguments that are the more permanent or that represent a current state.

On PICK and ROLL

Some folks like the words **PICK** and **ROLL**. They use these words to access elements from any level on the stack. We don't recommend them.

For one thing, **PICK** and **ROLL** encourage the programmer to think of the stack as an array, which it is not. If you have so many elements on the stack that you need **PICK** and **ROLL**, those elements should be in an array instead.

Second, they encourage the programmer to refer to arguments that have been left on the stack by higher-level, calling definitions without being explicitly *passed* as arguments. This makes the definition dependent on other definitions. That's unstructured—and dangerous.

Finally, the position of an element on the stack depends on what's above it, and the number of things above it can change constantly. For instance, if you have an address at the fourth stack position down, you can write

```
4 PICK @
```

to fetch its contents. But you must write

```
( n) 5 PICK !
```

because with "n" on the stack, the address is now in the fifth position.

Code like this is hard to read and harder to modify.

Make Stack Drawings

When you do have a cumbersome stack situation to solve, it's best to work it out with paper and pencil. Some people even make up forms, such as the one in Figure 7-1. Done formally like this (instead of on the back of your phone bill) stack commentaries serve as nice auxiliary documentation.

Stack Tips

TIP

Make sure that stack effects balance out under all possible control flows.

In the stack commentary for **CMOVE>** in Figure 7-1, the inner brace represents the contents of the **DO LOOP**. The stack depth upon exiting the loop is the same as upon entering it: one element. Within the outer braces, the stack result of the **IF** clause is the same as that of the **ELSE** clause: one element left over. (What that leftover element represents doesn't matter, as symbolized by the "x" next to **THEN**.)

Figure 7-1. *Example of a stack commentary.*

Word name: CMOVE>	Programmer: LPB	Date: 9/23/83
Operations:	**Stack effects:**	**Return stack:**
/ / / / / / / / / /	s d #	
?DUP IF	s d #	
1- DUP >R	s d #-1	#-1
+	s end-of-d	#-1
SWAP	end-of-d s	#-1
DUP	end-of-d s s	#-1
R>	end-of-d s s #-1	
+	end-of-d s end-of-s	
DO	end-of-d	
I C@	end-of-d last-char	
OVER	end-of-d last-char end-of-d	
C!	end-of-d	
1-	next-to-end-of-d	
-1 +LOOP	"	
ELSE	s d	
DROP	s	
THEN	×	
DROP ;		

TIP

When doing two things with the same number, perform the function that will go underneath first.

For example:

```
: COUNT  ( a -- a+1 # )  DUP C@  SWAP 1+  SWAP ;
```

(where you first get the count) is more efficiently written:

```
: COUNT  ( a -- a+1 # )  DUP 1+  SWAP C@ ;
```

(where you first compute the address).

You'll often find a definition which does some job and, if something goes wrong, returns an error-code indentifying the problem. Here's one way the stack interface might be designed:

```
( -- error-code f | -- t )
```

If the flag is true, the operation was successful. If the flag is false, it was unsuccessful and there's another value on the stack to indicate the nature of the error.

You'll find stack manipulation easier, though, if you redesign the interface to look like this:

```
( -- error-code | 0=no-error )
```

One value serves both as a flag and (in case of an error) the error code. Note that reverse-logic is used; non-zero indicates an error. You can use any values for the error codes except zero.

The Stylish Return Stack

What about this use of the return stack to hold temporary arguments? Is it good style or what?

Some people take great offense to its use. But the return stack offers the simplest solution to certain gnarly stack jams. Witness the definition of **CMOVE>** in the previous section.

If you decide to use the return stack for this purpose, remember that you are using a component of FORTH for a purpose other than that intended. (See the section called "Sharing Components," later in this chapter.)

Here's some suggestions to keep you from shooting yourself in the foot:

For every >R there must be a R> in the same definition. Sometimes the operators will appear to be symmetrical, but due to the control structure they aren't. For instance:

```
... BEGIN  ... >R ... WHILE ... R> ... REPEAT
```

If this construction is used in the outer loop of your application, everything will run fine until you exit (perhaps hours later) when you'll suddenly blow up. The problem? The last time through the loop, the resolving R has been skipped.

The Problem With Variables

Although we handle data of immediate interest on the stack, we depend on much information tucked away in variables, ready for recurring access. A piece of code can change the contents of a variable without necessarily having to know anything about how that data will be used, who will use it, or when and if it will be used. Another piece of code can fetch the contents of a variable and use it without knowing where that value came from.

For every word that pushes a value onto the stack, another word must consume that value. The stack gives us point-to-point communication, like the post office.

Variables, on the other hand, can be set by any command and accessed any number of times—or not at all—by any command. Variables are available for anyone who cares to look—like graffiti.

Thus variables can be used to reflect the current state of affairs.

Using currentness can simplify problems. In the Roman numeral example of Chapter Four, we used the variable COLUMN# to represent the current decimal-place; the words ONER, FIVER, and TENER depended on this information to determine which type of symbol to display. We didn't have to specify both descriptions every time, as in TENS ONER, TENS FIVER, etc.

On the other hand, currentness adds a new level of complexity. To make something current we must first define a variable or some type of data structure. We also must remember to initialize it, if there's any chance that part of our code will refer to it before another part has had a chance to set it.

A more serious problem with variables is that they are not "reentrant." On a multi-tasked FORTH system, each task which requires local variables must have its own copies. FORTH's USER variables serve this purpose. (See *Staring FORTH*, Chapter Nine, "FORTH Geography.")

Even within a single task, a definition that refers to a variable is harder to test, verify, and reuse in a different situation than one in which arguments are passed via the stack.

Suppose we are implementing a word-processor editor. We need a routine that calculates the number of characters between the current cursor position and the previous carriage-return/line-feed sequence. So we write a word that employs a **DO LOOP** starting at the current position (CURSOR @) and ending at the zeroth position, searching for the line feed character.

Once the loop has found the character sequence, we subtract its relative address from our current cursor position

```
its-position CURSOR @  SWAP -
```

to determine the distance between them.

Our word's stack effect is:

```
( -- distance-to-previous-cr/lf)
```

But in later coding we find we need a similar word to compute the distance from an arbitrary character—*not* the current cursor position—to the first previous line-feed character. We end up factoring out the "CURSOR @" and allowing the starting address to be passed as an argument on the stack, resulting in:

```
( starting-position -- distance-to-previous-cr/lf)
```

By factoring-out the reference to the variable, we made the definition more useful.

TIP

Unless it involves cluttering up the stack to the point of unreadability, try to pass arguments via the stack rather than pulling them out of variables.

Kogge:

Most of the modularity of FORTH comes from designing and treating FORTH words as "functions" in the mathematical sense. In my experience a FORTH programmer usually tries quite hard to avoid defining any but the most essential global variables (I have a friend who has the sign "Help stamp out variables" above his desk), and tries to write words with what is called "referential transparency," i.e., given the same stack inputs a word will always give the same stack ouputs regardless of the more global context in which it is executed.

In fact this property is exactly what we use when we test words in isolation. Words that do not have this property are significantly harder to test. In a sense a "named variable" whose value changes frequently is the next worst thing to the now "forbidden" GOTO.

"*Shot from a cannon on a fast-moving train, hurtling between the blades of a windmill, and expecting to grab a trapeze dangling from a hot-air balloon . . . I told you Ace, there were too many variables!*"

Earlier we suggested the use of local variables especially during the design phase, to eliminate stack traffic. It's important to note that in doing so, the variables were referred to only within the one definition. In our example, [BOX] receives four arguments from the stack and immediately loads them into local variables for its own use. The four variables are not referred to outside of this definition, and the word behaves safely as a function.

Programmers unaccustomed to a language in which data can be passed implicitly don't always utilize the stack as fully as they should. Michael Ham suggests the reason may be that beginning FORTH users don't trust the stack [1]. He admits to initially feeling safer about storing values into variables than leaving them on the stack. "No telling *what* might happen with all that thrashing about on the stack," he felt.

It took some time for him to appreciate that "if words keep properly to themselves, using the stack only for their expected input and output and cleaning up after themselves, they can be looked upon as sealed systems . . . I could put the count on the stack at the beginning of the loop, go through the complete routine for each group, and at the end the count would emerge, back on top of the stack, not a hair out of place."

Local and Global Variables/Initialization

As we saw earlier, a variable that is used exclusively within a single definition (or single lexicon), hidden from other code, is called a local variable. A variable used by more than one lexicon is called a global variable. As we've seen in an earlier chapter, a set of global variables that collectively describe a common interface between several lexicons is called an "interface lexicon."

FORTH makes no distinction between local and global variables. But FORTH programmers do.

Moore:

> We should be writing for the reader. If something is referred to only locally, a temporary variable just for accumulating a sum in, we should define it locally. It's handier to define it in the block where it's used, where you can see its comment.
>
> If it's used globally, we should collect things according to their logical function, and define them together on a separate screen. One per line with a comment.
>
> The question is, where do you initialize them? Some say on the same line, immediately following its definition. But that messes up the comments, and there isn't room for any decent comment. And it scatters the initialization all over the application.
>
> I tend to do all my initialization in the load screen. After I've loaded all my blocks, I initialize the things that have to be initialized. It might also set up color lookup tables or execute some initialization code.

If your program is destined to be target compiled, then it's easy to write a word at the point that encompasses all the initialization.

It can get much more elaborate. I've defined variables in ROM where the variables were all off in an array in high memory, and the initial values are in ROM, and I copy up the initial values at initialization time. But usually you're only initializing a few variables to anything other than zero.

Saving and Restoring a State

Variables have the characteristic that when you change their contents, you clobber the value that was there before. Let's look at some of the problems this can create, and some of the things we can do about them.

BASE is a variable that indicates the current number radix for all numeric input and output. The following words are commonly found in FORTH systems:

```
: DECIMAL    10 BASE ! ;
: HEX    16 BASE ! ;
```

Suppose we've written a word that displays a "dump" of memory. Ordinarily, we work in decimal mode, but we want the dump in hexadecimal. So we write:

```
: DUMP   ( a # )
    HEX   ...   ( code for the dump) ... DECIMAL ;
```

This works—most of the time. But there's a presumption that we want to come back to decimal mode. What if it had been working in hexadecimal, and wants to come back to hexadecimal? Before we change the base to **HEX**, we have to save its current value. When we're done dumping, we restore it.

This means we have to tuck away the saved value temporarily, while we format the dump. The return stack is one place to do this:

```
: DUMP   ( a # )
    BASE @ >R HEX   ( code for dump)  R> BASE ! ;
```

If things get too messy, we may have to define a temporary variable:

```
VARIABLE OLD-BASE
: DUMP   ( a # )
    BASE @   OLD-BASE !  HEX   ( code for dump )
    OLD-BASE @   BASE ! ;
```

How quickly things get complicated.

In this situation, if both the current and the old version of a variable belong only to your application (and not part of your system), and if this same situation comes up more than once, apply a technique of factoring:

```
: BURY    ( a)   DUP 2+   2 CMOVE ;
: EXHUME  ( a)   DUP 2+   SWAP 2 CMOVE ;
```

Then instead of defining two variables, such as CONDITION and OLD-CONDITION, define one double-length variable:

```
2VARIABLE CONDITION
```

Use BURY and EXHUME to save and restore the original value:

```
: DIDDLE    CONDITION BURY   17 CONDITION !   ( diddle )
   CONDITION EXHUME ;
```

BURY saves the "old" version of condition at CONDITION 2+.

You still have to be careful. Going back to our **DUMP** example, suppose you decided to add the friendly feature of letting the user exit the dump at any time by pressing the "escape" key. So inside the loop you build the test for a key being pressed, and if so execute **QUIT**. But what happens?

The user starts in decimal, then types **DUMP**. He exits **DUMP** midway through and finds himself, strangely, in hexadecimal.

In the simple case at hand, the best solution is to not use **QUIT**, but rather a controlled exit from the loop (via **LEAVE**, etc.) to the end of the definition where **BASE** is reset.

In very complex applications a controlled exit is often impractical, yet many variables must somehow be restored to a natural condition.

Moore responds to this example:

> You really get tied up in a knot. You're creating problems for yourself. If I want a hex dump I say **HEX DUMP**. If I want a decimal dump I say **DECIMAL DUMP**. I don't give **DUMP** the privilege of messing around with my environment.
>
> There's a philosophical choice between restoring a situation when you finish and establishing the situation when you start. For a long time I felt you should restore the situation when you're finished. And I would try to do that consistently everywhere. But it's hard to define "everywhere." So now I tend to establish the state before I start.
>
> If I have a word which cares where things are, it had better set them. If somebody else changes them, they don't have to worry about resetting them.
>
> There are more exits than there are entrances.

In cases in which I need to do the resetting before I'm done, I've found it useful to have a single word (which I call PRISTINE) to perform this resetting. I invoke PRISTINE:

- at the normal exit point of the application,
- at the point where the user may deliberately exit (just before **QUIT**)
- at any point where a fatal error may occur, causing an abort.

Finally, when you encounter this situation of having to save/restore a value, make sure it's not just a case of bad factoring. For example, suppose we have written:

```
: LONG    18 #HOLES ! ;
: SHORT    9 #HOLES ! ;
: GAME    #HOLES @  0 DO  I HOLE PLAY  LOOP ;
```

The current GAME is either LONG or SHORT.

Later we decide we need a word to play *any* number of holes. So we invoke GAME making sure not to clobber the current value of #HOLES:

```
: HOLES  ( n)  #HOLES @  SWAP #HOLES !  GAME  #HOLES ! ;
```

Because we needed HOLES after we'd defined GAME, it seemed to be of greater complexity; we built HOLES around GAME. But in fact—perhaps you see it already—rethinking is in order:

```
: HOLES ( n)  0 DO  I HOLE PLAY  LOOP ;
: GAME    #HOLES @ HOLES ;
```

We can build GAME around HOLES and avoid all this saving/restoring nonsense.

Application Stacks

In the last section we examined some ways to save and restore a *single* previous value. Some applications require *several* values to be saved and restored. You may often find the best solution to this problem in defining your own stack.

Here is the code for a user stack including very simple error checking (an error clears the stack):

```
CREATE STACK  12 ALLOT  \  { 2tos-pointer ! 10stack [5 cells] }
HERE CONSTANT STACK>
: INIT-STACK    STACK STACK ! ;   INIT-STACK
: ?BAD  ( ?)   IF ." STACK ERROR "  INIT-STACK  ABORT  THEN ;
```

```
: PUSH   ( n)    2 STACK +!   STACK @  DUP   STACK> = ?BAD   ! ;
: POP   ( -- n)   STACK @ @   -2 STACK +!   STACK @   STACK < ?BAD
```

The word PUSH takes a value from off of your data stack and "pushes" it onto this new stack. POP is the opposite, "popping" a value from off the new stack, and onto FORTH's data stack.

In a real application you might want to change the names PUSH and POP to better match their conceptual purposes.

Sharing Components

TIP

It's legal to use a component for an additional purpose besides its intended one, provided:
1. All uses of the component are mutually exclusive
2. Each interrupting use of the component restores the component to its previous state when finished.

Otherwise you need an additional component or level of complexity.

We've seen a simple example of this principle with the return stack. The return stack is a component of the FORTH system designed to hold return addresses, and thereby serve as an indication of where you've been and where you're going. To use the return stack as a holder for temporary values is possible, and in many cases desirable. Problems occur when one of the above restrictions is ignored.

In my text formatter the output can go invisible. This feature has two purposes: (1) for looking ahead to see whether something will fit, and (2) for formatting the table of contents (the entire document is formatted and page numbers are calculated without anything actually being displayed).

It was tempting to think that once having added the ability to make the output invisible, I could use this feature to serve both purposes. Unfortunately, the two purposes are not mutually exclusive.

Let's see what would happen if I tried to violate this rule. Imagine that the word DISPLAY does the output, and it's smart enough to know whether to be visible or invisible. The words VISIBLE and INVISIBLE set the state respectively.

My code for looking ahead will first execute INVISIBLE, then test-format the upcoming text to determine its length, and finally execute VISIBLE to restore things to the normal state.

This works fine.

Later I add the table-of-contents feature. First the code executes

INVISIBLE, then runs through the document determining page numbers etc.; then finally executes VISIBLE to restore things to normal.

The catch? Suppose I'm running a table of contents and I hit one of those places where I look ahead. When I finish looking ahead, I execute VISIBLE. Suddenly I start printing the document when I was supposed to be running the table of contents.

The solution? There are several.

One solution views the problem as being that the lookahead code is clobbering the visible/invisible flag, which may have been preset by table-of-contents. Therefore, the lookahead code should be responsible for saving, and later restoring, the flag.

Another solution involves keeping two separate variables—one to indicate we're looking ahead, the other to indicate we're printing the table of contents. The word DISPLAY requires that both flags be false in order to actually display anything.

There are two ways to accomplish the latter approach, depending on how you want to decompose the problem. First, we could nest one condition within the other:

```
: [DISPLAY]   ...
         ( the original definition, always does the output) ... ;
VARIABLE 'LOOKAHEAD?   ( t=looking-ahead)
: <DISPLAY>    'LOOKAHEAD? @ NOT IF   [DISPLAY]   THEN ;
VARIABLE 'TOC?   ( t=setting-table-of-contents)
: DISPLAY    'TOC? @ NOT IF   <DISPLAY>   THEN ;
```

DISPLAY checks that we're not setting the table of contents and invokes <DISPLAY>, which in turn checks that we're not looking ahead and invokes [DISPLAY].

In the development cycle, the word [DISPLAY] that always does the output was originally called DISPLAY. Then a new DISPLAY was defined to include the lookahead check, and the original definition was renamed [DISPLAY], thus adding a level of complexity backward without changing any of the code that used DISPLAY.

Finally, when the talbe-of-contents feature was added, a new DIS-PLAY was defined to include the table-of-contents check, and the previous DISPLAY was renamed <DISPLAY>.

That's one approach to the use of two variables. Another is to include both tests within a single word:

```
: DISPLAY    'LOOKAHEAD? @   'TOC @ OR   NOT IF [DISPLAY] THEN ;
```

But in this particular case, yet another approach can simplify the whole mess. We can use a single variable not as a flag, but as a counter.

We define:

```
VARIABLE 'INVISIBLE?   ( t=invisible)
: DISPLAY    'INVISIBLE? @  0= IF [DISPLAY] THEN ;
: INVISIBLE   1 'INVISIBLE? +! ;
: VISIBLE    -1 'INVISIBLE? +! ;
```

The lookahead code begins by invoking INVISIBLE which bumps the counter up one. Non-zero is "true," so DISPLAY will not do the output. After the lookahead, the code invokes VISIBLE which decrements the counter back to zero ("false").

The table-of-contents code also begins with VISIBLE and ends with INVISIBLE. If we're running the table of contents while we come upon a lookahead, the second invocation of VISIBLE raises the counter to two. The subsequent invocation of INVISIBLE decrements the counter to one, so we're still invisible, and will remain invisible until the table of contents has been run.

(Note that we must substitute 0= for **NOT**. The '83 Standard has changed **NOT** to mean one's complement, so that 1 **NOT** yields true. By the way, I think this was a mistake.)

This use of a counter may be dangerous, however. It requires parity of command usage: two VISIBLEs yields invisible. That is, unless VISIBLE clips the counter:

```
: VISIBLE    'INVISIBLE? @  1-  0 MAX  'INVISBLE? ! ;
```

The State Table

A single variable can express a single condition, either a flag, a value, or the address of a function.

A collection of conditions together represent the *state* of the application or of a particular component [2]. Some applications require the ability to save a current state, then later restore it, or perhaps to have a number of alternating states.

TIP

When the application requires handling a group of conditions simultaneously, use a state table, not separate variables.

Figure 7-2. *A collection of related variables.*

```
VARIABLE TOP
VARIABLE BOTTOM
VARIABLE LEFT
VARIABLE RIGHT
VARIABLE INSIDE
VARIABLE OUT
```

The simple case requires saving and restoring a state. Suppose we initially have six variables representing the state of a particular component, as shown in Figure 7-2.

Now suppose that we need to save all of them, so that further processing can take place, and later restore all of them. We could define:

```
: @STATE    ( -- top bottom left right inside out)
   TOP @  BOTTOM @  LEFT @  RIGHT @  INSIDE @  OUT @ ;
: !STATE    ( top bottom left right inside out -- )
   OUT !  INSIDE !  RIGHT !  LEFT !  BOTTOM !  TOP ! ;
```

thereby saving all the values on the stack until it's time to restore them. Or, we might define alternate variables for each of the variables above, in which to save each value separately.

But a preferred technique involves creating a table, with each element of the table referred to by name. Then creating a second table of the same length. As you can see in Figure 7-3, we can save the state by copying the table, called POINTERS, into the second table, called SAVED.

Figure 7-3. *Conceptual model for saving a state table.*

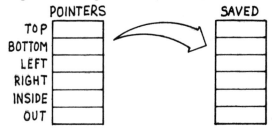

We've implemented this approach with the code in Figure 7-4.

Figure 7-4. *Implementation of save/restorable state table.*

```
O CONSTANT POINTERS  \ address of state table PATCHED LATER
: POSITION   ( o -- o+2 ) CREATE DUP ,  2+
   DOES>  ( -- a )  @  POINTERS + ;
O  \ initial offset
POSITION TOP
POSITION BOTTOM
POSITION LEFT
POSITION RIGHT
POSITION INSIDE
POSITION OUT
CONSTANT /POINTERS   \ final computed offset

HERE ' POINTERS >BODY !  /POINTERS ALLOT  \ real table
CREATE SAVED  /POINTERS ALLOT  \ saving place
: SAVE     POINTERS  SAVED  /POINTERS CMOVE ;
: RESTORE  SAVED  POINTERS  /POINTERS CMOVE ;
```

Notice in this implementation that the names of the pointers, TOP, BOTTOM, etc., always return the same address. There is only one location used to represent the current value of any state at any time.

Also notice that we define POINTERS (the name of the table) with CONSTANT, not with CREATE, using a dummy value of zero. This is because we refer to POINTERS in the defining word POSITION, but it's not until after we've defined all the field names that we know how big the table must be and can actually ALLOT it.

As soon as we create the field names, we define the size of the table as a constant /POINTERS. At last we reserve room for the table itself, patching its beginning address (HERE) into the constant POINTERS. (The word >**BODY** converts the address returned by tick into the address of the constant's value.) Thus POINTERS returns the address of the table allotted later, just as a name defined by CREATE returns the address of a table allotted directly below the name's header.

Although it's valid to patch the value of a CONSTANT at compile time, as we do here, there is a restriction of style:

TIP

A CONSTANT's value should never be changed once the application is compiled.

The case of alternating states is slightly more involved. In this situation we need to alternate back and forth between two (or more) states, never clobbering the conditions in each state when we jump to the other state. Figure 7-5 shows the conceptual model for this kind of state table.

Figure 7-5. *Conceptual model for alternating-states tables.*

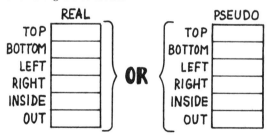

In this model, the names TOP, BOTTOM, etc., can be made to point into either of two tables, REAL or PSEUDO. By making the REAL table the current one, all the pointer names reference addresses in the REAL table; by making the PSEUDO table current, they address the PSEUDO table.

The code in Figure 7-6 implements this alternating states mechanism. The words WORKING and PRETENDING change the

Figure 7-6. *Implementation of alternating-states mechanism.*

```
VARIABLE 'POINTERS    \ pointer to state table
: POINTERS ( -- adr of current table)    'POINTERS @ ;
: POSITION    ( o -- o+2 ) CREATE DUP ,   2+
   DOES>  ( -- a )   @   POINTERS + ;
O \ initial offset
POSITION TOP
POSITION BOTTOM
POSITION LEFT
POSITION RIGHT
POSITION INSIDE
POSITION OUT
CONSTANT /POINTERS   \ final computed offset
CREATE REAL     /POINTERS ALLOT  \ real state table
CREATE PSEUDO   /POINTERS ALLOT  \ temporary state table
: WORKING       REAL 'POINTERS ! ;     WORKING
: PRETENDING    PSEUDO 'POINTERS ! ;
```

pointer appropriately. For instance:

```
WORKING
10 TOP !
TOP ?_10
PRETENDING
20 TOP !
TOP ?_20
WORKING
TOP ?_10
PRETENDING
TOP ?_20
```

The major difference with this latter approach is that names go through an extra level of indirection (POINTERS has been changed from a constant to a colon definition). The field names can be made to point to either of two state tables. Thus each name has slightly more work to do.

Also, in the former approach the names refer to fixed locations; a CMOVE is required each time we save or restore the values. In this approach, we have only to change a single pointer to change the current table.

Vectored Execution

Vectored execution extends the ideas of currentness and indirection beyond data, to functions. Just as we can save values and flags in variables, we can also save functions, because functions can be referred to by address.

The traditional techniques for implementing vectored execution are described in *Starting FORTH,* Chapter Nine. In this section we'll discuss a new syntax which I invented and which I think can be used in many circumstances more elegantly than the traditional methods.

The syntax is called DOER/MAKE. (If your system doesn't include these words, refer to Appendix B for code and implementation details.) It works like this: You define the word whose behavior will be vectorable with the defining word **DOER**, as in

```
DOER PLATFORM
```

Initially, the new word PLATFORM does nothing. Then you can write words that change what PLATFORM does by using the word **MAKE**:

```
: LEFTWING   MAKE PLATFORM  ." proponent " ;
: RIGHTWING  MAKE PLATFORM  ." opponent " ;
```

When you invoke LEFTWING, the phrase MAKE PLATFORM changes what PLATFORM will do. Now if you type PLATFORM, you'll see:

```
LEFTWING_ok
PLATFORM proponent ok
```

RIGHTWING will make PLATFORM display "opponent." You can use PLATFORM within another definition:

```
: SLOGAN    ." Our candidate is a longstanding "   PLATFORM
  ." of heavy taxation for business. " ;
```

The statement

```
LEFTWING SLOGAN
```

will display one campaign statement, while

```
RIGHTWING SLOGAN
```

will display another.

The "MAKE" code can be any FORTH code, as much or as long as you want; just remember to conclude it with semicolon. The semicolon at the end of LEFTWING serves for both LEFTWING and for the bit of code after MAKE. When MAKE redirects execution of the **DOER** word, it also *stops* execution of the word in which it appears.

When you invoke LEFTWING, for example, **MAKE** redirects PLATFORM and exits. Invoking LEFTWING does not cause "proponent" to be printed. Figure 7-7 demonstrates this point, using a conceptualized illustration of the dictionary.

If you want to *continue* execution, you can use the word ;AND in place of semicolon. ;AND terminates the code that the **DOER** word

Figure 7-7. *DOER and MAKE.*

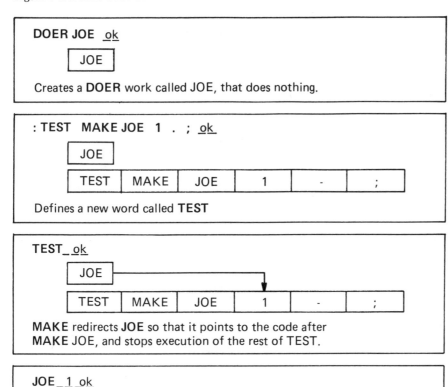

> **DOER JOE** <u>ok</u>
>
> | JOE |
> |---|
>
> Creates a **DOER** work called JOE, that does nothing.

> **: TEST MAKE JOE 1 . ;** <u>ok</u>
>
> | JOE |
> |---|
>
> | TEST | MAKE | JOE | 1 | - | ; |
> |---|---|---|---|---|---|
>
> Defines a new word called **TEST**

> **TEST** <u>ok</u>
>
> | JOE |
> |---|
>
> | TEST | MAKE | JOE | 1 | - | ; |
> |---|---|---|---|---|---|
>
> **MAKE** redirects **JOE** so that it points to the code after
> **MAKE** JOE, and stops execution of the rest of TEST.

> **JOE** <u>1 ok</u>
>
> Executes the code that JOE points to (**1** .).

points to, and resumes execution of the definition in which it appears, as you can see in Figure 7-8.

Finally, you can chain the "making" of **DOER** words in series by *not* using ;AND. Figure 7-9 explains this better than I could write about it.

Using DOER/MAKE

There are many occasions when the DOER/MAKE construct proves beneficial. They are:

1. To change the state of a function (when external testing of the state is not necessary). The words LEFTWING and RIGHTWING change the state of the word PLATFORM.
2. To factor out internal phrases from similar definitions, but within control structures such as loops.
   Consider the definition of a word called DUMP, designed to reveal the contents of a specified region of memory.

Figure 7-8. *Multiple MAKEs in parallel using ;AND.*

DOER SAM ok
DOER BIFF ok

| SAM | | BIFF |

Creates two **DOER** words that do nothing.

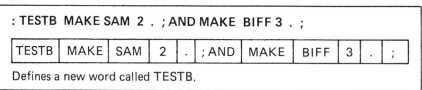

: TESTB MAKE SAM 2 . ; AND MAKE BIFF 3 . ;

| TESTB | MAKE | SAM | 2 | . | ; AND | MAKE | BIFF | 3 | . | ; |

Defines a new word called TESTB.

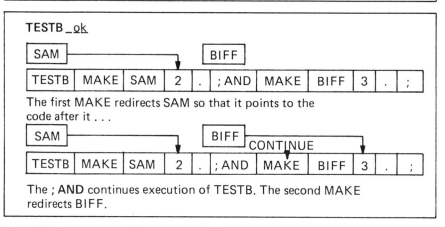

TESTB ok

The first MAKE redirects SAM so that it points to the code after it . . .

The ; AND continues execution of TESTB. The second MAKE redirects BIFF.

SAM 2 ok
BIFF 3 ok

Two **DOER** words have been redirected at the same time by the single word TESTB. SAM's code stops at ; AND.
BIFF's code stops at semicolon.

```
: DUMP  ( a # )
   0 DO  I 16 MOD 0=  IF   CR   DUP I +   5 U.R   2 SPACES   THEN
   DUP I +  @  6 U.R   2 +LOOP DROP ;
```

The problem arises when you write a definition called CDUMP, designed to format the output according to bytes, not cells:

```
: CDUMP  ( a # )
   0 DO  I 16 MOD 0=  IF   CR   DUP I +   5 U.R   2 SPACES   THEN
   DUP I +  C@   4 U.R   LOOP DROP ;
```

Figure 7-9. *Multiple MAKEs in series.*

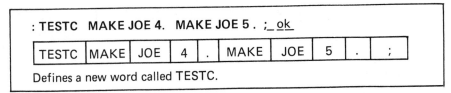

: TESTC MAKE JOE 4. MAKE JOE 5 . ;_ ok

| TESTC | MAKE | JOE | 4 | . | MAKE | JOE | 5 | . | ; |

Defines a new word called TESTC.

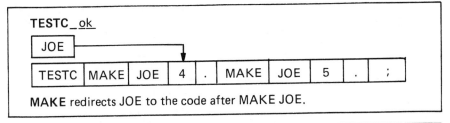

TESTC_ ok

| JOE |

| TESTC | MAKE | JOE | 4 | . | MAKE | JOE | 5 | . | ; |

MAKE redirects JOE to the code after MAKE JOE.

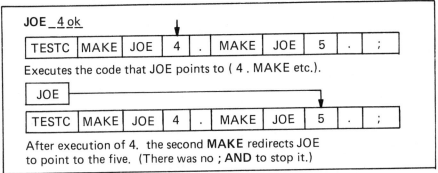

JOE _ 4 ok

| TESTC | MAKE | JOE | 4 | . | MAKE | JOE | 5 | . | ; |

Executes the code that JOE points to (4 . MAKE etc.).

| JOE |

| TESTC | MAKE | JOE | 4 | . | MAKE | JOE | 5 | . | ; |

After execution of 4. the second **MAKE** redirects JOE
to point to the five. (There was no ; **AND** to stop it.)

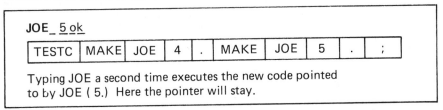

JOE_ 5 ok

| TESTC | MAKE | JOE | 4 | . | MAKE | JOE | 5 | . | ; |

Typing JOE a second time executes the new code pointed
to by JOE (5.) Here the pointer will stay.

The code within these two definitions is identical except for the fragments
in boldface. But factoring is difficult because the fragments occur inside the
DO LOOP.

Here's a solution to this problem, using **DOER/MAKE.** The code that
changes has been replaced with the word .UNIT, whose behavior is vectored by the code in DUMP and CDUMP. (Recognize that "1 +LOOP" has
the same effect as "LOOP".)

```
DOER .UNIT   ( a -- increment)   \ display byte or cell
: <DUMP>   ( a # )
    0 DO   I 16 MOD 0= IF CR  DUP I +  5 U.R  2 SPACES   THEN
    DUP I + .UNIT  +LOOP   DROP ;
: DUMP    ( a #)   MAKE .UNIT @  6 U.R  2 ;AND   <DUMP> ;
: CDUMP   ( a #)   MAKE .UNIT C@ 4 U.R  1 ;AND   <DUMP> ;
```

Notice how DUMP and CDUMP *set-up* the vector, then go on to *execute* the shell (the word <DUMP>).

3. To change the state of related functions by invoking a single command. For instance:

```
DOER TYPE'
DOER EMIT'
DOER SPACES'
DOER CR'
: VISIBLE        MAKE TYPE'    TYPE ;AND
                 MAKE EMIT'    EMIT ;AND
                 MAKE SPACES'    SPACES ;AND
                 MAKE CR'    CR ;
: INVISIBLE      MAKE TYPE'    2DROP ;AND
                 MAKE EMIT'    DROP ;AND
                 MAKE SPACES'    DROP ;AND
                 MAKE CR'    ;
```

Here we've defined a vectorable set of output words, each name having a "prime" mark at the end. VISIBLE sets them to their expected functions. INVISIBLE makes them no-ops, eating up the arguments that would normally be passed to them. Say INVISIBLE and any words defined in terms of these four output operators will *not* produce any output.

4. To change the state for the next occurrence only, then change the state (or reset it) again.

Suppose we're writing an adventure game. When the player first arrives at a particular room, the game will display a detailed description. If the player returns to the same room later, the game will show a shorter message. We write:

```
DOER ANNOUNCE
: LONG    MAKE ANNOUNCE
    CR ." You're in a large hall with a huge throne"
    CR  ." covered with a red velvet canopy. "
         MAKE ANNOUNCE
    CR ." You're in the throne room. " ;
```

The word ANNOUNCE will display either message. First we say LONG, to initialize ANNOUNCE to the long message. Now we can test ANNOUNCE, and find that it prints the long message. Having done that, however, it continues to "make" ANNOUNCE display the short message.

If we test ANNOUNCE a second time, it prints the short message. And it will for ever more, until we say LONG again.

In effect we're queuing behaviors. We can queue any number of behaviors, letting each one set the next. The following example (though not terribly practical) illustrates the point.

```
DOER WHERE
VARIABLE SHIRT
VARIABLE PANTS
VARIABLE DRESSER
VARIABLE CAR

: ORDER   \  specify search order
    MAKE WHERE  SHIRT   MAKE WHERE  PANTS
    MAKE WHERE  DRESSER   MAKE WHERE  CAR
    MAKE WHERE  0 ;

: HUNT   ( -- a!0 )  \  find location containing 17
    ORDER  5 0 DO  WHERE  DUP 0=  OVER @  17 =  OR  IF
        LEAVE  ELSE  DROP  THEN  LOOP ;
```

In this code we've created a list of variables, then defined an ORDER in which they are to be searched. The word HUNT looks through each of them, looking for the first one that contains a 17. HUNT returns either the address of the correct variable, or a zero if none have the value.

It does this by simply executing WHERE five times. Each time, WHERE returns a different address, as defined in ORDER, then finally zero.

We can even define a **DOER** word that toggles its own behavior endlessly:

```
DOER SPEECH
: ALTERNATE
    BEGIN  MAKE SPEECH  ." HELLO "
    MAKE SPEECH ." GOODBYE "
    0 UNTIL ;
```

5. To implement a forward reference. A forward reference is usually needed as a "hook," that is, a word invoked in a low-level definition but reserved for use by a component defined later in the listing.

To implement a forward reference, build the header of the word with **DOER**, before invoking its name.

```
DOER STILL-UNDEFINED
```

Later in the listing, use MAKE;

```
MAKE STILL-UNDEFINED  ALL THAT JAZZ ;
```

(Remember, MAKE can be used outside a colon definition.)

6. Recursion, direct or indirect.

Direct recursion occurs when a word invokes itself. A good example is the recursive definition of greatest-common-denominator:

$$\text{GCD of } a, b = \begin{array}{ll} a & \text{if } b = 0 \\ \text{GCD of } b, a \bmod b & \text{if } b > 0 \end{array}$$

This translates nicely into:

```
DOER GCD    ( a b -- gcd)
MAKE GCD    ?DUP  IF  DUP ROT ROT  MOD  GCD  THEN ;
```

Indirect recursion occurs when one word invokes a second word, while the second word invokes the first. This can be done using the form:

```
DOER B
: A    ... B ... ;
MAKE B   ... A ... ;
```

7. Debugging. I often define:

```
DOER SNAP
```

(short for SNAPSHOT), then edit SNAP into my application at a point where I want to see what's going on. For instance, with SNAP invoked inside the main loop of a keystroke interpreter, I can set it up to let me watch what's happening to a data structure as I enter keys. And I can change what SNAP does without having to recompile the loop.

The situations in which it's preferable to use the tick-and-execute approach are those in which you need control over the address of the vector, such as when vectoring through an element in a decision table, or attempting to save/restore the contents of the vector.

Summary

In this chapter we've examined the tradeoffs between using the stack and using variables and other data structures. Using the stack is preferable for testing and reusability, but too many values manipulated on the stack by a single definition hurts readability and writeability.

We also explored techniques for saving and restoring data structures, and concluded with a study of vectored execution using **DOER/MAKE**.

References

1. Michael Ham, "Why Novices Use So Many Variables," *FORTH Dimensions*, vol. 5, no. 4, November/December 1983.
2. Daniel Slater, "A State Space Approach to Robotics," *The Journal of FORTH Application and Research*, 1, 1 (September 1983), 17.

EIGHT

Minimizing Control Structures

Control structures aren't as important in FORTH as they are in other languages. FORTH programmers tend to write very complex applications in terms of short words, without much emphasis on **IF THEN** constructs.

There are several techniques for minimizing control structures. They include:

- computing or calculating
- hiding conditionals through re-factoring
- using structured exits
- vectoring
- redesigning.

In this chapter we'll examine these techniques for simplifying and eliminating control structures from your code.

What's So Bad about Control Structures?

Before we begin reeling off our list of tips, let's pause to examine why conditionals should be avoided in the first place.

The use of conditional structures adds complexity to your code. The more complex your code is, the harder it will be for you to read and to maintain. The more parts a machine has, the greater are its chances of breaking down. And the harder it is for someone to fix.

Moore tells this story:

> I recently went back to a company we had done some work for several years ago. They called me in because their program is now five years old, and it's gotten very complicated. They've had programmers going in and patching things, adding state variables and conditionals. Every statement that I recall being a simple thing five years ago, now has gotten very complicated. "If this, else if this, else if this" . . . and then the simple thing.
>
> Reading that statement now, it's impossible for me to figure out what it's doing and why. I'd have to remember what each variable indicated, why it

was relevant in this case, and then what was happening as a consequence of it—or not happening.

It started innocently. They had a special case they needed to worry about. To handle that special case, they put a conditional in one place. Then they discovered that they also needed one here, and here. And then a few more. Each incremental step only added a little confusion to the program. Since they were the programmers, they were right on top of it.

The net result was disastrous. In the end they had half a dozen flags. Test this one, reset it, set that one, and so on. As a result of this condition, you knew you had other conditions coming up you had to look out for. They created the logical equivalent of spaghetti code in spite of the opportunity for a structured program.

The complexity went far beyond what they had ever intended. But they'd committed themselves to going down this path, and they missed the simple solution that would have made it all unnecessary—having two words instead of one. You either say GO or you say PRETEND.

In most applications there are remarkably few times when you need to test the condition. For instance in a video game, you don't really say "If he presses Button A, then do this; if he presses Button B, then do something else. You don't go through that kind of logic.

If he presses the button, you do something. What you do is associated with the button, not with the logic.

Conditionals aren't bad in themselves—they are an essential construct. But a program with a lot of conditionals is clumsy and unreadable. All you can do is question each one. Every conditional should cause you to ask, "What am I doing wrong?"

What you're trying to do with the conditional can be done in a different way. The long-term consequences of the different way are preferable to the long-term consequences of the conditional.

Before we introduce some detailed techniques, let's look at three approaches to the use of conditionals in a particular example. Figure 8-1, Figure 8-2, and Figure 8-3 illustrate three versions of a design for an automatic teller machine.

The first example comes straight out of the School for Structured Programmers. The logic of the application depends on the correct nesting of IF statements.

Easy to read? Tell me under what condition the user's card gets eaten. To answer, you have to either count ELSEs from the bottom and match them with the same number of IFs from the top, or use a straightedge.

The second version, Figure 8-2, shows the improvement that using many small, named procedures can have on readibility. The user's card is eaten if the owner is not valid.

But even with this improvement, the design of each word depends completely on the *sequence* in which the tests must be performed. The supposedly "highest" level procedure is burdened with eliminating the worst-case, most trivial kind of event. And each test becomes responsible for invoking the next test.

Figure 8-1. *The structured approach.*

AUTOMATIC-TELLER

```
IF card is valid DO
    IF card owner is valid DO
        IF request withdrawal DO
            IF authorization code is valid DO
                query for amount
                IF request ≤ current balance DO
                    IF withdrawal ≤ available cash DO
                        vend currency
                        debit account
                    ELSE
                        message
                        terminate session
                ELSE
                    message
                    terminate session
            ELSE
                message
                terminate session
        ELSE
            IF authorization code is valid DO
                query for amount
                accept envelope through hatch
                credit account
            ELSE
                message
                terminate session
    ELSE
        eat card
ELSE
    message
END
```

The third version comes closest to the promise of FORTH. The highest level word expresses exactly what's happening conceptually, showing only the main path. Each of the subordinate words has its own error exit, not cluttering the reading of the main word. One test does not have to invoke the next test.

Also TRANSACT is designed around the fact that the user will make requests by pressing buttons on a keypad. No conditions are necessary. One button will initiate a withdrawal, another a deposit. This approach readily accommodates design changes later, such as the addition of a feature to transfer funds. (And this approach does *not* thereby become dependent on hardware. Details of the interface to the keypad may be hidden within the keypad lexicon, READ-BUTTON and BUTTON.)

Of course, FORTH will allow you to take any of the three approachs. Which do you prefer?

Figure 8-2. *Nesting conditionals within named procedures.*

<u>AUTOMATIC-TELLER</u>

```
PROCEDURE READ-CARD
      IF   card is readable  THEN   CHECK-OWNER
           ELSE  eject card  END

PROCEDURE CHECK-OWNER
      IF  owner is valid  THEN   CHECK-CODE
           ELSE   eat card  END

PROCEDURE CHECK-CODE
      IF   code entered matches owner  THEN   TRANSACT
           ELSE message, terminate session  END

PROCEDURE TRANSACT
      IF requests withdrawal  THEN  WITHDRAW
           ELSE  DEPOSIT END

PROCEDURE WITHDRAW
      Query
      If  request ≤ current balance  THEN  DISBURSE  END

PROCEDURE DISBURSE
      IF  disbursement ≤ available cash  THEN
              vend currency
              debit account
           ELSE   message  END

PROCEDURE DEPOSIT
      accept envelope
      credit account
```

How to Eliminate Control Structures

In this section we'll study numerous techniques for simplifying or avoiding conditionals. Most of them will produce code that is more readable, more maintainable, and more efficient. Some of the techniques produce code that is more efficient, but not always as readable. Remember, therefore: Not all of the tips will be applicable in all situations.

Using the Dictionary

TIP

Give each function its own definition.

Figure 8-3. *Refactoring and/or eliminating conditionals.*

AUTOMATIC-TELLER

```
: RUN
    READ-CARD  CHECK-OWNER  CHECK-CODE  TRANSACT  ;

: READ-CARD
    valid code sequence NOT readable  IF  eject card  QUIT
      THEN ;

: CHECK-OWNER
    owner is NOT valid  IF  eat card  QUIT  THEN ;

: CHECK-CODE
    code entered MISmatches owner's code  IF  message  QUIT
      THEN ;

: READ-BUTTON  ( -- adr-of-button's-function}
    ( device-dependent primitive} ;

: TRANSACT
    READ-BUTTON  EXECUTE ;

1 BUTTON WITHDRAW

2 BUTTON DEPOSIT

: WITHDRAW
    Query
    request < current balance  IF  DISBURSE  THEN ;

: DISBURSE
    disbursement < available cash  IF
        vend currency
        debit account
      ELSE  message  THEN  ;

: DEPOSIT
    accept envelope
    credit account ;
```

By using the FORTH dictionary properly, we're not actually eliminating conditionals; we're merely factoring them out from our application code. The FORTH dictionary is a giant string case statement. The match and execute functions are hidden within the FORTH system.

Moore:

In my accounting package, if you receive a check from somebody, you type the amount, the check number, the word FROM, and the person's name:

```
200.00 127 FROM ALLIED
```

The word FROM takes care of that situation. If you want to bill someone, you type the amount, the invoice number, the word BILL and the person's name:

```
1000.00 280 BILL TECHNITECH
```

. . . One word for each situation. The dictionary is making the decision.

This notion pervades FORTH itself. To add a pair of single-length numbers we use the command +. To add a pair of double-length numbers we use the command **D+**. A less efficient, more complex approach would be a single command that somehow "knows" which type of numbers are being added.

FORTH is efficient because all these words—**FROM** and **BILL** and + and **D+**—can be implemented without any need for testing and branching.

TIP

Use dumb words.

This isn't advice for TV writers. It's another instance of using the dictionary. A "dumb" word is one that is not state-dependent, but instead, has the same behavior all the time ("referentially transparent").

A dumb word is unambiguous, and therefore, more trustworthy.

A few common FORTH words have been the source of controversy recently over this issue. One such word is ." which prints a string. In its simplest form, it's allowed only inside a colon definition:

```
: TEST    ." THIS IS A STRING " ;
```

Actually, this version of the word does *not* print a string. It *compiles* a string, along with the address of another definition that does the printing at run time.

This is the dumb version of the word. If you use it outside a colon definition, it will uselessly compile the string, not at all what a beginner might expect.

To solve this problem, the FIG model added a test inside ." that determined whether the system was currently compiling or interpreting. In the first case, ." would compile the string and the address of the primitives; in the second case it would **TYPE** it.

." became two completely different words housed together in one definition with an **IF ELSE THEN** structure. The flag that indicates whether FORTH is compiling or interpreting is called **STATE**. Since the ." depends on **STATE**, it is said to be "**STATE**-dependent," literally.

The command *appeared* to behave the same inside and outside a colon definition. This duplicity proved useful in afternoon introductions to FORTH, but the serious student soon learned there's more to it than that.

Suppose a student wants to write a new word called **B.''** (for ''bright-dot-quote'') to display a string in bright characters on her display, to be used like this:

```
." INSERT DISK IN "  B." LEFT "  ." DRIVE "
```

She might expect to define **B.''** as

```
: B."   BRIGHT  ."  NORMAL ;
```

that is, change the video mode to bright, print the string, then reset the mode to normal.

She tries it. Immediately the illusion is destroyed; the deception is revealed; the definition won't work.

To solve her problem, the programmer will have to study the definition of (.'') in her own system. I'm not going to get sidetracked here with explaining how (.'') works—my point is that smartness isn't all it appears to be.

Incidentally, there's a different syntactical approach to our student's problem, one that does not require having two separate words, .'' and B.'' to print strings. Change the system's (.'') so that it always sets the mode to normal after typing, even though it will already be normal most of the time. With this syntax, the programmer need merely precede the emphasized string with the simple word BRIGHT.

```
." INSERT DISK IN "  BRIGHT ." LEFT "  ." DRIVE "
```

The '83 Standard now specifies a dumb .'' and, for those cases where an interpretive version is wanted, the new word .(has been added. Happily, in this new standard we're using the dictionary to make a decision by having two separate words.

The word ' (tick) has a similar history. It was **STATE**-dependent in fig-FORTH, and is now dumb in the '83 Standard. Tick shares with dot-quote the characteristic that a programmer might want to reuse either of these words in a higher-level definition and have them behave in the same way they do normally.

TIP

Words should not depend on **STATE** if a programmer might ever want to invoke them from within a higher-level definition and expect them to behave as they do interpretively.

ASCII works well as a STATE-dependent word, and so does **MAKE**. (See Appendix C.)

Nesting and Combining Conditionals

TIP

Don't test for something that has already been excluded.

Take this example, please:

```
: PROCESS-KEY
   KEY   DUP   LEFT-ARROW   =   IF CURSOR-LEFT    THEN
         DUP   RIGHT-ARROW  =   IF CURSOR-RIGHT   THEN
         DUP   UP-ARROW     =   IF CURSOR-UP      THEN
               DOWN-ARROW   =   IF CURSOR-DOWN    THEN ;
```

This version is inefficient because all four tests must be made regardless of the outcome of any of them. If the key pressed was the left-arrow key, there's no need to check if it was some other key.

Instead, you can nest the conditionals, like this:

```
: PROCESS-KEY
   KEY   DUP   LEFT-ARROW   =   IF CURSOR-LEFT    ELSE
         DUP   RIGHT-ARROW  =   IF CURSOR-RIGHT   ELSE
         DUP   UP-ARROW     =   IF CURSOR-UP      ELSE
                                   CURSOR-DOWN
         THEN THEN THEN   DROP ;
```

TIP

Combine booleans of similar weight.

Many instances of doubly-nested **IF THEN** structures can be simplified by combining the flags with logical operators before making the decision. Here's a doubly-nested test:

```
: ?PLAY    SATURDAY? IF   WORK FINISHED? IF
     GO PARTY    THEN    THEN ;
```

The above code uses nested **IF**s to make sure that it's both Saturday and the chores are done before it boogies on down. Instead, let's combine the conditions logically and make a single decision:

```
: ?PLAY    SATURDAY?  WORK FINISHED? AND   IF
     GO PARTY    THEN ;
```

It's simpler and more readable.

The logical "or" situation, when implemented with **IF THENs**, is even clumsier:

```
: ?RISE    PHONE RINGS? IF  UP GET   THEN
         ALARM-CLOCK RINGS?  IF UP GET THEN ;
```

This is much more elegantly written as

```
: ?RISE  PHONE RINGS?  ALARM RINGS? OR  IF  UP GET THEN ;
```

One exception to this rule arises when the speed penalty for checking some of the conditions is too great.
    We might write

```
: ?CHOW-MEIN   BEAN-SPROUTS?  CHOW-MEIN RECIPE?  AND IF
    CHOW-MEIN PREPARE   THEN ;
```

But suppose it's going to take us a long time to hunt through our recipe file to see if there's anything on chow mein. Obviously there's no point in undertaking the search if we have no bean sprouts in the fridge. It would be more efficient to write

```
: ?CHOW-MEIN   BEAN-SPROUTS? IF  CHOW-MEIN RECIPE? IF
    CHOW-MEIN PREPARE THEN    THEN ;
```

We don't bother looking for the recipe if there are no sprouts.
    Another exception arises if any term is probably not true. By eliminating such a condition first, you avoid having to try the other conditions.

TIP

When multiple conditions have dissimilar weights (in likelihood or calculation time) nest conditionals with the term that is least likely to be true or
easiest to calculate on the outside.

Trying to improve performance in this way is more difficult with the OR construct. For instance, in the definition

```
: ?RISE  PHONE RINGS?  ALARM RINGS? OR  IF  UP GET THEN ;
```

we're testing for the phone and the alarm, even though only one of them needs to ring for us to get up. Now suppose it were much more difficult to determine that the alarm clock was ringing. We could write

```
: ?RISE    PHONE RINGS? IF  UP GET  ELSE
         ALARM-CLOCK  RINGS?  IF UP GET THEN THEN  ;
```

If the first condition is true, we don't waste time evaluating the second. We have to get up to answer the phone anyway.

The repetition of UP GET is ugly—not nearly as readable as the solution using **OR**—but in some cases desirable.

Choosing Control Structures

TIP

The most elegant code is that which most closely matches the problem. Choose the control structure that most closely matches the control-flow problem.

Case Statements

A particular class of problem involves selecting one of several possible paths of execution according to a numeric argument. For instance, we want the word .SUIT to take a number representing a suit of playing cards, 0 through 3, and display the name of the suit. We might define this word using nested **IF ELSE THENs**, like this:

```
: .SUIT   ( suit -- )
   DUP   0=  IF   ." HEARTS  "    ELSE
   DUP   1 = IF   ." SPADES  "    ELSE
   DUP   2 = IF   ." DIAMONDS " ELSE
                  ." CLUBS  "
   THEN THEN THEN   DROP ;
```

We can solve this problem more elegantly by using a "case statement." Here's the same definition, rewritten using the "Eacker case statement" format, named after Dr. Charles E. Eacker, the gentleman who proposed it [1].

```
: .SUIT   ( suit -- )
   CASE
   0 OF    ." HEARTS  "     ENDOF
   1 OF    ." SPADES  "     ENDOF
   2 OF    ." DIAMONDS " ENDOF
   3 OF    ." CLUBS  "     ENDOF        ENDCASE ;
```

The case statement's value lies exclusively in its readability and writeability. There's no efficiency improvement either in object memory or in execution speed. In fact, the case statement compiles much the same code as the nested **IF THEN** statements. A case statement is a good example of compile-time factoring.

Should all FORTH systems include such a case statement? That's a matter of controversy. The problem is twofold. First, the instances in which a case statement is actually needed are rare—rare enough to question its value. If there are only a few cases, a nested **IF ELSE THEN** construct will work as well, though perhaps not as readably. If there are many cases, a decision table is more flexible.

Second, many case-like problems are not quite appropriate for the case structure. The Eaker case statement assumes that you're testing for equality against a number on the stack. In the instance of .SUIT, we have contiguous integers from zero to three. It's more efficient to use the integer to calculate an offset and directly jump to the right code.

In the case of our Tiny Editor, later in this chapter, we have not but two dimensions of possibilities. The case statement doesn't match that problem either.

Personally, I consider the case statement an elegant solution to a misguided problem: attempting an algorithmic expression of what is more aptly described in a decision table.

A case statement ought to be part of the application when useful, but not part of the system.

Looping Structures

The right looping structure can eliminate extra conditionals.

Moore:

> Many times conditionals are used to get out of loops. That particular use can be avoided by having loops with multiple exit points.
>
> This is a live topic, because of the multiple **WHILE** construct which is in polyFORTH but hasn't percolated up to FORTH '83. It's a simple way of defining multiple **WHILE**s in the same **REPEAT**.
>
> Also Dean Sanderson [of FORTH, Inc.] has invented a new construct that introduces two exit points to a **DO LOOP**. Given that construction you'll have fewer tests. Very often I leave a truth value on the stack, and if I'm leaving a loop early, I change the truth value to remind myself that I left the loop early. Then later I'll have an **IF** to see whether I left the loop early, and it's just clumsy.
>
> Once you've made a decision, you shouldn't have to make it again. With the proper looping constructs you won't need to remember where you came from, so more conditionals will go away.
>
> This is not completely popular because it's rather unstructured. Or perhaps it is elaborately structured. The value is that you get simpler programs. And it costs nothing.

Indeed, this is a live topic. As of this writing it's too early to make any specific proposals for new loop constructs. Check your system's documentation to see what it offers in the way of exotic looping structures. Or, depending on the needs of your application, consider adding your own conditional constructs. It's not that hard in FORTH.

I'm not even sure whether this use of multiple exits doesn't violate the doctrine of structured programming. In a **BEGIN WHILE REPEAT** loop with multiple **WHILE**s, all the exits bring you to a common "continue" point: the **REPEAT**. But with Sanderson's construct, you can exit the loop by jumping *past* the end of the loop, continuing at an **ELSE**. There are two possible "continue" points.

This is "less structured," if we can be permitted to say that. And yet the definition will always conclude at its semicolon and return to the word that invoked it. In that sense it is well-structured; the module has one entry point and one exit point.

When you want to execute special code only if you did *not* leave the loop prematurely, this approach seems the most natural structure to use. (We'll see an example of this in a later section, "Using Structured Exits.")

TIP

Favor counts over terminators.

FORTH handles strings by saving the length of the string in the first byte. This makes it easier to type, move, or do practically anything with the string. With the address and count on the stack, the definition of **TYPE** can be coded:

```
: TYPE   ( a #)   OVER + SWAP DO   I C@ EMIT   LOOP ;
```

(Although **TYPE** really ought to be written in machine code.)

This definition uses no overt conditional. **LOOP** actually hides the conditional since each loop checks the index and returns to **DO** if it has not yet reached the limit.

If a delimiter were used, let's say ASCII null (zero), the definition would have to be written:

```
: TYPE   ( a)   BEGIN DUP C@   ?DUP WHILE   EMIT   1+
    REPEAT   DROP ;
```

An extra test is needed on each pass of the loop. (**WHILE** is a conditional operator.)

Optimization note: The use of **?DUP** in this solution is expensive in terms of time because it contains an extra decision itself. A faster definition would be:

```
: TYPE   ( a)   BEGIN DUP C@   DUP WHILE   EMIT   1+
    REPEAT   2DROP ;
```

The '83 Standard applied this principle to **INTERPRET** which now accepts a count rather than looking for a terminator.

The flip side of this coin is certain data structures in which it's easiest to *link* the structures together. Each record points to the next (or previous) record. The last (or first) record in the chain can be indicated with a zero in its link field.

If you have a link field, you have to fetch it anyway. You might as well test for zero. You don't need to keep a counter of how many records there are. If you decrement a counter to decide whether to terminate, you're making more work for yourself. (This is the technique used to implement FORTH's dictionary as a linked list.)

Calculating Results

TIP

Don't decide, calculate.

Many times conditional control structures are applied mistakenly to situations in which the difference in outcome results from a difference in numbers. If numbers are involved, we can calculate them. (In Chapter Four see the section called "Calculations vs. Data Structures vs. Logic.")

TIP

Use booleans as hybrid values.

This is a fascinating corollary to the previous tip, "Don't decide, calculate." The idea is that booleans, which the computer represents as numbers, can efficiently be used to effect numeric decisions. Here's one example, found in many FORTH systems:

```
: S>D  ( n -- d)  \ sign extend s to d
      DUP 0<  IF -1  ELSE  0 THEN ;
```

(The purpose of this definition is to convert a single-length number to double-length. A double-length number is represented as two 16-bit values on the stack, the high-order part on top. Converting a positive integer to double-length merely means adding a zero onto the stack, to represent its high-order part. But converting a negative integer to double-length requires "sign extension"; that is, the high-order part should be all ones.)

The above definition tests whether the single-length number is negative. If so, it pushes a negative one onto the stack; otherwise a zero.

But notice that the outcome is merely arithmetic; there's no change in process. We can take advantage of this fact by using the boolean itself:

```
: S>D  ( n -- d)  \ sign extend s to d
      DUP  0< ;
```

This version pushes a zero or negative one onto the stack without a moment's (in)decision.

(In pre-1983 systems, the definition would be:

```
: S>D   ( n -- d)   \ sign extend s to d
     DUP   0< NEGATE ;
```

See Appendix C.)

We can do even more with "hybrid values":

TIP

To effect a decision with a numeric outcome, use **AND**.

In the case of a decision that produces either zero or a non-zero "n," the traditional phrase

```
( ? )  IF  n  ELSE  0  THEN
```

is equivalent to the simpler statement

```
( ? )   n AND
```

Again, the secret is that "false" is represented by -1 (all ones) in '83 FORTH systems. **AND**ing "n" with the flag will either produce "n" (all bits intact) or "0" (all bits cleared).

To restate with an example:

```
( ? )   IF  200  ELSE  0  THEN
```

is the same as

```
( ? )    200 AND
```

Take a look at this example:

```
n   a b <   IF   45 +   THEN
```

This phrase either adds 45 to "n" or doesn't, depending on the relative sizes of "a" and "b." Since "adding 45 or not" is the same as "adding 45 or adding 0," the difference between the two outcomes is purely numeric. We can rid ourselves of a decision, and simply compute:

```
n   a b <   45 AND   +
```

Moore:

> The "45 AND" is faster than the IF, and certainly more graceful. It's simpler. If you form a habit of looking for instances where you're calculating this value from that value, then usually by doing arithmetic on the logic you get the same result more cleanly.
>
> I don't know what you call this. It has no terminology; it's merely doing arithmetic with truth values. But it's perfectly valid, and someday boolean algebra and arithmetic expressions will accommodate it.
>
> In books you often see a lot of piece-wise linear approximations that fail to express things clearly. For instance the expression
>
> ```
> x = 0 for t < 0
> x = 1 for t ≥ 0
> ```
>
> This would be equivalent to
>
> ```
> t   0<  1 AND
> ```
>
> as a single expression, not a piece-wise expression.

I call these flags "hybrid values" because they are booleans (truth values) being applied as data (numeric values). Also, I don't know what else to call them.

We can eliminate numeric **ELSE** clauses as well (where both results are non-zero), by factoring out the difference between the two results. For instance,

```
: STEPPERS   'TESTING? @  IF  150 ELSE 151   THEN  LOAD ;
```

can be simplified to

```
: STEPPERS   150  'TESTING? @  1 AND +  LOAD ;
```

This approach works here because conceptually we want to either load Screen 150, or if testing, the next screen past it.

A Note on Tricks

This sort of approach is often labelled a "trick." In the computing industry at large, tricks have a bad rep.

A trick is simply taking advantage of certain properties of operation. Tricks are used widely in engineering applications. Chimneys eliminate smoke by taking advantage of the fact that heat rises. Automobile tires provide traction by taking advantage of gravity.

Arithmetic Logic Units (ALUs) take advantage of the fact that subtracting a number is the same as adding its two's complement.

These tricks allow simpler, more efficient designs. What justifies their use is that the assumptions are certain to remain true.

The use of tricks becomes dangerous when a trick depends on something likely to change, or when the thing it depends on is not protected by information hiding.

Also, tricks become difficult to read when the assumptions on which they're based aren't understood or explained. In the case of replacing conditionals with AND, once this technique becomes part of every programmer's vocabulary, code can become *more* readable. In the case of a trick that is specific to a specific application, such as the order in which data are arranged in a table, the listing must clearly document the assumption used by the trick.

TIP

Use **MIN** and **MAX** for clipping.

Suppose we want to decrement the contents of the variable VALUE, but we don't want the value to go below zero:

```
-1 VALUE +!   VALUE @   -1 = IF   0 VALUE !   THEN
```

This is more simply written:

```
VALUE @   1-   0 MAX   VALUE !
```

In this case the conditional is factored within the word **MAX**.

Using Decision Tables

TIP

Use decision tables.

We introduced these in Chapter Two. A decision table is a structure that contains either data (a "data table") or addresses of functions (a "function table") arranged according to any number of dimensions. Each dimension represents all the possible, mutually exclusive states of a particular aspect of the problem. At the intersection of the "true" states of each dimension lies the desired element: the piece of data or the function to be performed.

A decision table is clearly a better choice than a conditional structure when the problem has multiple dimensions.

One-Dimensional Data Table

Here's an example of a simple, one-dimensional data table. Our application has a flag called 'FREEWAY? which is true when we're referring to freeways, false when we're referring to city streets.

Let's construct the word SPEED—LIMIT, which returns the speed limit depending on the current state. Using **IF THEN** we would write:

```
: SPEED-LIMIT  ( -- speed-limit)
      'FREEWAY? @  IF  55  ELSE  25   THEN ;
```

We might eliminate the **IF THEN** by using a hybrid value with **AND**:

```
: SPEED-LIMIT   25  'FREEWAY? @  30 AND + ;
```

But this approach doesn't match our conceptual model of the problem and therefore isn't very readable.

Let's try a data table. This is a one-dimensional table, with only two elements, so there's not much to it:

```
CREATE LIMITS   25 ,  55 ,
```

The word SPEED—LIMIT? now must apply the boolean to offset into the data table:

```
: SPEED-LIMIT  ( -- speed-limit)
     LIMITS  'FREEWAY? @  2 AND  +  @ ;
```

Have we gained anything over the **IF THEN** approach? Probably not, with so simple a problem.

What we have done, though, is to factor out the decision-making process from the data itself. This becomes more cost-effective when we have more than one set of data related to the same decision. Suppose we also had

```
CREATE #LANES   4 ,  10 ,
```

representing the number of lanes on a city street and on a freeway. We can use identical code to compute the current number of lanes:

```
: #LANES?  ( -- #lanes)
     #LANES  'FREEWAY? @  2 AND  +  @ ;
```

Applying techniques of factoring, we simplify this to:

```
: ROAD  ( for-freeway  for-city ) CREATE  ,  ,
     DOES>  ( -- data )  'FREEWAY? @  2 AND  +  @ ;
```

```
55 25 ROAD SPEED-LIMIT?
10  4 ROAD #LANES?
```

Another example of the one-dimensional data table is the "superstring" (*Starting FORTH*, Chapter Ten).

Two-Dimensional Data Table

In Chapter Two we presented a phone-rate problem. Figure 8-4 gives one solution to the problem, using a two-dimensional data structure.

In this problem, each dimension of the data table consists of three mutually exclusive states. Therefore a simple boolean (true/false) is inadequate. Each dimension of this problem is implemented in a different way.

The current rate, which depends on the time of day, is stored as an address, representing one of the three rate-structure sub-tables. We can say

```
    FULL RATE !
```

or

```
    LOWER RATE !
```

etc.

Figure 8-4. *A solution to the phone rate problem.*

```
\ Telephone rates                                    03/30/84
CREATE FULL      30 ,  20 ,   12 ,
CREATE LOWER     22 ,  15 ,   10 ,
CREATE LOWEST    12 ,   9 ,    6 ,
VARIABLE RATE    \ points to FULL, LOWER or LOWEST
                 \ depending on time of day
FULL RATE !  \ for instance
: CHARGE   ( o -- ) CREATE ,
   DOES>  ( -- rate )   @ RATE @ +  @ ;
0 CHARGE 1MINUTE   \ rate for first minute
2 CHARGE +MINUTES  \ rate for each additional minute
4 CHARGE /MILES    \ rate per each 100 miles


\ Telephone rates                                    03/30/84
VARIABLE OPERATOR? \ 90 if operator assisted; else 0
VARIABLE #MILES  \ hundreds of miles
: ?ASSISTANCE  ( direct-dial charge -- total charge)
   OPERATOR? @  + ;
: MILEAGE  ( -- charge )  #MILES @  /MILES * ;
: FIRST  ( -- charge )  1MINUTE  ?ASSISTANCE  MILEAGE + ;
: ADDITIONAL  ( -- charge)  +MINUTES   MILEAGE + ;
: TOTAL  ( #minutes -- total charge)
   1- ADDITIONAL * FIRST + ;
```

The current charge, either first minute, additional minute, or per-mile, is expressed as an offset into the table (0, 2, or 4).

An optimization note: we've implemented the two-dimensional table as a set of three one-dimensional tables, each pointed to by RATE. This approach eliminates the need for a multiplication that would otherwise be needed to implement a two-dimensional structure. The multiplication can be prohibitively slow in certain cases.

Two-Dimensional Decision Table

We'll hark back to our Tiny Editor example in Chapter Three to illustrate a two-dimensional decision table.

In Figure 8-5 we're constructing a table of functions to be performed when various keys are pressed. The effect is similar to that of a case statement, but there are two modes, Normal Mode and Insert Mode. Each key has a different behavior depending on the current mode.

The first screen implements the change of the modes. If we invoke

```
NORMAL MODE#  !
```

we'll go into Normal Mode.

```
INSERTING MODE#  !
```

enters Inserting Mode.

The next screen constructs the function table, called FUNCTIONS. The table consists of the ASCII value of a key followed by the address of the routine to be performed when in Normal Mode, followed by the address of the routine to be performed when in Insert Mode, when that key is pressed. Then comes the second key, followed by the next pair of addresses, and so on.

In the third screen, the word 'FUNCTION takes a key value, searches through the FUNCTIONS table for a match, then returns the address of the cell containing the match. (We preset the variable MATCHED to point to the last row of the table—the functions we want when *any* character is pressed.)

The word ACTION invokes 'FUNCTION, then adds the contents of the variable MODE#. Since MODE# will contain either a 2 or a 4, by adding this offset we're now pointing into the table at the address of the routine we want to perform. A simple

```
@ EXECUTE
```

will perform the routine (or @**EXECUTE** if you have it).

In fig-FORTH, change the definition of IS to:

```
: IS    [COMPILE] ' CFA , ;
```

Figure 8-5. *Implementation of the Tiny Editor.*

```
Screen # 30
  0 \ Tiny Editor
  1 2 CONSTANT NORMAL       \ offset in FUNCTIONS
  2 4 CONSTANT INSERTING    \         "
  3 6 CONSTANT /KEY         \ bytes in table for each key
  4 VARIABLE MODE#          \ current offset into table
  5 NORMAL MODE# !
  6 : INSERT-OFF   NORMAL    MODE# ! ;
  7 : INSERT-ON    INSERTING MODE# ! ;
  8
  9 VARIABLE ESCAPE?         \ t=time-to-leave-loop
 10 : ESCAPE   TRUE ESCAPE? ! ;
 11
 12
 13
 14
 15
```

```
Screen # 31
  0 \ Tiny Editor                 function table              07/29/83
  1 : IS    ' , ; \    function   ( -- )      ( for '83 standard)
  2 CREATE FUNCTIONS
  3 \ keys                  normal mode         insert mode
  4  4 ,  ( ctrl-D)         IS DELETE           IS INSERT-OFF
  5  9 ,  ( ctrl-I)         IS INSERT-ON        IS INSERT-OFF
  6  8 ,  ( backspace)      IS BACKWARD         IS INSERT<
  7 60 ,  ( left arrow)     IS BACKWARD         IS INSERT-OFF
  8 62 ,  ( right arrow)    IS FORWARD          IS INSERT-OFF
  9 27 ,  ( return)         IS ESCAPE           IS INSERT-OFF
 10  0 ,  ( no match)       IS OVERWRITE        IS INSERT
 11 HERE /KEY -  CONSTANT 'NOMATCH  \  adr of no-match key
 12
 13
 14
 15
```

```
Screen # 32
  0 \ Tiny Editor cont'd                                      07/29/83
  1 VARIABLE MATCHED
  2 : 'FUNCTION  ( key -- adr-of-match )  'NOMATCH  MATCHED !
  3    'NOMATCH FUNCTIONS DO   DUP  I @ =   IF
  4      I MATCHED !  LEAVE   THEN  /KEY +LOOP  DROP
  5    MATCHED @ ;
  6 : ACTION  ( key -- )  'FUNCTION  MODE# @ +  @  EXECUTE ;
  7 : GO   FALSE ESCAPE? !  BEGIN  KEY ACTION  ESCAPE? @ UNTIL ;
  8
  9
 10
 11
 12
 13
 14
 15
```

In 79-Standard FORTHs, use:

```
: IS    [COMPILE] '  , ;
```

We've also used non-redundancy at compile time in the definition just below the function table:

```
HERE /KEY -  CONSTANT 'NOMATCH  \  adr of no-match key
```

We're making a constant out of the last row in the function table. (At the moment we invoke **HERE**, it's pointing to the next free cell after the last table entry has been filled in. Six bytes back is the last row.) We now have two words:

```
FUNCTIONS   ( adr of beginning of function table )
'NOMATCH    ( adr of "no-match" row; these are the
              routines for any key not in the table)
```

We use these names to supply the addresses passed to **DO**:

```
'NOMATCH FUNCTION DO
```

to set up a loop that runs from the first row of the table to the last. We don't have to know how many rows lie in the table. We could even delete a row or add a row to the table, without having to change any other piece of code, even the code that searches through the table.

Similarly the constant /KEY hides information about the number of columns in the table.

Incidentally, the approach to 'FUNCTION taken in the listing is a quick-and-dirty one; it uses a local variable to simplify stack manipulation. A simpler solution that uses no local variable is:

```
: 'FUNCTION   ( key -- adr of match )
    'NOMATCH SWAP  'NOMATCH FUNCTIONS DO  DUP
      I @ =  IF SWAP DROP I SWAP  LEAVE  THEN
    /KEY +LOOP  DROP ;
```

(We'll offer still another solution later in this chapter, under "Using Structured Exits.")

Decision Tables for Speed

We've stated that if you can calculate a value instead of looking it up in a table, you should do so. The exception is where the requirements for speed justify the extra complexity of a table.

Here is an example that computes powers of two to 8-bit precision:

```
CREATE TWOS
    1 C,   2 C,   4 C,   8 C,   16 C,   32 C,
: 2** ( n -- 2 to the n)
    TWOS + C@ ;
```

Instead of computing the answer by multiplying two times itself "n" times, the answers are all pre-computed and placed in a table. We can use simple addition to offset into the table and get the answer.

In general, addition is much faster than multiplication.

Moore provides another example:

If you want to compute trig functions, say for a graphics display, you don't need much resolution. A seven-bit trig function is probably plenty. A table look-up of 128 numbers is faster than anything else you're going to be able to do. For low-frequency function calculations, decision tables are great.

But if you have to interpolate, you have to calculate a function anyway. You're probably better off calculating a slightly more complicated function and avoiding the table lookup.

Redesigning

TIP

One change at the bottom can save ten decisions at the top.

In our interview with Moore at the beginning of the chapter, he mentioned that much conditional testing could have been eliminated from an application if it had been redesigned so that there were two words instead of one: "You either say GO or you say PRETEND."

It's easier to perform a simple, consistent algorithm while changing the context of your environment than to choose from several algorithms while keeping a fixed environment.

Recall from Chapter One our example of the word APPLES. This was originally defined as a variable; it was referred to many times throughout the application by words that incremented the number of apples (when shipments arrive), decremented the number (when apples are sold), and checked the current number (for inventory control).

When it became necessary to handle a second type of apples, the *wrong* approach would have been to add that complexity to all the shipment/sales/inventory words. The *right* approach was the one we took: to add the complexity "at the bottom"; that is, to APPLES itself.

This principle can be realized in many ways. In Chapter Seven (under "The State Table") we used state tables to implement the words

WORKING and PRETENDING, which changed the meaning of a group of variables. Later in that chapter, we used vectored execution to define VISIBLE and INVISIBLE, to change the meanings of TYPE', EMIT', SPACES' and CR' and thereby easily change all the formatting code that uses them.

TIP

Don't test for something that can't possibly happen.

Many contemporary programmers are error-checking-happy.

There's no need for a function to check an argument passed by another component in the system. The calling program should bear the responsibility for not exceeding the limits of the called component.

TIP

Reexamine the algorithm.

Moore:

> A lot of conditionals arise from fuzzy thinking about the problem. In servo-control theory, a lot of people think that the algorithm for the servo ought to be different when the distance is great than when it is close. Far away, you're in slew mode; closer to the target you're in decelerate mode; very close you're in hunt mode. You have to test how far you are to know which algorithm to apply.

> I've worked out a non-linear servo-control algorithm that will handle full range. This approach eliminates the glitches at the transitioning points between one mode and the other. It eliminates the logic necessary to decide which algorithm to use. It eliminates your having to empirically determine the transition points. And of course, you have a much simpler program with one algorithm instead of three.

> Instead of trying to get rid of conditionals, you're best to question the underlying theory that led to the conditionals.

TIP

Avoid the need for special handling.

One example we mentioned earlier in the book: if you keep the user out of trouble you won't have to continually test whether the user has gotten into trouble.

Moore:

> Another good example is writing assemblers. Very often, even though an opcode may not have a register associated with it, pretending that it has a register—say, Register 0—might simplify the code. Doing arithmetic by introducing bit patterns that needn't exist simplifies the solution. Just substitute zeros and keep on doing arithmetic that you might have avoided by testing for zero and not doing it.
>
> It's another instance of the "don't care." If you don't care, then give it a dummy value and use it anyway.

Anytime you run into a special case, try to find an algorithm for which the special case becomes a normal case.

TIP

Use properties of the component.

A well-designed component—hardware or software—will let you implement a corresponding lexicon in a clean, efficient manner. The character graphics set from the old Epson MX-80 printer (although now obsolete) illustrates the point well. Figure 8-6 shows the graphics characters produced by the ASCII codes 160 to 223.

Figure 8-6. *The Epson MX-80 graphics character set.*

160	161	162	163	164	165	166	167
168	169	170	171	172	173	174	175
176	177	178	179	180	181	182	183
184	185	186	187	188	189	190	191
192	193	194	195	196	197	198	199
200	201	202	203	204	205	206	207
208	209	210	211	212	213	214	215
216	217	218	219	220	221	222	223

Each graphics character is a different combination of six tiny boxes, either filled in or left blank. Suppose in our application we want to use these characters to create a design. For each character, we know what we want in each of the six positions—we must produce the appropriate ASCII character for the printer.

A little bit of looking will tell you there's a very sensible pattern involved. Assuming we have a six-byte table in which each byte represents a pixel in the pattern:

PIXELS

0	1
2	3
4	5

and assuming that each byte contains hex FF if the pixel is "on;" zero if it is "off," then here's how little code it takes to compute the character:

```
CREATE PIXELS  6 ALLOT
: PIXEL  ( i -- a )   PIXELS + ;
: CHARACTER  ( -- graphics character)
   160   6 0 DO  I PIXEL C@  I 2** AND  +  LOOP ;
```

(We introduced 2** a few tips back.)

No decisions are necessary in the definition of CHARACTER. The graphics character is simply computed.

Note: to use the same algorithm to translate a set of six adjoining pixels in a large grid, we can merely redefine PIXEL. That's an example of adding indirection backwards, and of good decomposition.

Unfortunately, external components are not always designed well. For instance, The IBM Personal Computer uses a similar scheme for graphics characters on its video display, but without any discernible correspondence between the ASCII values and the pattern of pixels. The only way to produce the ASCII value is by matching patterns in a lookup table.

Moore:

> The 68000 assembler is another example you can break your heart over, looking for a good way to express those op-codes with the minimal number of operators. All the evidence suggests there is no good solution. The people who designed the 68000 didn't have assemblers in mind. And they could have made things a lot easier, at no cost to themselves.

By using properties of a component in this way, your code becomes dependent on those properties and thus on the component itself. This is excusable, though, because all the dependent code is confined to a single lexicon, which can easily be changed if necessary.

Using Structured Exits

TIP

Use the structured exit.

In the chapter on factoring we demonstrated the possibility of factoring out a control structure using this technique:

```
: CONDITIONALLY   A B OR  C AND  IF  NOT R> DROP   THEN ;
: ACTIVE   CONDITIONALLY   TUMBLE JUGGLE JUMP ;
: LAZY   CONDITIONALLY SIT  EAT  SLEEP ;
```

FORTH allows us to alter the control flow by directly manipulating the return stack. (If in doubt, see *Starting FORTH*, Chapter Nine.) Indiscreet application of this trick can lead to unstructured code with nasty side effect. But the disciplined use of the structured exit can actually simplify code, and thereby improve readability and maintainability.

Moore:

> More and more I've come to favor R> DROP to alter the flow of control. It's similar to the effect of an **ABORT"**, which has an **IF THEN** built in it. But that's only one **IF THEN** in the system, not at every error.
>
> I either abort or I don't abort. If I don't abort, I continue. If I do abort, I don't have to thread my way through the path. I short-circuit the whole thing.
>
> The alternative is burdening the rest of the application with checking whether an error occurred. That's an inconvenience.

The "abort route" circumvents the normal paths of control flow under special conditions. FORTH provides this capability with the words **ABORT"** and **QUIT**.

The "structured exit" extends the concept by allowing the immediate termination of a single word, without quitting the entire application.

This technique should not be confused with the use of GOTO, which is unstructured to the extreme. With GOTO you can go anywhere, inside or outside the current module. With this technique, you effectively jump directly to the final exit point of the module (the semicolon) and resume execution of the calling word.

The word **EXIT** terminates the definition in which the word appears. The phrase **R>DROP** terminates the definition that *called* the definition in which the phrase appears; thus it has the same effect but can be used one level down. Here are some examples of both approaches.

If you have an **IF ELSE THEN** phrase in which no code follows **THEN**, like this:

```
... HUNGRY?  IF  EAT-IT  ELSE  FREEZE-IT  THEN ;
```

you can eliminate **ELSE** by using **EXIT**:

```
... HUNGRY?  IF EAT-IT EXIT  THEN  FREEZE-IT ;
```

(If the condition is true, we eat and run; **EXIT** acts like a semicolon. If the condition is false, we skip to **THEN** and FREEZE-IT.)

The use of **EXIT** here is more efficient, saving two bytes and extra code to perform, but it is not as readable.

Moore comments on the value, and danger, of this technique:

> Especially if your conditionals are getting elaborate, it's handy to jump out in the middle without having to match all your **THEN**s at the end. In one application I had a word that went like this:

```
: TESTING
    SIMPLE   1CONDITION IF ... EXIT THEN
             2CONDITION IF ... EXIT THEN
             3CONDITION IF ... EXIT THEN ;
```

> SIMPLE handled the simple cases. SIMPLE ended up with **R > DROP**. These other conditions were the more complex ones.
>
> Everyone exited at the same point without having to painfully match all the **IF**s, **ELSE**s, and **THEN**s. The final result, if none of the conditions matched, was an error condition.
>
> It was bad code, difficult to debug. But it reflected the nature of the problem. There wasn't any better scheme to handle it. The **EXIT** and **R > DROP** at least kept things manageable.

Programmers sometimes also use **EXIT** to get out of a complicated **BEGIN** loop in a graceful way. Or we might use a related technique in the **DO LOOP** that we wrote for 'FUNCTION in our Tiny Editor, earlier in this chapter. In this word, we are searching through a series of locations looking for a match. If we find a match, we want to return the address where we found it; if we don't find a match, we want the address of the last row of the functions table.

We can introduce the word LEAP (see Appendix C), which will work like **EXIT** (it will simulate a semicolon). Now we can write:

```
: 'FUNCTION  ( key -- adr of match )
   'NOMATCH FUNCTIONS DO  DUP  I @ =  IF  DROP I LEAP
   THEN  /KEY +LOOP  DROP  'NOMATCH ;
```

If we find a match we LEAP, not to **+LOOP**, but right out of the definition, leaving I (the address at which we found it) on the stack. If we don't find a match, we fall through the loop and execute

```
DROP  'NOMATCH
```

which drops the key# being searched for, then leaves the address of the last row!

As we've seen, there may be times when a premature exit is appropriate, even multiple exit points and multiple "continue" points. Remember though, this use of **EXIT** and **R> DROP** is *not consistent* with structured programming in the strictest sense, and requires great care.

For instance, you may have a value on the stack at the beginning of a definition which is consumed at the end. A premature **EXIT** will leave the unwanted value on the stack.

Fooling with the return stack is like playing with fire. You can get burned. But how convenient it is to have fire.

Employing Good Timing

TIP

Take the action when you know you need to, not later.

Any time you set a flag, ask yourself why you're setting it. If the answer is, "So I'll know to do such-and-such later," then ask yourself if you can do such-and-such *now*. A little restructuring can greatly simplify your design.

TIP

Don't put off till run time what you can compile today.

Any time you can make a decision prior to compiling an application, do.

Suppose you had two versions of an array: one that did bounds checking for your protection during development and one that ran faster, though unprotected for the actual application.

Keep the two versions in different screens. When you compile your application, load only the version you need.

By the way, if you follow this suggestion, you may go crazy editing parentheses in and out of your load blocks to change which version gets loaded each time. Instead, write throw-away definitions that make the decisions for you. For instance (as already previewed in another context):

```
: STEPPERS    150  'TESTING? @  1 AND +   LOAD ;
```

TIP

DUP a flag, don't recreate it.

Sometimes you need a flag to indicate whether or not a previous piece of code was invoked. The following definition leaves a flag which indicates that DO-IT was done:

```
: DID-I?   ( -- t=I-did)
    SHOULD-I? IF  DO-IT  TRUE  ELSE  FALSE  THEN ;
```

This can be simplified to:

```
: DID-I?   ( -- t=I-did)
      SHOULD-I? DUP  IF  DO-IT  THEN ;
```

TIP

Don't set a flag, set the data.

If the only purpose to setting a flag is so that later some code can decide between one number and another, you're better off saving the number itself.

The "colors" example in Chapter Six's section called "Factoring Criteria" illustrates this point.

The purpose of the word LIGHT is to set a flag which indicates whether we want the intensity bit to be set or not. While we could have written

```
: LIGHT    TRUE 'LIGHT? ! ;
```

to set the flag, and

```
'LIGHT? @ IF  8 OR   THEN   ...
```

to use the flag, this approach is not quite as simple as putting the intensity bit-mask itself in the variable:

```
: LIGHT    8 'LIGHT? ! ;
```

and then simply writing

```
'LIGHT? @  OR ...
```

to use it.

TIP

Don't set a flag, set the function. (Vector.)

This tip is similar to the previous one, and lives under the same restriction. If the only purpose to setting a flag is so that later some code can decide between one function and another, you're better off saving the address of the function itself.

For instance, the code for transmitting a character to a printer is different than for slapping a character onto a video display. A poor implementation would define:

```
VARIABLE DEVICE   ( 0=video | 1=printer)
: VIDEO    FALSE DEVICE ! ;
: PRINTER   TRUE DEVICE ! ;
: TYPE   ( a # -- ) DEVICE @ IF
    ( ...code for printer...) ELSE
    ( ...code for video...)   THEN ;
```

This is bad because you're deciding which function to perform every time you type a string.

A preferable implementation would use vectored execution. For instance:

```
DOER TYPE   ( a # -- )
: VIDEO    MAKE TYPE   ( ...code for video...) ;
: PRINTER   MAKE TYPE   ( ...code for printer...) ;
```

This is better because TYPE doesn't have to decide which code to use, it already knows.

(On a multi-tasked system, the printer and monitor tasks would each have their own copies of an execution vector for TYPE stored in a user variable.)

The above example also illustrates the limitation of this tip. In our second version, we have no simple way of knowing whether our current device is the printer or the video screen. We might need to know, for instance, to decide whether to clear the screen or issue a formfeed. Then we're making an additional use of the state, and our rule no longer applies.

A flag would, in fact, allow the simplest implementation of additional state-dependent operations. In the case of TYPE, however, we're concerned about speed. We type strings so often, we can't afford to waste time doing it. The best solution here might be to set the function of TYPE and also set a flag:

```
DOER TYPE
: VIDEO    0 DEVICE !  MAKE TYPE
    ( ...code for video...) ;
: PRINTER   1 DEVICE !  MAKE TYPE
    ( ...code for printer...) ;
```

Thus TYPE already knows which code to execute, but other definitions will refer to the flag.

Another possibility is to write a word that fetches the parameter of the **DOER** word TYPE (the pointer to the current code) and compares it against the address of PRINTER. If it's less than the address of PRINTER, we're using the VIDEO routine; otherwise we're using the PRINTER routine.

If changing the state involves changing a small number of functions, you can still use DOER/MAKE. Here are definitions of three memory-move operators that can be shut off together.

```
DOER !'   ( vectorable ! )
DOER CMOVE'   ( vectorable CMOVE )
DOER FILL'   ( vectorable FILL )
: STORING    MAKE !'  !  ;AND
             MAKE CMOVE'   CMOVE ;AND
             MAKE FILL'   FILL ;
: -STORING   MAKE !'   2DROP ;AND
             MAKE CMOVE'   2DROP DROP ;AND
             MAKE FILL'   2DROP DROP ;
```

But if a large number of functions need to be vectored, a state table would be preferable.

A corollary to this rule introduces the "structured exit hook," a **DOER** word vectored to perform a structured exit.

```
DOER HESITATE   ( the exit hook)
: DISSOLVE   HESITATE   FILE-DIVORCE ;

( ... Much later in the listing:)
: RELENT   MAKE HESITATE   SEND-FLOWERS   R> DROP ;
```

By default, HESITATE does nothing. If we invoke DISSOLVE, we'll end up in court. But if we RELENT before we DISSOLVE, we'll send flowers, then jump clear to the semicolon, cancelling that court order before our partner ever finds out.

This approach is especially appropriate when the cancellation must be performed by a function defined much later in the listing (decomposition by sequential complexity). Increased complexity of the earlier code is limited solely to defining the hook and invoking it at the right spot.

Simplifying

I've saved this tip for last because it exemplifies the rewards of opting for simplicity. While other tips concern maintainability, performance, compactness, etc., this tip relates to the sort of satisfaction that Thoreau sought at Walden Pond.

Try to avoid altogether saving flags in memory.

A flag on the stack is quite different from a flag in memory. Flags on the stack can simply be determined (by reading the hardware, calculating, or whatever), pushed onto the stack, then consumed by the control structure. A short life with no complications.

But save a flag in memory and watch what happens. In addition to having the flag itself, you now have the complexity of a location for the flag. The location must be:

- created
- initialized (even before anything actually changes)
- reset (otherwise, passing a flag to a command leaves the flag in that current state).

Because flags in memory are variables, they are not reentrant.

An example of a case in which we might reconsider the need for a flag is one we've seen several times already. In our "colors" example we made the assumption that the best syntax would be:

```
LIGHT BLUE
```

that is, the adjective LIGHT preceding the color. Fine. But remember the code to implement that version? Compare it with the simplicity of this approach:

```
0 CONSTANT BLACK     1 CONSTANT BLUE     2 CONSTANT GREEN
3 CONSTANT CYAN      4 CONSTANT RED      5 CONSTANT MAGENTA
6 CONSTANT BROWN     7 CONSTANT GRAY
: LIGHT    ( color -- color )  8 OR ;
```

In this version we've reversed the syntax, so that we now say

```
BLUE LIGHT
```

We establish the color, then we modify the color.

We've eliminated the need for a variable, for code to fetch from the variable and more code to reset the variable when we're done. And the code is so simple it's impossible not to understand.

When I first wrote these commands, I took the English-like approach. "BLUE LIGHT" sounded backwards, not at all acceptable. That was before my conversations with Chuck Moore.

Moore's philosophy is persuasive:

> I would distinguish between reading nicely in English and reading nicely. In other languages such as Spanish, adjectives follow nouns. We should be independent of details like which language we're thinking in.
>
> It depends on your intention: simplicity, or emulation of English. English is not such a superb language that we should follow it slavishly.

If I were selling my "colors" words in a package for graphic artists, I would take the trouble to create the flag. But writing these words for my own use, if I had to do it over again, I'd favor the Moore-ish influence, and use "BLUE LIGHT."

Summary

The use of logic and conditionals as a significant structural element in programming leads to overly-complicated, difficult-to-maintain, and inefficient code. In this chapter we've discussed several ways to minimize, optimize or eliminate unnecessary conditional structures.

As a final note, FORTH's downplaying of conditionals is not shared by most contemporary languages. In fact, the Japanese are basing their fifth-generation computer project on a language called PROLOG—for PROgramming in LOGic—in which one programs entirely in logic. It will be interesting to see the battle-lines forming as we ponder the question:

> To **IF** or not to **IF**

In this book we've covered the first six steps of the software development cycle, exploring both the philosophical questions of designing software and practical considerations of implementing robust, efficient, readable software.

We have not discussed optimization, validation, debugging, documenting, project management, FORTH development tools, assembler definitions, uses and abuses of recursion, developing multiprogrammed applications, or target compilation.

But that's another story.

References

1. Charles Eaker, "Just in Case," *FORTH Dimensions* II/3, p. 37.

1. You have the word CHOOSE which takes an argument "n" and returns a random number between 0 and n-1. The result is always positive or zero. You can use CHOOSE to produce a flag; the phrase

   2 CHOOSE

   produces a random flag of zero or one (false or true).
2. Write a phrase to choose a number at random between 0 and 19 (inclusive) *or* between -20 and 0.

EPILOGUE

FORTH's Effect on Thinking

> FORTH is like the Tao: it is a Way, and is realized when followed. Its
> fragility is its strength; its simplicity is its direction *(Michael Ham, win-*
> *ning entry in Mountain View Press's contest to describe FORTH in twenty-*
> *five words or less).*

To help extract something of the FORTH philosophy, I conducted a poll
among several FORTH users in which I asked, "How has FORTH affected your thinking? Have you found yourself applying 'FORTH-like'
principles in other areas?"

Here are some of the replies:

Mark Bernstein is president of Eastgate Systems Inc. in Cam-
bridge, Massachusetts, and holds a doctorate from the department of
chemistry at Harvard University.

> I first met FORTH while working in laser chemistry. I was trying to build a
> rather complicated controller for a new laser spectrometer. The original
> plans called for a big green box full of electronics, The Interface. Nobody
> had built this particular kind of instrument before—that's why we were
> doing it—and the list of things we wanted the computer to handle changed
> every couple of weeks.

> After a few months, I had hundreds of pages of assembly-language
> routines, three big circuit boards filled with ICs, and a 70-odd pin System
> Bus. Day by day, everything got more fragile and harder to fix. The wiring
> on the circuit boards frayed, the connectors got loose, the assembler code
> grew ever more tangled.

> FORTH was an obvious solution to the software problem, since it provided
> a decent environment in which to build and maintain a complex and rapidly-
> changing program. But the essence of good FORTH programming is the
> art of factoring procedures into useful, free-standing words. The idea of the
> FORTH word had unexpected implications for laboratory hardware design.

> Instead of building a big, monolithic, all-purpose Interface, I found myself
> building piles of simple little boxes which worked a lot like FORTH words:
> they had a fixed set of standard inputs and standard outputs, they per-
> formed just one function, they were designed to connect up to each other
> without much effort, and they were simple enough that you could tell what
> a box did just by looking at its label.

> . . . The idea of "human scale" is, I think, today's seminal concept in soft-
> ware design. This isn't specifically a FORTH development; the great joy of

UNIX, in its youth at least, was that you could read it (since it was written in C), understand it (since it was small), and modify it (since it was simple). FORTH shares these virtues, although it's designed to tackle a different sort of problem.

Because FORTH is small, and because FORTH gives its users control over their machines, FORTH lets humans control their applications. It's just silly to expect scientists to sit in front of a lab computer playing "twenty-questions" with packaged software. FORTH, used properly, lets a scientist instruct the computer instead of letting the computer instruct the scientist.

In the same sense that in baseball, a batter is supposed to feel the bat as an extension of himself, FORTH is human-scaled, and helps convince you that the computer's achievements, and its failures, are also your own.

Raymond E. Dessy is Professor of Chemistry at Virginia Polytechnic Institute and State University, Blacksburg, Virginia.

As I attempted to understand the nature and structure of the language C, I found myself drawing upon the knowledge I had of the organization and approach of FORTH. This permitted me to understand convoluted, or high-fog-coefficient sections describing C.

I have found the FORTH approach is an ideal platform upon which to build an understanding and an educational framework for other languages and operating system concepts.

Jerry Boutelle is owner of Nautilus Systems in Santa Cruz, California, which markets the Nautilus Cross-compiler.

FORTH has changed my thinking in many ways. Since learning FORTH I've coded in other languages, including assembler, BASIC and FORTRAN. I've found that I used the same kind of decomposition we do in FORTH, in the sense of creating words and grouping them together. For example, in handling strings I would define subroutines analogous to CMOVE, —TRAILING, FILL, etc.

More fundamentally, FORTH has reaffirmed my faith in simplicity. Most people go out and attack problems with complicated tools. But simpler tools are available and more useful.

I try to simplify all the aspects of my life. There's a quote I like from *Tao Te Ching* by the Chinese philosopher Lao Tzu: "To attain knowledge, add things every day; to obtain wisdom, remove things every day."

APPENDIX A

Overview
of FORTH
(For Newcomers)

The Dictionary

FORTH is expressed in words (and numbers) and is separated by spaces:

```
HAND OPEN   ARM LOWER   HAND CLOSE   ARM RAISE
```

Such commands may be typed directly from the keyboard, or edited onto mass storage then "**LOAD**"ed.

All words, whether included with the system or user-defined, exist in the "dictionary," a linked list. A "defining word," is used to add new names to the dictionary. One defining word is : (pronounced "colon"), which is used to define a new word in terms of previously-defined words. Here is how one might define a new word called LIFT:

```
: LIFT   HAND OPEN   ARM LOWER   HAND CLOSE   ARM RAISE ;
```

The ; terminates the definition. The new word LIFT may now be used instead of the long sequence of words that comprise its definition.

FORTH words can be nested like this indefinitely. Writing a FORTH application consists of building increasingly powerful definitions, such as this one, in terms of previously defined ones.

Another defining word is **CODE,** which is used in place of colon to define a command in terms of machine instructions for the native processor. Words defined with **CODE** are indistinguishable to the user from words defined with colon. **CODE** definitions are needed only for the most time-critical portions of an application, if at all.

Data Structures

Still another defining word is **CONSTANT,** which is used like this:

```
17 CONSTANT SEVENTEEN
```

The new word SEVENTEEN can now be used in place of the actual number 17.

The defining word VARIABLE creates a location for temporary data. VARIABLE is used like this:

```
VARIABLE BANANAS
```

This reserves a location which is identified by the name BANANAS.

Fetching the contents of this location is the job of the word @ (pronounced "fetch"). For instance,

```
BANANAS @
```

fetches the contents of the variable BANANAS. Its counterpart is ! (pronounced "store"), which stores a value into the location, as in:

```
100 BANANAS !
```

FORTH also provides a word to increment the current value by the given value; for instance, the phrase

```
2 BANANAS +!
```

increments the count by two, making it 102.

FORTH provides many other data structure operators, but more importantly, it also provides the tools necessary for the programmer to create any type of data structure needed for the application.

The Stack

In FORTH, variables and arrays are used for saving values that may be required by many routines and/or at unpredictable times. They are *not* used for the local passing of data between definitions. For this, FORTH employs a much simpler mechanism: the data stack.

When you type a number, it goes on the stack. When you invoke a word which has numeric input, it will take it from the stack. Thus the phrase

```
17 SPACES
```

will display seventeen blanks on the current output device. "17" pushes the binary value 17 onto the stack; the word **SPACES** consumes it.

A constant also pushes its value onto the stack; thus the phrase:

```
SEVENTEEN SPACES
```

has the same effect.

The stack operates on a "last-in, first-out" (LIFO) basis. This means that data can be passed between words in an orderly, modular way, consistent with the nesting of colon definitions.

For instance, a definition called GRID might invoke the phrase 17 SPACES. This temporary activity on the stack will be transparent to any other definition that invokes GRID because the value placed on the stack is removed before the definition of GRID ends. The calling definition might have placed some numbers of its own on the stack prior to calling GRID. These will remain on the stack, unharmed, until GRID has been executed and calling definition continues.

Control Structures

FORTH provides all the control structures needed for structured, GOTO-less programming.

The syntax of the **IF THEN** construct is as follows:

```
...  ( flag )  IF   KNOCK   THEN   OPEN ...
```

The "flag" is a value on the stack, consumed by IF. A non-zero value indicates true, zero indicates false. A true flag causes the code after **IF** (in this case, the word KNOCK) to be executed. The word **THEN** marks the end of the conditional phrase; execution resumes with the word OPEN. A false flag causes the code between **IF** and **THEN** to *not* be executed. In either case, OPEN will be performed.

The word **ELSE** allows an alternate phrase to be executed in the false case. In the phrase:

```
( flag )  IF   KNOCK   ELSE   RING   THEN   OPEN ...
```

the word KNOCK will be performed if the flag is true, otherwise the word RING will be performed. Either way, execution will continue starting with OPEN.

FORTH also provides for indexed loops in the form

```
( limit)  ( index)  DO ... LOOP
```

and indefinite loops in the forms:

```
... BEGIN  ...   ( flag)  UNTIL
```

and

```
... BEGIN ...  ( flag)  WHILE ...  REPEAT ;
```

For a complete introduction to the FORTH command set, read *Starting FORTH*, published by Prentice-Hall.

APPENDIX B

Defining DOER/MAKE

If your system doesn't have DOER and MAKE already defined, this appendix is meant to help you install them and, if necessary, understand how they work. Because by its nature this construct is system dependent, I've included several different implementations at the end of this appendix in the hope that one of them will work for you. If not, and if this section doesn't give you enough information to get them running, you probably have an unusual system. Please don't ask me for help; ask your FORTH vendor.

Here's how it works. **DOER** is a defining word that creates an entry with one cell in its parameter field. That cell contains the vector address, and is initialized to point to a no-op word called **NOTHING**.

Children of **DOER** will execute the **DOES** > code of **DOER**, which does only two things: fetch the vector address and place it on the return stack. That's all. FORTH execution then continues with this address on the return stack, which will cause the vectored function to be performed. It's like saying (in '83-Standard)

```
' NOTHING >BODY >R <return>
```

which executes NOTHING. (This trick only works with colon definitions.)

Here's an illustration of the dictionary entry created when we enter

DOER JOE

	pfa of
JOE	NOTHING
header	parameter
	field

Now suppose we define:

```
: TEST    MAKE JOE   CR ;
```

that is, we define a word that can vector JOE to do a carriage return.

Here's a picture of the compiled definition of TEST:

| | adr of | | | adr of | adr of | adr of |
| TEST | (MAKE) | 0 | | JOE | CR | EXIT |

header   MARKER

Let's look at the code for **MAKE**. Since we're using **MAKE** inside a colon definition, **STATE** will be true, and we'll execute the phrase:

```
COMPILE (MAKE)  HERE MARKER !  0 ,
```

We can see how **MAKE** has compiled the address of the run-time routine, **(MAKE)**, followed by a zero. (We'll explain what the zero is for, and why we save its address in a the variable **MARKER**, later).

    Now let's look at what **(MAKE)** does when we execute our new definition **TEST**:

`R>`	Gets an address from the return stack. This address points to the cell just past **(MAKE)**, where the zero is.
`DUP 2+`	Gets the address of the second cell after **(MAKE)**, where the address of **JOE** is.
`DUP 2+`	Gets the address of the third cell after **(MAKE)**, where the code we want to execute begins. The stack now has: ('marker, 'joe, 'code --)
`SWAP @ >BODY`	Fetches the contents of the address pointing to JOE (i.e., gets the address of JOE) and computes JOE's pfa, where the vector address goes.
`!`	Stores the address where the new code begins (**CR**, etc.) into the vector address of JOE.
	Now JOE points inside the definition of TEST. When we type JOE, we'll do a carriage return.
`@ ?DUP IF >R THEN`	Fetches the contents of the cell containing zero. Since the cell does contain zero, the IF THEN statement is not performed.

That's the basic idea. But what about that cell containing zero? That's for the use of **;AND**. Suppose we changed TEST to read:

```
: TEST   MAKE JOE  CR ;AND SPACE ;
```

That is, when we invoke TEST we'll vector JOE to do a **CR**, and we'll do a **SPACE** right now. Here's what this new version of TEST will look like:

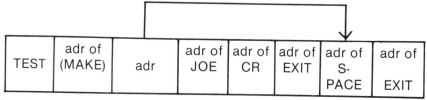

| TEST | adr of (MAKE) | adr | adr of JOE | adr of CR | adr of EXIT | adr of S-PACE | adr of EXIT |

header   MARKER

Here's the definition of **;AND**:

```
: ;AND   COMPILE EXIT   HERE MARKER @ ! ;      IMMEDIATE
```

We can see that **;AND** has compiled an **EXIT**, just as semicolon would.

Next, recall that **MAKE** saved the address of that cell in a variable called **MARKER**. Now **;AND** stores **HERE** (the location of the second string of code beginning with **SPACE)** into the cell previously containing zero. Now **(MAKE)** has a pointer to the place to resume execution. The phrase

```
IF  >R THEN
```

will leave on the return stack the address of the code beginning with **SPACE**. Thus execution will skip over the code between **MAKE** and **;AND** and continue with the remainder of the definition up to semicolon.

The word **UNDO** ticks the name of a **DOER** word, and stores the address of **NOTHING** into it.

One final note: on some systems you may encounter a problem. If you use **MAKE** outside of a colon definition to create a forward reference, you may not be able to find the most recently defined word. For instance, if you have:

```
: REFRAIN     DO-DAH   DO-DAH ;
MAKE SONG     CHORUS   REFRAIN ;
```

your system might think that REFRAIN has not been defined. The problem is due to the placement of SMUDGE. As a solution, try rearranging the order of definitions or, if necessary, put the MAKE code inside a definition which you then execute:

```
: SETUP    MAKE SONG   CHORUS   REFRAIN ;   SETUP
```

In Laboratory Microsystems PC/FORTH 2.0, the UNSMUDGE on line 9 handles the problem. This problem does not arise with the Laxen/Perry/Harris model.

The final screen is an example of using **DOER/MAKE**. After loading the block, enter

```
RECITAL
```

then enter

```
WHY?
```

followed by return, as many times as you like (you'll get a different
reason each time).


```
Screen # 21
  0 ( DOER/MAKE    Shadow screen                      LPB 12/05/83 )
  1 NOTHING      A no-op
  2 DOER         Defines a word whose behavior is vectorable.
  3 MARKER       Saves adr for optional continuation pointer.
  4 (MAKE)       Stuffs the address of further code into the
  5                parameter field of a doer word.
  6 MAKE         Used interpretively:  MAKE doer-name  forth-code ;
  7              or inside a definition:
  8                 : def   MAKE doer-name  forth-code ;
  9              Vectors the doer-name word to the forth-code.
 10 ;AND         Allows continuation of the "making" definition
 11 UNDO         Usage:  UNDO doer-name ; makes it safe to execute
 12
 13
 14
 15
```

```
Screen # 22
  0 \ DOER/MAKE    FORTH-83 Laxen/Perry/Harris model  LPB 12/05/83
  1 : NOTHING ;
  2 : DOER    CREATE  ['] NOTHING  >BODY ,   DOES> @ >R ;
  3 VARIABLE MARKER
  4 : (MAKE)   R> DUP 2+  DUP 2+  SWAP @  >BODY !
  5     @ ?DUP IF >R THEN ;
  6 : MAKE    STATE @ IF ( compiling)
  7    COMPILE (MAKE)  HERE MARKER !  0 ,
  8    ELSE  HERE  [COMPILE] '  >BODY !
  9    [COMPILE] ]  THEN ;   IMMEDIATE
 10 : ;AND    COMPILE EXIT  HERE MARKER @ ! ;   IMMEDIATE
 11 : UNDO    ['] NOTHING  >BODY  [COMPILE] '  >BODY ! ;
 12
 13 \ The code in this screen is in the public domain.
 14
 15
```

```
Screen # 23
  0 ( DOER/MAKE    FORTH-83 Lab. Micro PC/FORTH 2.0   LPB 12/05/83 )
  1 : NOTHING   ;
  2 : DOER    CREATE  ['] NOTHING  >BODY ,   DOES> @ >R ;
  3 VARIABLE MARKER
  4 : (MAKE)   R> DUP 2+  DUP 2+  SWAP @  >BODY !
  5     @ ?DUP IF >R THEN ;
  6 : MAKE    STATE @ IF ( compiling)
  7    COMPILE (MAKE)  HERE MARKER !  0 ,
  8    ELSE  HERE  [COMPILE] '  >BODY !
  9    [COMPILE] ] UNSMUDGE  THEN ;   IMMEDIATE
 10 : ;AND    COMPILE EXIT  HERE MARKER @ ! ;  IMMEDIATE
 11 : UNDO    ['] NOTHING  >BODY  [COMPILE] '  >BODY ! ;
 12
 13 ( The code in this screen is in the public domain.)
 14
 15
```

```
Screen # 24
 0 ( DOER/MAKE    FIG model                        LPB 12/05/83 )
 1 : NOTHING    ;
 2 : DOES-PFA   ( pfa -- pfa of child of <BUILDS-DOES> )  2+ ;
 3 : DOER    <BUILDS ' NOTHING ,  DOES> @ >R ;
 4 0 VARIABLE MARKER
 5 : (MAKE)   R>  DUP 2+  DUP 2+  SWAP @  2+ DOES-PFA !
 6   @ -DUP IF >R THEN ;
 7 : MAKE  STATE @ IF ( compiling)
 8   COMPILE (MAKE)  HERE  MARKER !  0 ,
 9   ELSE  HERE  [COMPILE] ' DOES-PFA !
10   SMUDGE    [COMPILE] ] THEN ; IMMEDIATE
11 : ;AND    COMPILE ;S  HERE MARKER @ ! ;  IMMEDIATE
12 : UNDO    ' NOTHING [COMPILE] ' DOES-PFA ! ;
13 ;S
14 The code in this screen is in the public domain.
15


Screen # 25
 0 ( DOER/MAKE   79-Standard  MVP FORTH          LPB 12/05/83 )
 1 : NOTHING ;
 2 : DOER    CREATE  ' NOTHING  ,  DOES> @ >R ;
 3 VARIABLE MARKER
 4 : (MAKE)   R>  DUP 2+  DUP 2+  SWAP @  2+ ( pfa) !
 5   @ ?DUP IF >R THEN ;
 6 : MAKE    STATE @ IF ( compiling)
 7   COMPILE (MAKE)  HERE MARKER !  0 ,
 8   ELSE  HERE  [COMPILE] ' !
 9   [COMPILE] ]  THEN ;   IMMEDIATE
10 : ;AND    COMPILE EXIT  HERE MARKER @ ! ;   IMMEDIATE
11 : UNDO    ['] NOTHING  [COMPILE] ' ! ;
12
13 ( 238 )
14 ( The code in this screen is in the public domain.)
15


Screen # 26
 0 ( TODDLER: Example of DOER/MAKE                  12/01/83 )
 1 DOER WHY?
 2 : RECITAL
 3   CR ." Your daddy is standing on the table.  Ask him 'WHY?' "
 4   MAKE WHY? ." To change the light bulb."
 5   BEGIN
 6   MAKE WHY?  ." Because it's burned out."
 7   MAKE WHY?  ." Because it was old."
 8   MAKE WHY?  ." Because we put it in there a long time ago."
 9   MAKE WHY?  ." Because it was dark!"
10   MAKE WHY?  ." Because it was night time!!"
11   MAKE WHY?  ." Stop saying WHY?"
12   MAKE WHY?  ." Because it's driving me crazy."
13   MAKE WHY?  ." Just let me change this light bulb!"
14   F UNTIL ;
15 : WHY?   CR  WHY?  QUIT ;
```

APPENDIX C

Other Utilities Described in This Book

This appendix is here to help you define some of the words referred to in this book that may not exist in your system. Definitions are given in FORTH-83 Standard.

From Chapter 4

A definition of **ASCII** that will work in '83 Standard is:

```
: ASCII  ( -- c)  \  Compile:  c   ( -- )
\ Interpret:   c   ( -- c)
      BL WORD 1+ C@  STATE @
      IF [COMPILE] LITERAL  THEN ; IMMEDIATE
```

From Chapter 5

The word \ can be defined as:

```
: \  ( skip rest of line)
     >IN @  64 /  1+  64 *  >IN ! ; IMMEDIATE
```

If you decide not to use **EXIT** to terminate a screeen, you can define \S as:

```
: \S   1024 >IN ! ;
```

The word **FH** can be defined simply as:

```
: FH  \   ( offset -- offset-block)    "from here"
      BLK @ + ;
```

This factoring allows you to use FH in many ways, e.g.:

```
: TEST   [ 1 FH ] LITERAL LOAD ;
```

or

```
: SEE   [ 2 FH ] LITERAL LIST ;
```

A slightly more complicated version of FH also lets you edit or load a screen with a phrase such as "14 FH LIST", relative to the screen that you just listed (SCR):

```
: FH   \   ( offset -- offset-block)   "from here"
      BLK @   ?DUP O= IF   SCR @   THEN   + ;
```

BL is a simple constant:

```
32 CONSTANT BL
```

TRUE and **FALSE** can be defined as:

```
O CONSTANT FALSE
-1 CONSTANT TRUE
```

(FORTH's control words such as IF and UNTIL interpret zero as "false" and any non-zero value as "true." Before FORTH '83, the convention was to indicate "true" with the value 1. Starting with FORTH '83, however, "true" is indicated with hex FF, which is the signed number -1 (all bits set).

WITHIN can be defined in high level like this:

```
: WITHIN   ( n lo hi+1 -- ?)
      >R   1- OVER <   SWAP R>   < AND ;
```

From Chapter 8

The implementation of **LEAP** will depend on how your system implements **DO LOOPs**. If **DO** keeps two items on the return stack (the index and the limit), **LEAP** must drop both of them plus one more return—stack item to exit:

```
: LEAP   R> R> 2DROP   R> DROP ;
```

If **DO** keeps *three* items on the return stack, it must be defined:

```
: LEAP   R> R> 2DROP   R> R> 2DROP ;
```

APPENDIX D

Answers to "Further Thinking" Problems

Chapter 3

1. The answer depends on whether you believe that other components will need to "know" the numeric code associated with each key. Usually this would *not* be the case. The simpler, more compact form is therefore preferable. Also in the first version, to add a new key would require a change in two places.

2. The problem with the words RAM-ALLOT and THERE are that they are *time-dependent:* we must execute them in a particular order. Our solution then will be to devise an interface to the RAM allocation pointer that is not dependent on order; the way to do this is to have a *single* word which does both functions transparently.

   Our word's syntax will be:

   ```
   : RAM-ALLOT   ( #bytes-to-allot -- starting-adr) ... ;
     ... ;
   ```

   This syntax will remain the same whether we define it to allocate growing upward:

   ```
   : RAM-ALLOT   ( #bytes-to-allot -- starting-adr)
       >RAM @   DUP ROT +   >RAM ! ;
   ```

   or to allocate growing downward:

   ```
   : RAM-ALLOT   ( #bytes-to-allot -- starting-adr)
       >RAM @   SWAP -   DUP >RAM ! ;
   ```

Chapter 4

4. Our solution is as follows:

```
\ CARDS                    Shuffle                         6-20-83
52 CONSTANT #CARDS
CREATE DECK   #CARDS ALLOT    \   one card per byte
```

```
: INIT-DECK
    #CARDS 0 DO  I   DECK I + C!   LOOP ;
INIT-DECK
: 'CSWAP  ( a1 a2 -- )  \  swap bytes at a1 and a2
    2DUP C@  SWAP C@  ROT C!   SWAP C! ;
: SHUFFLE    \  shuffle deck of cards
    #CARDS 0 DO  DECK I +   DECK  #CARDS CHOOSE +
        'CSWAP  LOOP ;
```

Chapter 8

1. This will work:

       20 CHOOSE   2 CHOOSE   IF NEGATE THEN

   But this is simpler:

       40 CHOOSE   20 -

APPENDIX E

Summary of
Style Conventions

The contents of this Appendix are in the public domain. We encourage publication without restriction, provided that you credit the source.

Spacing and Indentation Guidelines

1 space between the colon and the name

2 spaces between the name and the comment*

2 spaces, or a carriage return, after the comment and before the definition*

3 spaces between the name and definition if no comment is used

3 spaces indentation on each subsequent line (or multiples of 3 for nested indentation)

1 space between words/numbers within a phrase

2 or 3 spaces between phrases

1 space between the last word and the semicolon

1 space between semicolon and **IMMEDIATE** (if invoked)

No blank lines between definitions, except to separate distinct groups of definitions

Stack-Comment Abbreviations

n	single-length signed number
d	double-length signed number
u	single-length unsigned number
ud	double-length unsigned number
t	triple-length
q	quadruple-length
c	7-bit character value
b	8-bit byte
?	boolean flag; or:

*An often-seen alternative calls for 1 space between the name and comment and 3 between the comment and the definition. A more liberal technique uses 3 spaces before and after the comment. Whatever you choose, be consistent.

t=	true
f=	false
a or adr	address
acf	address of code field
apf	address of parameter field
'	(as prefix) address of
s d	(as a pair) source destination
lo hi	lower-limit upper-limit (inclusive)
#	count
o	offset
i	index
m	mask
x	don't care (data structure notation)

An "offset" is a difference expressed in absolute units, such as bytes.

An "index" is a difference expressed in logical units, such as elements or records.

Input-Stream Comment Designations

c	single character, blank-delimited
name	sequence of characters, blank delimited
text	sequence of characters, delimited by non-blank

Follow "text" with the actual delimiter required; e.g., text" or text).

Samples of Good Commenting Style

Here are two sample screens to illustrate good commenting style.

```
Screen # 126
   0 \ Formatter          Data Structures -- p.2          06/06/83
   1   6 CONSTANT TMARGIN \ line# where body of text begins)
   2 55 CONSTANT BMARGIN \ line# where body of text ends)
   3
   4 CREATE HEADER   82 ALLOT
   5    { 11eft-cnt | 1right-cnt | 80header }
   6 CREATE FOOTER   82 ALLOT
   7    { 11eft-cnt | 1right-cnt | 80footer }
   8
   9 VARIABLE ACROSS     \ formatter's current horizontal position
  10 VARIABLE DOWNWARD \ formatter's current vertical position
  11 VARIABLE LEFT       \ current primary left margin
  12 VARIABLE WALL       \ current primary right margin
  13 VARIABLE WALL-WAS \ WALL when curr. line started being formt'd
  14
  15
```

```
Screen # 127
  0 \ Formatter          positioning -- p.1                06/06/83
  1 : SKIP  ( n)  ACROSS +! ;
  2 : NEWLEFT  \ reset left margin
  3    LEFT @  PERMANENT @ +  TEMPORARY @ +  ACROSS ! ;
  4 : \LINE  \ begin new line
  5    DOOR  CR'  1 DOWNWARD +!  NEWLEFT  WALL @  WALL-WAS ! ;
  6 : AT-TOP?  ( -- t=at-top)  TMARGIN  DOWNWARD @ = ;
  7 : >TMARGIN  \ move from crease to TMARGIN
  8    0 DOWNWARD !  BEGIN  \LINE  AT-TOP? UNTIL ;
  9
 10
 11
 12
 13
 14
 15
```

Naming Conventions

Meaning	Form	Example
Arithmetic		
integer 1	1name	1+
integer 2	2name	2*
takes relative input parameters	+name	+DRAW
takes scaled input parameters	*name	*DRAW
Compilation		
start of "high-level" code	name:	CASE:
end of "high-level" code	;name	;CODE
put something into dictionary	name,	C,
executes at compile time	[name]	[COMPILE]
slightly different	name' (prime)	CR'
internal form or primitive	(name)	(TYPE)
	or < name>	< TYPE>
compiling word run-time part:		
systems with no folding	lower-case	if
systems with folding	(NAME)	(IF)
defining word	:name	:COLOR
block-number where overlay begins	namING	DISKING
Data Structures		
table or array	names	EMPLOYEES
total number of elements	#name	#EMPLOYEES
current item number (variable)	name#	EMPLOYEE#
sets current item	(n) name	13 EMPLOYEE
advance to next element	+name	+EMPLOYEE
size of offset to item from beginning of structure	name+	DATE+
size of (bytes per) (short for BYTES/name)	/name	/EMPLOYEE

Meaning	Form	Example
index pointer	> name	>IN
convert address of structure to address of item	> name	>BODY
file index	(name)	(PEOPLE)
file pointer	−name	−JOB
initialize structure	0name	0RECORD

Direction, Conversion

backwards	name<	SLIDE<
forwards	name>	CMOVE>
from	< name	< TAPE
to	> name	> TAPE
convert to	name >name	FEET> METERS
downward	\name	\LINE
upward	/name	/LINE
open	{name	{FILE
close	}name	}FILE

Logic, Control

return boolean value	name?	SHORT?
returns reversed boolean	−name?	−SHORT?
address of boolean	'name?	'SHORT?
operates conditionally	?name	?DUP (maybe DUP)
enable	+name	+CLOCK
or, absence of symbol	name	BLINKING
disable	−name	−CLOCK −BLINKING

Memory

save value of	@name	@CURSOR
restore value of	!name	!CURSOR
store into	name!	SECONDS!
fetch from	name@	INDEX@
name of buffer	:name	:INSERT
address of name	'name	'S
address of pointer to name	'name	'TYPE
exchange, especially bytes	> name<	>MOVE<

Numeric Types

byte length	Cname	C@
2 cell size, 2's complement integer encoding	Dname	D+
mixed 16 and 32-bit operator	Mname	M*
3 cell size	Tname	T*
4 cell size	Qname	Q*
unsigned encoding	Uname	U.

Meaning	Form	Example
Output, Printing		
print item	.name	.S
print numeric (name denotes type)	name.	D. , U.
print right justified	name.R	U.R
Quantity		
"per"	/name	/SIDE
Sequencing		
start	< name	< #
end	name >˙	# >
Text		
string follows delimited by ''	name''	ABORT'' text''
text or string operator	''name	''COMPARE
(similar to $ prefix in BASIC		
superstring array	''name''	''COLORS''

How to Pronounce the Symbols

!	store
@	fetch
#	sharp (or "number," as in #RECORDS)
$	dollar
%	percent
^	caret
&	ampersand
*	star
(	left paren; paren
)	right paren; paren
—	dash; not
+	plus
=	equals
{ }	faces (traditionally called "curly brackets")
[ ]	square brackets
''	quote
'	as prefix: tick; as suffix: prime
~	tilde
|	bar
\	backslash. (also "under," "down," and "skip")
/	slash. (also "up")
<	less-than
	left dart
>	greater-than
	right dart
?	question (some prefer "query")
,	comma
.	dot

INDEX